14/40 ·

Previous pages: A fisherman off Cape Cornwall

Left: Market porters at Billingsgate in London, a photograph taken in 1954

INTRODUCTION

You can, repeat can, eat fish! We know that they are good for us, not to mention wonderful to cook with. The Food Standards Agency (FSA) recommends that we should eat at least two portions a week as part of a healthy diet, one of which should be oily fish like mackerel, herring or salmon. Oily fish are rich in Omega3, the polyunsaturated fatty acids that protect against heart disease, high blood pressure and kidney disorders, and are good for the skin, bone joints and brain tissue. The worst thing we could do would be to give up eating fish: for the sake of our health, and for the sake of our fishermen. We need to support our local fisheries because in the UK alone the livelihoods of more than 135,000 people both on the catching side and on-shore depend on the fishing industry. Living in Cornwall as I do, I know that many fishermen come from small communities with fragile economies where fishing has been a way of life for generations.

But how do we know which types of fish we can enjoy with a clear conscience? Every week the media seems to bombard us with the tragic news that fisheries worldwide are in danger of collapsing from over-fishing. Before I attempt to answer the question, we need to look back into history to understand how the oceans have reached their current sad state.

In 1497 the Genoese explorer John Cabot stumbled across the Grand Banks fisheries off the coast of Newfoundland as he attempted to find a new route to the spice riches of the Orient. The waters were so teeming with codfish, he reported, that to catch them, all his men had to do was hang a wicker basket over the side of the ship and it would come up laden. Two centuries later English skippers were still talking about cod shoals 'so thick by the shore that we hardly have been able to row a boat thro' them'. Some fish were 6 or 7 feet long and weighed up to 200lbs.

This rich harvest continued through the centuries until the arrival in the spring of 1954 of a new Scottish fishing boat. The *Fairtry* was no ordinary vessel: at 280 feet long and with a gross weight of 2,600 tons, it was more than four times the size of the largest trawlers that it began fishing alongside. The era of factory fishing had arrived and the Atlantic cod fishery, the most bountiful the world had ever known, was doomed from that moment. The distant-water factory trawlers were ruthlessly efficient. Equipped with increasingly sophisticated technology – sonar, radar, echograms – they could locate and catch entire shoals of fish with ease. Below deck were on-board processing plants and huge banks of freezers to keep their catch fresh while they continued pursuing fish around the clock, in all weathers, for months on end. Every major fishing nation got in on the act.

By the 1970s the Soviets had 400 factory trawlers, the Japanese 125, Spain 75 and France and Britain 40 each. According to the UN's Food and Agriculture Organisation (FAO) one factory ship could haul in as much cod in an hour as a typical 16th-century boat could land in a season. And it wasn't only cod that suffered; stocks of other groundfish such as halibut and haddock were decimated. The sea was a free-for-all, with fleets flying the flags of their countries, competing for fish thousands of miles from home.

In 1982, the UN adopted the Convention on the Law of the Sea, which allows countries bordering the sea to claim exclusive economic zones reaching 200 nautical miles into open waters. These areas include the highly productive continental shelves of roughly 200 metres in depth where most fish live out their lives. The Convention ended centuries of fighting over coastal fishing grounds, but it placed the responsibility for managing marine fisheries squarely on maritime countries. Unfortunately, no nation has faced up to its responsibilities. Some countries have continued to build new offshore fleets of even bigger, more powerful and more efficient boats to replace those of foreign nations pushed out by the Convention, and have begun to fish more extensively in their own territories, thus providing less opportunity for

The harbour at Boscastle in Cornwall, in 1894

foreign fleets to fish the excess, as sanctioned by the Convention. Other countries have been pressed to accept agreements that allow foreign fleets to fish their waters, again sanctioned by the Convention. The end result has been more fishing than ever, because bigger foreign fleets have no incentive to preserve local marine resources and, in fact, are subsidised by their own countries to catch as much fish as they can. In 1992, the Grand Banks cod fishery collapsed, leaving its cod population commercially extinct. Thousands of Canadian fishermen lost their jobs and their way of life.

However, the destruction is not limited to the Grand Banks. According to the World Wildlife Fund (WWF), over 70 per cent of fish stocks across the globe are either fully depleted or over-exploited. Hauls of commercially desirable species are dwindling and the sizes of the individual fish are getting smaller; a large number are captured before they even have time to mature. Trawlers trailing dredges the size of football pitches have literally scraped the bottom of the sea clean, harvesting an entire eco-system along with the catch of the day.

There is almost nothing left in the North Sea, Irish, Baltic or Bering Seas. In fact, 70 per cent of the commercial fish stocks in European waters have been over-fished to the point

where they are now considered 'outside safe biological limits'. In other words, the fish cannot reproduce rapidly enough to keep pace with their harvest. As stocks have collapsed, fishing grounds been closed and quotas slashed, European boats have simply changed course to chase fish wherever they are, be it Africa or Antarctica. The EU has been very busy buying up fishing rights from developing countries: between 1993 and 1997 one billion euros were spent. Instead of putting our house in order, we are causing problems in developing countries by depleting their fish stocks as well. The waters off the African states of Mauritania, Somalia and Mozambique, for example, have provided fish for their coastal communities for centuries; now they are the hunting ground for European factory fleets and face a severe over-fishing crisis.

These satellite-guided giants are also fishing in ever deeper waters, taking fish species about which we know very little. No one has a clue as to what happens if a species of deep-water fish is heavily targeted. According to the WWF many newly discovered species could face extinction before being properly researched. Marine biologists now believe that deep-water species have far slower life cycles than pelagic species (fish that inhabit the upper levels of the sea). For example, a species such as the orange roughy

may not mature and reproduce until it is over 30 years old and, even then, may produce only a limited number of offspring. Sadly stocks of this wonderful fish are thought to have declined by 76 per cent in only 12 years and have been almost wiped out in British waters. The WWF says that the EU has ignored the advice of its own scientists to ban deep-sea fishing, but must do so before it is too late.

But why, if fish are becoming so scarce, are bigger and more technologically advanced vessels being built? The answer is that the fishing industry is heavily subsidised and the EU dishes out funds for many reasons. A key aim of the Common Fisheries Policy has been to reduce the fishing fleet, so between 1995 and 2000 the EU spent millions of euros on subsidies for scrapping fishing boats, but also invested millions of euros in new vessels. This money, on top of the money put forward by member states' own governments and the fishing industry itself, meant that much more money was spent on new vessels than on decommissioning existing ones. The UK has actually been more forward-thinking on this point and hasn't given subsidies for new vessels since 1997, but until this policy is accepted by all member states, larger modern vessels will continue to be built.

But surely the much-publicised quota system is designed to stop over-fishing by

Newlyn Fish Market in Cornwall, a photograph taken in 1906

EU member states? The fact is it just doesn't work. The International Council for the Exploration of the Seas (ICES) based in Denmark, offers advice regarding the condition of fish stocks and hence suitable quotas and total allowable catches (TAC) to maintain them species by species, but historically, this advice has been largely overruled. When the EU tries to enforce low TACs and quotas, member states with the strongest fishing lobby, such as Spain, Portugal and France, do everything they can to block the move.

The UK has fared particularly badly in the fight for fishing rights. After the cod wars of the 1970s the UK sold off 60 per cent of its fishing waters, and when we joined the Common Market, as the EU was then called, much of our fishing fleet was working in distant waters rather than those of Europe. With the first Common Fisheries Policy (CFP) of 1973, access rights and quotas were based on the patterns of fishing existing at the time, so the UK was left with very little.

However, even if adequate quotas were put in place and obeyed, the rules regarding by-catch (the fish caught at the same time but without a quota) and the catching of under-sized fish would still create immense problems. By law, these fish must be thrown back. Where many different species swim together, fishermen are bound to catch a large number that they cannot land. It is estimated that at least 25 per cent caught each year are thrown back – a huge number. Unfortunately, most of these will be dead or irrevocably damaged. In mixed fisheries such as those of the West Country, a Newlyn or Brixham fisherman with a quota for pursuing pollack could face throwing up to 40 tonnes of cod back into the sea as it becomes the by-catch or 'discard': perfect and endangered cod thrown over the side, dead or dying. Another by-catch horror story that crops up every year in Devon and Cornwall is the wholesale slaughter of dolphins believed to be linked with the winter sea bass pair-trawling, which is carried out as the bass move up the English Channel for spawning from January to March. The fishery is blamed because the pair-trawlers nets are so gigantic (you can fit seven jumbo jets into one net) and the dolphins don't realise they are caught until they try and come up for air, so they drown. DEFRA banned pair-netting in 2004, affecting just seven Scottish boats, but this has not stopped the dozens of French and Spanish pair-trawlers. Local pressure groups have called for an EU total ban, but so far it has not moved.

As wild fish become increasingly scarce the gap between demand and supply will have to be supplemented by aquaculture, or fish farming. The UN's FAO believes that by 2020 more than half the world's fish will come from farms, but as environmentalists have pointed out, this is unlikely to mean a respite for wild stocks unless the farmed fish do not consume fishmeal. Nearly all the highly valued fish, like cod, haddock, turbot and bass, are carnivorous and with heavy restrictions on fishing, fleets are increasingly turning their attention to catching varieties categorised as industrial, which have no quotas, to sell to the manufacturers of food for the fish farming business. Currently 11 million tonnes of wild fish a year (12 per cent of the total caught) are destined to become fish pellets and this will include fish that are perfectly fit for human consumption, such as juvenile herring, sardines, anchovies and mackerel. Salmon farms actually consume more fish than they produce: it can take 1.35kg (3lb) fish meal to yield 450g (1lb) of salmon.

The future must lie in developing feeds that contain less fish and more plant-based material for carnivorous fish and raising more varieties of herbivorous fish, such as carp and tilapia (a freshwater fish mainly farmed in China at the moment). The farming of shellfish, such as oysters, mussels, clams and scallops, could also be expanded as they do not require industrial fishmeal.

A fascinating fish-farming project is taking place in Wakefield in Yorkshire, where

Castle Hill Fish Market, Scarborough, North Yorkshire, *c.* **1880**

a private environmental company is using waste cardboard to feed worms which in turn are fed to sturgeon, once a common fish in British waters. The fish are good eating and also provide caviar. Yorkshire caviar is now on the market at just over half the price of Beluga!

Recent research for the UK's Seafish Industry Authority reveals consumers have 'overall negative attitudes' towards fish farming due to a decade of bad publicity in the salmon industry. Intensive fish farms have created serious environmental problems. If cages are not placed in areas where there are strong currents of clean water, the waste, uneaten food, and chemicals for controlling parasites and disease can pollute a wide area around the fish farm. According to the WWF, pollution from the farms on the west coast of Scotland, which has the world's third largest salmon farming industry, is comparable to the sewage input of up to 9.4 million people, poisoning the surrounding waters and destroying delicate marine habitats. Marine biologists say siting farms at the mouths of deep-sea lochs is a major problem because there is not enough tidal flush to remove the pollutants and sweep them out to sea. Diseases then proliferate, including sea lice, and it is common for farmed fish to escape, spreading these diseases to the already vulnerable wild stock that are also being

weakened through interbreeding with escaped fish.

The recent scare about the discovery of high quantities of potentially cancer-causing chemicals known as dioxins and poly-chlorinated biphenyls (PCBs) in farmed salmon from Scotland was catastrophic news for fish farming in Britain. The chemicals found do not come from the water the salmon swim in, but from the food they eat, which is manufactured from wild fish caught on the bottom of the seas around Britain, pre-dominantly in the North Sea where some of the nastiest chemicals from the industrial and farming revolution have washed and settled in the mud. These chemicals can pollute other fish too and may even find their way into fish-oil supplements. The FSA keeps a careful eye on those for sale in the UK and has assured the public that farmed salmon is within the safety levels set by the World Health Organisation and the EU. It argues that the known benefits of eating one portion of oily fish a week outweigh any possible risks.

The relatively new development of organic fish farming has set out to alleviate some of the problems of aquaculture. Lower stock densities, around half that of intensive farms, and careful siting of cages, often much further out at sea where the water currents spread the wastes more efficiently, is significant in

controlling disease. The fish are healthier and better able to resist infection and some are fed on the by-products of the commercial fish industry rather than industrial fishmeal, which could be seen as a more sustainable way of feeding. But, the Soil Association admits organic aquaculture is not without its problems and that the regulations and practices will need 'considerable evolution and refinement in years to come'.

Although there are other factors contributing to the lack of fish in our oceans, like pollution and climate change, proper management of fish resources will go a long way to alleviating these problems. At least the EU realises that its Common Fisheries Policy is not working and for the first time conservation is going to be on the top of its list of concerns. The EU is calling for 'an immediate and significant reduction in fishing effort'. Conservation bodies say that grants and government subsidies that keep too many boats on the seas chasing too few fish will have to be abolished and fishermen receive incentives to change to more sustainable fishing methods. We need to learn more from Norwegian, Icelandic and Faroese fisheries where the industry has put more money into research and grants for highly selective fishing gear to avoid damage to non-target marine species and habitat.

Gutting fish outside a factory in Whitby, North Yorkshire, a photograph taken in 1959

Creating 'no-take zones' may be another key to preserving the world's fisheries. These are areas of sea where fishing is either banned or restricted to allow the fish to mature and breed. Countries that have embraced marine regeneration like New Zealand, Australia and Canada have amassed compelling evidence that no-take zones vastly improve fish stocks. When fishing was resumed after both World Wars, it was noted that the numbers of fish were significantly increased. But scientists have estimated that up to a third of the world's oceans will need to be designated as marine protected areas if the global fishing industry is to be saved: the total area currently protected constitutes a mere 0.01% of the ocean surface. There are 490,000 square miles of commercial fishing grounds around the UK, but only one statutory no-take zone so far, a two-mile zone around Lundy off the coast of North Devon, set up by English Nature in 2003. The lobster fishermen of St Agnes in Cornwall agreed in 1997 to a voluntary no-take zone, while the fishermen of the Isle of Arran are hoping to set up Scotland's first official no-take zone in Lamlash Bay, once famous for its haddock. Whatever measures are taken, there will have to be much more effective policing of fishing waters and harsher enforcing of regulations.

Environmental groups are calling for clearer labelling and fish traceability will become a requirement of EU food law in 2005. A project known as Tracefish has established a set of international standards enabling the traceability of both wild and farmed fish and seafood from catcher, or farmer, to retailer. So we should soon be able to choose eco-friendly fish with much more knowledge and confidence. As always, we consumers can be a powerful force.

Author's Acknowledgements

I have always loved eating fish, but life in Cornwall has encouraged in me a great respect for fishermen and their families. I have been very aware of what is happening at sea and how fragile are their livelihoods, so I wanted to write this book to bring attention to the difficulties while encouraging everyone to eat more fish.

Fishermen, government bodies and environmental scientists are not always in accord, so I am offering you a personal view of the situation today. All three groups have given me help and I am very grateful for their opinions, information and advice. They are too many to mention individually, although a special 'thank you' must go to Bernadette Clarke of the Marine Conservation Society.

The National Trust has been as supportive as ever, and I had great fun talking to coastal and river wardens, property managers and chefs. My publisher and editor, Margaret Willes, has offered me much encouragement, patience and understanding. As always it has been a joy working with her and her staff, in particular her assistants Andrew Cummins and Grant Berry who have tracked down the old photographs that are such a feature of the book. These black and white images present a powerful contrast to the food photography that has been accomplished through the skills of Maxine Clark, Helen Purchas, Maggie Jary and Mark Kensett of Imagen. I am also grateful to Stuart Smith for his clever designer's eye.

Most of the book was expertly typed by Caroline Magne, who lives in the Western Isles of Scotland. My handwritten manuscript winged its way by helicopter to the Isle of Harris, and I owe her a huge debt of gratitude, as I do to Jackie Smith who completed the work.

Lastly, but by no means least, how would I have managed this book without the men in my life? So, thank you Peter, a non-fish lover, and Alan for 'living fish' with me for the last year.

Sara Paston-Williams

MARINE CONSERVATION SOCIETY TOP 20 SPECIES TO AVOID

This list is correct at the time of going to press. However, the list is updated on a regular basis. Please check the website, www.fishonline.org or their publication *The Good Fish Guide* **for the most recent information.**

Atlantic Cod (from over-fished stocks)
Species listed by World Conservation Union (IUCN). Some stocks close to collapse, e.g. North Sea. *Alternatively try: Line-caught fish from Icelandic waters*

Atlantic Salmon Wild stocks reduced by 50% in last 20 years. *Alternatively try: Wild Pacific salmon or responsibly and/or organically farmed Atlantic salmon*

Chilean Seabass (Patagonian Toothfish)
Species threatened with extinction by illegal fishing. Also high levels of seabird by-catch

Dogfish/Spurdog Species listed by IUCN

European Hake Species heavily over-fished and now scarce. *Alternatively try: South African hake*

European Sea Bass Trawl fisheries target pre-spawning & spawning fish. Also high levels of cetacean by-catch. *Alternatively try: Line-caught or farmed fish*

Grouper Many species are listed by IUCN

Haddock (from over-fished stocks) Species listed by IUCN. *Alternatively try: Line-caught from Icelandic & Faroese waters*

North Atlantic Halibut Species listed by IUCN *Alternatively try: Line caught Pacific species. Halibut also farmed*

Ling Deep-water species and habitat vulnerable to impacts of exploitation and trawling

Marlin Many species are listed by IUCN

Monkfish Long-lived species vulnerable to exploitation. Mature females extremely rare

Orange Roughy Very long-lived species vulnerable to exploitation

Shark Long-lived species vulnerable to exploitation

Skates and Rays Long-lived species vulnerable to exploitation

Snapper Some species listed by IUCN, others over-exploited locally

Sturgeon Long-lived species vulnerable to exploitation. 5 of the 6 Caspian Sea species listed by IUCN

Swordfish Species listed by IUCN

Tuna All commercially-fished species listed by IUCN except skipjack and yellowfin which is over-fished

Warm-water or tropical prawns High by-catch levels and habitat destruction

25 SPECIES TO EAT WITH A CLEARER CONSCIENCE

Bream (black or sea bream) No assessment of stocks but no evidence that fishery in the Channel is unsustainable. *Precautions: Avoid eating immature fish less than at least 20cms and during the spawning season of April to May*

Brill No specific information available but, like turbot, remains a relatively scarce species in many areas. *Precautions: Avoid eating immature fish and during spawning season in spring and summer*

Brown Crab Although some stocks are over-fished, the method of capture – potting – is selective and restrictive licensing is proposed to improve management in coastal waters. *Precautions: Avoid eating egg-bearing or 'berried' females and undersized crabs*

Catfish (Wolfish) No information available on stock status as species not assessed. However it is a slow- growing fish and would be easily affected by over-fishing. *Precautions: Avoid eating immature fish and during the spawning season in winter*

Clam Stocks vulnerable to local over-exploitation. *Precautions: Only eat clams harvested by traditional methods, i.e. tongs, rakes or hand-picking*

Cockle Stocks vulnerable to local over-exploitation. *Precautions: Choose cockles harvested legally using sustainable methods (such as hand-gathering) only. Avoid eating cockles gathered during the breeding season of May to August*

Coley (Staithe) Stocks in North Sea and waters west of Scotland are within safe biological limits. *Precautions: To avoid issues associated with trawl fisheries, i.e. discarding , by-catch etc. , eat only line-caught fish above the length at which it matures, i.e. 40-50cm*

Dab Caught mainly in trawls and Danish seines. Because species has no commercial value, many are likely to be discarded. *Precautions: Avoid eating immature fish and during spawning season in spring and early summer*

Dover sole Eastern Channel and Irish Sea stocks within safe biological limits. *Precautions: Avoid eating immature fish and during the spawning season in spring and early summer*

Flounder Not an important food fish. No information available on stock status. *Precautions: Avoid eating immature fish and during the spawning season in spring*

Gurnard Species characterised by fast growth rate and early sexual maturity at a large size *Precautions: Avoid eating immature fish and during spawning season in summer*

Herring Stock rebuilt after collapse in 1970s to sustainable levels. *Precautions: Be aware that depending upon fishing method some fisheries*

are associated with by-catch of marine mammals

Langoustine Langoustine stocks are mostly inside safe biological limits e.g. North Sea. *Precautions: Increase the sustainability of the fish you eat by choosing pot- or creel-caught langoustines rather than trawl caught*

Lemon Sole No information available on stock size although no evidence of over-fishing. *Precautions: Avoid eating fish caught by beam-trawlers which damage seabed and fish with smaller mesh sizes*

Lobster Although some stocks are over-fished the method of capture – potting – is selective and restrictive licensing is proposed to improve management in coastal waters. *Precautions: Avoid eating egg-bearing or 'berried' females and undersized lobsters.*

Mackerel Handline fishery in South West England certified by Marine Stewardship Council as an environmentally responsible fishery. *Precautions: Avoid eating immature fish and during spawning season March to July. Only eat line-caught fish*

Megrim Although a common flat fish, only the Western stock is assessed and this is considered to be within safe biological limits but harvested at high levels. *Precautions: Avoid eating immature fish and during spawning season January to April*

Mussel Mussel cultivation is widespread and regarded as a low-impact method of mariculture. *Precautions: Avoid mussels that have been dredged*

Oyster Oyster cultivation is widespread and regarded as a low-impact method of mariculture. *Precautions: Avoid oysters that have been dredged*

Pollack No information available on stock status as species not assessed. *Precautions: Avoid eating immature fish and during spawning season January to April*

Routing No information available on stock status as species not assessed. *Precautions: Avoid eating immature fish and during spawning season March to April*

Red Mullet No information available on stock status as species not assessed. *Precautions: Avoid eating immature fish and during spawning season in summer*

Scallop Scallop cultivation is widespread and regarded as a low-impact method of mariculture. *Precautions: Avoid scallops that have been dredged. Choose dive-caught or cultivated ones only*

Turbot No information available on stock status. It is a highly valuable food fish and demand is high. *Precautions: Avoid eating immature fish and during spawning season in spring and summer*

Witch No information available on stock status. *Precautions: Avoid eating immature fish and during spawning season in summer*

HOW TO CHOOSE ECO-FRIENDLY FISH

1   If possible, buy from a responsible and knowledgeable fishmonger. Quiz him/her about the stock. Ask for as local a catch as possible to support local fisheries and ask how it was caught.

2   If you shop in your local supermarket, buy from the fresh fish counter, if it has one, and avoid the pre-packed fish on the shelves. The more environmentally friendly and sustainable fish is sold here, because it tends to be more expensive and we 'buy with our eyes, not according to price' from the fresh fish counter. If we buy more of this fish, the chances are the supermarket will not stock so much of the pre-packed.

3   Avoid the top 20 species listed by the Marine Conservation Society (MCS), the UK's national charity set up in 1983, dedicated to the protection of the marine environment and its wildlife (see p.235). The Society is regularly consulted by the government for its views on a range of marine issues, including fisheries. Its former Fisheries Officer, Bernadette Clarke, has produced the highly acclaimed *Good Fish Guide*.

4   Widen your taste in fish to take the pressure off the most popular species – cod, haddock, plaice, salmon and prawns – and to encourage fishermen to diversify. The MCS lists 25 species to eat with a clearer conscience (see opposite).

5   Look out for eco-labels, or labels of sustainability. Probably the best known is the 'blue tick' of the Marine Stewardship Council (MSC) which features on some packaged products sourced from fisheries certified by the Council. The MSC is a global non-profit-making body founded in 1996 to promote sustainable fishing practices. Their programme is gathering momentum with over 150 product lines worldwide and over 70 in Europe. DEFRA has plans to fund more UK fisheries to become accredited and if more customers ask for the 'blue tick', more suppliers will try to buy it.

6   Do not buy juvenile fish. Always choose large specimens which have had the chance to breed. Avoid eating whitebait – yes, I know it's delicious and I miss it too – because it is the fry (the young) of oily fish, like herrings.

7   Ask for 'line-caught' fish, which generally means long-line caught (rod and line is probably the most eco-friendly, but rare these days). This method of capture is more selective and causes less damage to the seabed and fish stocks. Again, there are degrees of responsibility: long-line fishing can kill seabirds (the albatross is facing extinction partly because of this – birds dive for the bait and get hooked and drown). If you want to be really caring, try and find out whether the lines are weighted, which means they sink faster than the seabirds can swoop.

8   Always buy shellfish from managed fisheries harvested by licensed fishermen. Illegal harvesting causes huge problems both environmental and social.

9   Only buy cod and haddock from the Iceland/Norway belt where the stock levels are currently good and management is considered to be sustainable. After the cod wars of the 1970s Iceland hung on to its fishing waters and has a 200-mile exclusion zone where no one else is allowed to fish. It is generally accepted to be a good fishery. As a rule, if your cod and haddock have been processed through Hull or Grimsby (as has 90 per cent of the fish for fish and chip shops), it is pretty certain to be from the tightly protected fisheries of Iceland, Norway and the Faroes. This is the sort of information a good fishmonger or his supplier will know. A new 'Ocean Wild' assurance mark will be appearing in more supermarkets and fishmongers denoting fillets of cod and haddock frozen at sea off Iceland and the Barents Sea.

10   Do not buy wild Atlantic salmon, which are threatened with virtual extinction because of over-fishing. Ask for Pacific salmon, which are widely available, especially those from the Marine Stewardship Council-certified Alaskan fishery. When buying farmed salmon, choose organic, or at least look for responsibly farmed. Scottish Quality Salmon is dedicated to improving the quality and sustainability of farmed salmon and now represents two-thirds of the Scottish industry. Look for their Tartan Quality Mark in the UK. Every salmon carrying this mark can be traced back to source through a unique number printed on the gill tag on a whole fish, or labels on pre-packed fresh portions. Also look out for the RSPCA's blue Freedom Food welfare mark, the first ever in aquaculture, awarded to salmon produced by Loch Duart Ltd, a small Scottish company who worked closely with the RSPCA for three years to develop the Society's new salmon standards.

HOW TO CHOOSE FRESH FISH

Once you have chosen your eco-friendly fish, it is absolutely vital to be able to judge whether it is fresh or not. I follow the advice of Chris Leftwich, the Chief Inspector to the Worshipful Company of Fishmongers, who has been in charge of quality control at London's Billingsgate Fish Market for over 16 years. The market runs training courses on fish cookery, preparation, handling, quality and recognition.

Smell
Don't be afraid to use your nose. Smell the gills of a whole fish, or smell the flesh of fillets. Really fresh fish may smell slightly of the sea, but it should be that lovely sea-salty tang that hits you when you stand on the seashore. Stale fish have a strong unpleasant fishy smell.

Appearance
Skin should have a bright, glossy sheen with bright colours. Stale fish loses it colour and becomes dull. Its scales become dry and dull-looking and are easily detached from the skin (don't confuse this with fish, such as herrings and pilchards, whose scales naturally come away from the skin quite easily). Any slime on stale fish is cloudy, and thick, whereas on fresh fish that are naturally more slimy than others, such as skate and lemon sole, it will be reflective, not opaque.

Gills should be a nice bright red colour. As the fish goes off they will change to a dark red, then brown or purple and be covered in thick, yellowish slime.

Eyes should be bright and clear with black pupils. The eyes of poor-quality fish will be dull, cloudy and sunk into their sockets. Discolouration will have taken place. (Beware, however, the herring family whose eyes are often blood-red even when fresh.)

Flesh should be firm and elastic to the touch. The flesh of white fish should be white and not discoloured. Stale fish will be soft or flabby and will pit easily under gentle pressure with the fingers. Once again, be careful when examining hake or whiting whose flesh is naturally soft – rely on your nose instead.

Insides If the fish are whole, but have been gutted, the inside of the belly feels sticky when it is not fresh and eventually will feel quite gritty. Any retained blood will be badly discoloured and the flesh along the backbone will be pink or red.

THE SOUTH WEST

The very beauty of the rugged coastlines of Cornwall and Devon made them vulnerable to unsightly development as the tourist industry got underway in the late 19th century. The prime example of this in Cornwall was Tintagel, where the attraction of a healthy family holiday and strong connections with King Arthur proved a heady combination. To save Tintagel from becoming a large seaside resort, the headland of Barras Head was bought by public subscription and given to the National Trust in 1897, the first English coastal property to be provided such protection. Over the hundred years since, the Trust's coastal holdings have grown spectacularly. In Cornwall the National Trust currently owns 161 miles of coast, in Devon 111, and it also looks after parts of the coast of Somerset and Dorset, as well as the islands of St Michael's Mount, Lundy and Brownsea, and the Isle of Purbeck, which isn't an island at all. There are simply too many places to mention here, but they will emerge in the recipes in this chapter.

Until the 19th century, the South-West, particularly Cornwall, was remote and inaccessible. The standard of living was amongst the lowest in the United Kingdom, with fish representing an unusually important staple of the diet. In small ports all the way around the coastline, families relied for their fortunes on the skill and perseverance of their fishermen. Long hours, wild weather and treacherous seas were accepted as occupational hazards, for 'no dole, no fish, no money'. The history of Cornish fishing is distinctive for the overwhelming importance of one type of fish – the pilchard – which was caught by seine-netting, a method originally unique to Cornwall and parts of Devon.

Given that the South-West is a peninsula, it comes as no surprise that its fishing industry is currently worth £165 million per annum, accounting directly for nearly 2,000 jobs and around the same number in indirect employment. Newlyn, in Cornwall, is the biggest fishing port in England, bringing in about £19 million of fish a year. Sadly, 80-90 per cent of this catch is then exported to mainland Europe, resulting in an enormous loss in revenue to local producers. The Devon ports of Brixham and Plymouth are the next largest ports, while the fish market at Looe in Cornwall has the first electronic auction system offering full traceability.

The fishing is one of the most diverse in Europe, from small inshore punts to beam trawlers, catching over 60 different species. Rather than relentlessly pursuing just one or two species, the cause of so many difficulties in the North Sea, local fishermen are able to switch according to abundance or season. This can also be frustrating, for when the quota for one species is taken up, inevitably the banned fish is also caught, leaving little choice but to throw it back, dead, into the sea. However, less than half of the total fish landed is of quota species, the rest being 'non pressure stocks', like brown crab, line-caught coley or saithe, and cuttle-fish, now providing vital earnings to both fishermen and merchants at Brixham and Plymouth each winter and spring.

The rising temperature of the waters around the South-West Peninsula is thought to be caused by global warming. Traditional species such as mackerel do not thrive in this temperature, so Cornish fish smokers have to source their mackerel from the colder waters around the Shetlands and Norway where the fish grow bigger. But more unusual species are beginning to appear, such as blue-fin tuna. A Newlyn fish-seller has recently been given a grant to increase tuna-fishing. At the moment, two 350kg (700lb) fish worth around £1,000 are landed per trip, but it is hoped that in a few years there may be two or three boats, involved in sustainable fishing as the blue-fin tuna is on the endangered list.

Over the past few years, the South West's Sea Fisheries Committees have set up numerous initiatives to create new shellfish areas in the estuaries all around the coast, so providing re-employment for their members. But these developments are not always popular with visitors and pleasure boat owners: the dilemma facing the people of Tintagel back in the 19th century is with us still. For example, the idyllic Cornish village of Helford, huddled on the southern shore of the River Fal, a popular venue for sailing, still has eighteen small working boats potting for crabs and lobsters, and they need a new landing quay. And again the National Trust is involved – not this time as the solution, but as a stakeholder, because the organisation holds a covenant over the land involved.

Previous pages: St Michael's Mount, Cornwall
Left: Newlyn fisherman, a photograph taken in 1906

GRIDDLED SEA BASS WITH GINGER AND PURPLE SPROUTING BROCCOLI
(serves 4)

There is an active small sustainable fishery at Beesands in Start Bay, South Devon, where the National Trust has recently acquired land at Tinsey Head. This consists of 2 cliff-top farms which act as a dramatic background to the beach, where the small fishing boats are hauled. All the catch is taken by the fishmonger in the village – mainly bass and flatfish netted from nearby Skerry's Bank, a shallow shingle bank at Start Point.

In this recipe sea bass is combined with purple sprouting broccoli which is grown all over the South-West in early spring, and is so much more delicious than calabrese. Red mullet or trout could also be used.

4 responsibly netted, line-caught or
responsibly farmed sea bass, about
280g (10oz) each, cleaned and scaled
2 teaspoons fresh ginger, finely chopped
2 tablespoons dark soy sauce
2 tablespoons sesame oil
2 tablespoons sunflower oil
2 tablespoons rice wine vinegar
1 teaspoon chilli sauce
sea salt and freshly ground black pepper
olive oil for brushing
about 16 stalks of purple sprouting
broccoli
1 unwaxed lemon, cut into 4 wedges

Put the ginger, soy sauce, sesame and sunflower oils, wine vinegar and chilli sauce into a screw-topped jar. Season and shake vigorously. Set aside.

To cook the fish, cut 3 diagonal slashes across the thick part of both sides. Brush with olive oil and season. Heat a griddle or frying pan and brush with a little olive oil. Cook the fish for about 5 minutes, then turn over and cook for another 5 minutes. Meanwhile, steam the broccoli or boil for 5 minutes until tender.

To serve, divide the broccoli between 4 warmed plates and top with the fish. Drizzle with the dressing and accompany with lemon wedges.

CRAB AND SAFFRON BREAD AND BUTTER PUDDING
(serves 4)

In East Devon, the National Trust protects 3 miles of magnificent coast between Salcombe Hill and Branscombe, part of the land designated by the Countryside Commission as the East Devon Heritage Coast. In Branscombe village itself, the National Trust owns several cottages, the last thatched working forge in England and a recently restored water-powered mill that probably supplied the flour for the old thatched bakery, also owned by the Trust. Until 1987 this was the last traditional working bakery in Devon and I remember it well – the bread was wonderful and it was fascinating to watch it being baked in the wood-fired oven. The old baking equipment has been preserved in the baking room while the rest of the building now serves as a tea-room. The National Trust also owns a working brewery in the village that is not open to the public, but helps support the local economy.

Branscombe has one full-time fisherman left, John Hughes, who has just one boat in which he takes people fishing for mackerel and bass. He pots for crabs, then sells them freshly boiled from his cottage above the beach.

You will need the meat from one medium brown or edible crab for this recipe, which celebrates both the crab and bread of Branscombe. It is best prepared at least 2 hours before cooking. As a guide, a 1.35kg (3lb) brown crab will yield about 450g (1lb) meat. Mussels, prawns or soft herring roes could be used instead.

about 225g (8oz) crab meat, separated
into white and dark
8 slices of day-old bread
about 200g (7oz) butter
sea salt, black pepper and cayenne pepper
3 large free-range eggs
good pinch saffron strands, soaked in 1
tablespoon hot water for 30 minutes
300ml (½ pt) whole milk
60ml (2fl oz) double cream
a pinch ground ginger
1 tablespoon fresh chives, finely chopped

Butter an ovenproof serving dish lightly, then butter the slices of bread generously. Season the 2 types of crab meat with salt, black pepper and cayenne, then spread 4 slices of bread with the dark crab meat. Top with the white crab meat and make into sandwiches. Cut each into 4 triangles and arrange in the dish. Beat together the eggs, saffron and water, milk, cream, ginger and chives. Season to taste.

Pour carefully over the bread in the dish – the liquid should just cover it. Add more milk if it doesn't.

Leave to stand for at least 1 hour, preferably longer, then place in a roasting tin filled with enough hot water to be level with the top of the custard. Bake in a pre-heated oven at 150°C/300°F/GM2 for about 1½ hours, or until the top is crisp and golden, but the custard is still creamy and slightly wobbly.

Rest for about 20 minutes before serving with a crisp, green salad.

Right: Crab and Saffron Bread and Butter Pudding

SAFFRON

Saffron is the most expensive and highly prized spice in the world – 150,000 flowers are needed to produce 1 kilo of saffron. It is the deep red-orange stamen of the purple crocus, 3 of which are removed from the centre of each flower by hand and dried over charcoal fires. The word saffron comes from the Arabic 'zafaran', meaning yellow, and over the last few years the spice has become very fashionable.

Today saffron is grown commercially in Spain, Morocco, Iran and India, although at one time it was grown in Britain, hence Saffron Walden in Essex, where it formed part of a triple rotation of crops with teasel and coriander. It is still widely used by bakers in Cornwall where, according to legend, saffron was introduced by the Phoenicians who landed on the Cornish coast in search of tin. Little historical evidence supports this theory, but culinary history is surely enlivened by such myths! There is no reason why you can't grow your own supply of genuine saffron, and all for the price of the crocus corms. C.sativus prefers a warm, sunny situation in dry sandy soil, but is ideal for planting in containers and window boxes.

Saffron is sold in stamen or powdered form, but in Cornwall we prefer the stamens, which have more flavour and look more attractive in recipes.

CORNISH CRAB PASTIES
(serves 6)

Fish pasties have been made by generations of West Country fishermen's wives, usually from herrings, small mackerel or pilchards. Crab was not often put into pasties, but special crab and lobster pies were served to shareholders in the Cornish mines on Accounting Day. The main room of the mine's counting house would be cleared and a feast was prepared by the wives of the clerks and officials. Starry-gazey (see box below) and conger-eel pies were served alongside the shellfish pies as well as joints of beef and mutton.

Cornwall's oldest working beam engine, used for pumping water from underground and for winching men and ore, has been restored by the National Trust and is steaming again after 60 idle years. In its tiny house perched dramatically on the cliff edge near St Just, the famous Levant engine conjures up those days when the tin and copper mining industry dominated Cornish life. Half a mile along the cliff is Geevor Mine, which closed in 1991, now a fascinating museum.

Crab pasties are rich and delicious and wonderful for picnics. Use the meat from the brown crab or the spider crab, which is plentiful in Cornwall, but mostly disappears to France where it is particularly popular. Known locally as Granfer Jenkin, the spider crab emerges from winter retirement in May. It can be used in any crab recipe and is very sweet and fragrant although you get less meat per crab as the claws are smaller. Many stocks of the brown or edible are now over-fished and smaller crabs, just above the minimum sizes, now dominate the landings. Don't ever buy or eat 'berried' or egg-bearing females, as their sale is illegal and damages stock.

For the pastry
> 350g (12oz) plain flour
> ¹/₂ teaspoon salt
> 175g (6oz) unsalted butter, diced
> 1 free-range egg, beaten, for glazing

For the filling
> 50g (2oz) unsalted butter
> 4 spring onions, finely chopped
> 100g (3¹/₂ oz) any firm white fish fillet, finely chopped
> 200g (7oz) mixed white and dark crabmeat
> grated rind and juice of 1 unwaxed lime
> 1 tablespoon fresh parsley, finely chopped
> ¹/₂ teaspoon fresh thyme, finely chopped
> a pinch of cayenne pepper
> sea salt and freshly ground black pepper

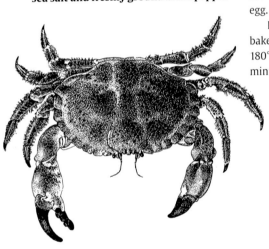

Sieve the flour and salt into a mixing bowl and rub in the butter until the mixture resembles fine breadcrumbs. Add enough cold water to form a soft dough, then knead lightly. Wrap in clingfilm and chill for about 30 minutes.

Pre-heat the oven to 200°C/400°F/GM6 and grease a baking sheet.

To prepare the filling, fry the spring onions in the butter until soft, then mix with all the other ingredients. Season to taste.

Roll out the chilled pastry to about 2.5mm (¹/₈ in) thick, then, using a 15 cm (6in) plate, cut out 6 circles. Pile 1¹/₂ tablespoons of the filling in the middle of each. Brush the rims of pastry with beaten egg, then bring the edges together over the filling. Firmly pinch together and crimp the edges to form a scalloped crest. Make 2 small holes to allow the steam to escape and brush with beaten egg.

Place on the prepared baking sheet and bake for 20 minutes. Reduce the heat to 180°C/350°F/GM4 and bake for a further 20 minutes until golden brown. Serve hot or cold.

TOM BAWCOCK'S STARRYGAZEY PIE
The only true survivor of this pie is made in Mousehole, near Penzance. The story goes that 200 years ago there had been a spell of very bad weather when the boats had been unable to put to sea. The people of Mousehole were starving. At last, a local fisherman, Tom Bawcock, chanced the weather and took his boat out, returning with a catch of 7 kinds of fish. This miracle is celebrated each year on 23 December when a huge fish pie is made with the heads sticking out of the pastry, and shared out in the local pub with much drinking and singing.

The legend may have evolved from an older feast traditionally held during the third week of December by fishermen, with the different kinds of fish representing hopes of plentiful and varied catches in the year ahead.

Left: Engine houses of the Botallack Mine near St Just, Cornwall
Right: Dolly Pentreath's House in Mousehole, Cornwall, an early 20th-century photograph. Dolly, a fishwife who hawked from village to village, was the last native Cornish speaker

PLYMOUTH JOHN DORY WITH CIDER, APPLES AND CREAM
(serves 4)

Plymouth Sound in South Devon has been designated a Special Area of Conservation as well as a Special Protection Area because of its marine and bird life. The area involved runs from the Yealm Estuary, where the National Trust owns land, including Wembury Beach where the Devon Wildlife Trust runs a Marine Conservation Centre, across to Rame Head in south-east Cornwall. Any fishing that takes place within this area has to be sustainable and environmentally friendly.

Plymouth was one of the old sail-trawler ports with fishing grounds around the Eddystone Lighthouse. Smacks went up to 40 miles out for catches of hake, conger, dory, halibut, sole, turbot, red mullet, brill and skate. In the 1870s, Plymouth smacks worked in Mount's Bay in Cornwall, landing catches at Newlyn for the last Penzance to Paddington train at 3.50pm. The Great Western Railway rates were 60 shillings per ton for cod or mackerel and 45 shillings for herring.

Today Plymouth still has an active fishery landing catches on the Barbican Quay including John Dory, which is known as 'Plymouth's proudest fish'. Although it's a valuable species, John Dory is generally taken as a by-catch in trawls, so it is not landed in large quantities. Unfortunately, immature fish can be caught in the nets, so select larger John Dory at the fishmongers. It is indeed an excellent, firm-fleshed fish, responding well to simple cooking such as grilling and frying. Catfish bass, gurnard, or sole may be used instead.

4 medium or large John Dory fillets, skinned
40g (1½oz) flour, seasoned with sea salt and freshly ground black pepper
about 80g (3oz) clarified butter
2 Cox's apples, peeled and cut into 8 wedges
caster sugar for sprinkling
1 tablespoon fresh fennel, chopped
1 tablespoon fresh tarragon, chopped
1 tablespoon fresh parsley, chopped
1 tablespoon lemon juice
150ml (¼pt) dry cider or white wine
sea salt and freshly ground black pepper
2 tablespoons clotted cream

Coat the fish fillets with seasoned flour, patting to remove excess.

In a heavy frying pan, melt 25g (1oz) of the butter. Once bubbling, fry the apple quickly for a minute or two until golden brown on both sides. Sprinkle with a little caster sugar and baste with the butter to give a slightly caramelised finish. Remove and keep warm in a low oven. Wipe out the pan, then heat the remaining butter until foaming. Add the fish, skinned side down. Fry over brisk heat for 2-3 minutes until golden brown, then flip over and cook the other side for about 1 minute. Remove the fish and place on 4 warm serving dishes. Add the herbs, lemon juice and cider to the pan and bring to the boil. Simmer for a few minutes. Adjust the seasoning if necessary, then stir in the cream. Cook for another minute until the sauce is smooth, then pour over the waiting fish. Garnish each plate with the fried apple wedges and serve at once.

POTATO PANCAKES WITH TAMAR SMOKED EEL, CRISP BACON AND HORSERADISH
(serves 4 as a starter for lunch)

Based in the historic Georgian port of Charlestown on the south coast of Cornwall, Martin and Sarah Pumphrey have been smoking fish to a very high standard for 30 years. One of their specialities is hot-smoked eel, mostly from the River Tamar Estuary, caught by Alan Jewett, who lives an idyllic lifestyle on his houseboat between Saltash and Cotehele. Alan believes in sustainable fishing and although he is inundated with requests for elver (baby eels), he will not supply them.

Mature, or silver, eels are best for smoking. Plump and juicy with a rich succulent flesh, the eel turns silver in autumn as it is ready to starts its extraordinary, exhausting journey downstream to its breeding grounds in the faraway Sargasso Sea.

Please don't be put off by the thought of eating eel – smoked eel is the most delicious of all smoked fish and is beginning to replace salmon as a gourmand's treat.

225g (8oz) smoked eel fillets, skinned
6 very thin rashers, oak-smoked streaky bacon

For the potato pancakes
450g (1lb) floury potatoes, peeled and cut into large chunks
50ml (2fl oz) full-fat milk
2 heaped tablespoons potato flour, or ordinary flour
3 free-range whole eggs
4 free-range egg whites
2½ tablespoons double cream
sea salt and freshly ground black pepper
a little clarified unsalted butter for frying

For the horseradish cream
150ml (5fl oz) double or sour cream or crème fraîche
about 10cm (4in) piece of fresh horseradish root, or use preserved grated horseradish to taste
squeeze of lemon juice
sea salt
fresh chives, finely chopped

Steam the potatoes until tender, then mash in a bowl. Whisk in the milk, flour, eggs, egg whites and cream, and season to taste. To cook the pancakes, heat a little clarified butter in a non-stick frying pan. Add 1 tablespoon of batter and, keeping the heat moderate to high, fry for about 2 minutes, until it begins to bubble and brown at the edges, then turn over with a palette knife. The cooked surface should be mottled with pale brown blisters and have a thin golden ring around the edge. Finish cooking for a further 1 or 2 minutes, then transfer to a large warm plate and keep warm in a very low oven uncovered, while you make the rest. (If your pan is big enough, fry several at a time.)

Grill the bacon until very crisp.

For the horseradish cream, finely grate horseradish root into a bowl. Whip the cream, then stir in the horseradish a teaspoon at a time, tasting as you go, until it is right for you – there is no going back! Stir in lemon juice and salt to taste.

To serve, allow 3 pancakes per person. Cut the eel into 12 pieces and arrange on the pancakes. Top with half a bacon rasher and a dollop of horseradish cream. Sprinkle with chives.

NB: If you don't want to make your own horseradish cream, buy a good-quality jar.

OLD HARRY'S FISH CRUMBLE
(serves 4-6)

Old Harry and Old Harry's Wife are a set of eroding chalk rocks once part of the main cliff face at Ballard Down in Studland, Dorset. Old Harry himself was a notorious pirate who tricked ships into sailing onto the rocks surrounding those named after him. The rocks stand in a prominent position at one end of Studland Bay at the start of the Dorset Jurassic Coast World Heritage Site and on the South West Coastal Path. This is an area of outstanding natural beauty, part of the 37,000-hectare (90,000-acre) Purbeck and Corfe Castle Estates owned by the National Trust. The heathland behind Studland Beach is a National Nature Reserve of particular interest in winter because of its variety of over-wintering birds. The whole area is very popular even on a grey day.

There are plenty of anglers fishing off National Trust land here, but few commercial fishermen – they work out of Swanage and Poole, except in the winter, when some have moorings at Studland where there is more protection from the weather. The fishermen net for bass in the winter, catch plaice, flounders and grey mullet and pot for lobsters, brown crabs and spider crabs (the latter are sent straight off to France). The local National Trust warden remembers collecting buckets of mackerel from the beach where they had leapt out of the water to escape a predator – the shoals were so huge – but today there are few, although further west at Chesil Beach there are plenty.

This homely fish crumble using locally smoked haddock was invented by Neil Godfrey, a previous manager, and Peter Yeates, the chef, for visitors to the National Trust's Knoll Beach Café, where it is a favourite.

750g (1lb 10oz) undyed smoked, line-caught haddock or cod from Icelandic or Faroese waters
600ml (1pt) full-cream milk
90g (3oz) butter
60g (2oz) self-raising flour
100g (3½oz) mature Cheddar, grated
25g (1oz) fresh parsley, finely chopped
4-6 free-range eggs, hard boiled for 8 minutes and sliced
sea salt and freshly ground black pepper

For the crumble
200g (7oz) self-raising flour
100g (3½oz) butter, chilled and diced
sea salt and freshly ground black pepper
200g (7oz) mature Cheddar, finely grated

Poach the fish in the milk for about 5 minutes until tender. Drain the fish reserving the liquor for the sauce. Remove all the skin and bones and flake into large chunks.

Melt the butter in a pan, then stir in the flour. Cook for a few minutes without browning, then slowly stir in the reserved cooking liquor. Bring slowly to the boil stirring all the time, to make a thick white sauce. Reduce the heat and add the cheese and parsley. Season to taste, then simmer gently for a few minutes. Arrange the fish in a deep ovenproof dish and pour over three-quarters of the sauce. Cover with the slices of hard-boiled eggs and pour over the remaining sauce.

Pre-heat the oven to 210°C/425°F/GM7.

To make the crumble, sieve the flour into a bowl. Rub in the butter with your fingertips, then mix in the grated cheese. Season with salt and pepper, then sprinkle over the top of the fish, making sure all the sauce is covered.

Bake for 25-30 minutes or until the crumble is golden and the dish is piping hot.

Serve with warm crusty bread and fresh garden peas.

Left: Old Harry Rocks on the Corfe Castle Estate, Dorset
Above: The ruins of the Norman fortifications of Corfe Castle, dominating the ridge that runs across the Isle of Purbeck

ST MICHAEL'S MOUNT SEAFOOD PANCAKES
(makes about 12)

Much of the history of St Michael's Mount is shrouded in legend, but we know for certain that a chapel was built here by Edward the Confessor in the 11th century as an offshoot of the Benedictine Abbey of Mont St Michel in Normandy. The castle dates from the 14th century with many subsequent additions. In the 15th century the causeway was built to Marazion on the mainland, and a harbour established with houses and fish cellars. Today about 30 people live permanently on the island, many working as ferrymen or 'hobblers'.

The castle is currently the Trust's fifth most visited property: 225,000 people climbed the Pilgrim's Steps in 2003, while three times as many visit the village and harbour. This is one of the most popular dishes served in the Sail Loft Restaurant on the island. Any combination of white fish and shellfish can be used; including a little smoked fish will improve the flavour.

For the pancakes
125g (4oz) plain flour
pinch of salt
1 egg
300ml (½ pt) milk, or milk and water
sunflower oil for frying

For the filling
125g (4½oz) crab meat, brown and white mixed
225g (8oz) white fish, cooked
125g (4½oz) prawns, shelled
125g (4½oz) mushrooms, chopped
1 tablespoon fresh chives, chopped
1 tablespoon fresh parsley, chopped
300ml (½ pt) velouté sauce (see p.220)
sea salt
cayenne pepper
2 tablespoons double cream
50g (1¾oz) Cheddar cheese, grated

Sieve the flour and salt together into a basin. Make a well in the centre and add the egg. Stir, then beat in the milk gradually until thick and smooth. Leave the batter to stand in a cool place for at least 30 minutes. Heat a little oil in a small frying-pan until it begins to smoke. Add 60ml (2fl oz) of batter and cook over a high heat for about 2 minutes until the pancake is lightly browned on the bottom and set firm. Turn over and brown the other side quickly. Slide on to a plate and continue in the same way with the rest of the batter. Stack the pancakes on top of each other between sheets of greaseproof paper or foil and keep warm.

Divide the crab meat, flaked white fish, prawns and mushrooms amongst the pancakes. Sprinkle with the herbs and top with a spoonful of sauce, reserving most of it for later. Season well and roll up neatly. Place the rolled pancakes in a lightly buttered ovenproof dish and heat through in a moderate oven (180°C/350°F/GM4) for about 20 minutes. Mix the remaining sauce with the cream and pour over the pancakes. Sprinkle with cheese and continue to bake in a slightly hotter oven (200°C/400°F/GM6) until the top is brown and bubbling. Serve immediately with a mixed salad.

THE FOX AND GOOSE STEAK AND SEAWEED PIE
(serves 6-8)

Set in the beautiful North Devon village of Parracombe, not far from National Trust-owned coastline between Woody Bay and Trentishoe, the Fox and Goose is getting quite a name for itself. Landlord Phil Reed-Evans is a great believer in local produce including fish, which he tries to buy from day-boats or local fishermen.

In 2002, he reached the semi-finals of the British Meat Steak Pie of the Year competition with his popular steak and seaweed pie. The seaweed is laver, which is always associated with Wales (p.154), but it is available all around the coast and is collected by locals from many beaches on the North Devon coast.

Here is Phil's award-winning recipe exactly as he sent it.

2kg (4½lb) best quality chuck steak, cut into 2.5cm (1in) chunks
2 or 3 tablespoons beef dripping
450g (1lb) ready prepared laver
1.2 litres (2 pts) home-made beef stock

For the pastry
225g (8oz) self-raising flour
110g (4oz) butter
4 teaspoons dried parsley or 3 tablespoons fresh, finely chopped
4 teaspoons fresh thyme
4 teaspoons fresh sage, chopped
225g (8oz) fresh mashed potato
1 beaten egg for glazing

Toss the meat in seasoned flour, then brown in the beef dripping in a large pan a little at a time. Add the seaweed and beef stock and bring to simmering point. Simmer gently for about 2 hours, or until the meat is tender.

Meanwhile make the pastry by rubbing the butter into the flour. Stir in the herbs, then knead in the mashed potato. Cover with clingfilm and chill for 20 minutes.

When the meat is cooked, transfer it to a large pie dish. Roll out the pastry and cover the meat. Decorate with scraps of pastry if you wish and make a small steam-hole in the centre. Glaze with beaten egg and bake in a pre-heated oven at 200°C/400°F/GM6 for about 30 minutes, until the pastry is golden brown.

PENBERTH MACKEREL AND SAMPHIRE STEW
(serves 4)

Penberth, near Land's End, is perhaps Cornwall's most delightful little fishing cove – a lively working place typical of the small fishing communities once common in the county, with mackerel and shellfish boats tightly moored against the waves that sweep up the slipways. The headland and cove with much of the valley behind were transferred to the National Trust in 1957. The scattered granite cottages are let to working families with businesses in the valley: daffodils and violets are grown for market in many of the small sheltered valley fields or 'quillets'. The fishermen go out in their small boats with hooks and lines to 'feather' for mackerel in the summer when the fish move inshore to feed on other small fish rather than plankton. They fish until September when the mackerel begin to disperse for their winter rest in the deep water.

This stew combines mackerel with other Cornish summer delights – new potatoes, fresh peas and samphire.

4 very fresh line-caught mackerel, filleted and cut into large chunks
400 ml (14fl oz) dry cider
600ml (1pt) fish stock (see p.222)
450g (1lb) new potatoes, scrubbed and cut into chunks
900g (2lbs) fresh peas in the pod
225g (8oz) samphire, untrimmed
8 spring onions, trimmed and cut into 5cm (2in) lengths
2 tablespoons fresh mint, chopped
3 sprigs fresh lemon thyme

For the aïoli
2 large garlic cloves, crushed with salt
a good pinch of saffron threads, pounded to a powder
1 large free-range egg yolk, beaten
150ml (5fl oz) olive oil
sea salt and freshly ground black pepper

Bring the cider to the boil in a large pan. Pour on the stock and bring back to the boil. Add the potato chunks and peas and simmer for 7 minutes. Add the spring onions, 1 tablespoon of the chopped mint and the leaves from one sprig of lemon thyme. Simmer for a further 2 minutes.

Wash and trim the samphire – only use the very tender little branches. (This quantity will give you about 150g [5½oz].) Add the samphire to the stew and bring back to the boil. Take off a ladle of the liquor and reserve. Slip the mackerel chunks into the stew and cook very gently for a further 2 minutes, then switch off the heat, cover and set the pan aside.

To make the aïoli, cream the garlic and saffron into the beaten egg yolk, then beat in the oil very gradually to make a thick emulsion. Add the remaining mint and the leaves from the two sprigs of thyme. Stir the reserved ladle of stew liquor slowly into the aïoli, then stir this into the mackerel stew itself.

Let the finished stew stand, covered, by the side of the stove for 5 minutes to let the flavours infuse, then check the seasoning.

Serve in soup plates with chunks of bread for an informal meal.

THE CORNISH MACKEREL FISHERY

Although mackerel is fished all around the coast of Cornwall, Newlyn near Penzance has always been the great centre – sometimes taking as much as half the total English catch. In the spring of 1838, over 120 boats, known locally as drivers, were engaged in the mackerel fishery at Newlyn, Mousehole and Porthleven. With the opening of the Cornwall railway a new and important market was developed for the spring catch. By 1884, the number of mackerel drivers had increased to nearly 400, employing 2,700 men. Newlyn became the local depot for this trade and the great fleet of drivers had permanent moorings off the shore before the harbour was built. Each vessel kept a 4-oared boat at these moorings to land the catches. The Mousehole mackerel drivers, on the other hand, liked 3-oared jolly boats to bring their fish ashore. Each of these was in the charge of a boy, 10-14 years old, who was known as a 'yawler'. While the season lasted, he was the absolute slave of the lugger who employed him.

The first 'up-country' trawlers began to frequent the western waters as far back as 1843, but the disastrous effects of trawl fishing were not fully appreciated until much later. Once the railways had come to Cornwall there was a vast increase in the number of visiting trawlers over the best mackerel grounds, day and night, from February to April, frequently fouling and cutting the nets of the local boats. The trawlers were followed by large steam drifters, and the fate of the famous Mount's Bay fleet of sailing drivers was sealed.

Mackerel taken in the spring were mostly consumed fresh; those caught in the autumn, of better quality due to their higher oil content, were salted in great numbers for winter use.

Fishing boats pulled up on the shore at Penberth, Cornwall

PORTHLEVEN SMOKED MACKEREL WITH RED CABBAGE (serves 6)

Porthleven, close to the National Trust's extensive Penrose Estate, means 'smooth harbour', which must surely have been an old Cornish joke, for it faces south west into Mount's Bay and the teeth of the prevailing wind. Even in a moderate sea, entering the harbour has always been difficult. The present harbour was finished in 1825 and by 1848 there were 63 boats engaged in the mackerel and pilchard fisheries. The Porthleven drifter fleet was one of the top three in Cornwall along with Newlyn and St Ives.

The village has grown out of all recognition, but the harbour area is still delightful and there is an active fishing fleet in the summer bringing in a variety of fish, including mackerel, which is smoked in the quayside smokehouse.

In this recipe the combination of smoked mackerel and red cabbage is excellent. The Cornish enjoy red cabbage, particularly when it is pickled.

> 6 fillets undyed smoked, line-caught mackerel
> 1 tablespoon sunflower oil
> 2 red onions, peeled and sliced
> 1 medium red cabbage, core removed and finely chopped
> 3 tablespoons red wine
> 1 firm English dessert apple, grated
> 2 tablespoons dark brown sugar
> sea salt and freshly ground black pepper
> 1 tablespoon fresh parsley, chopped

Heat the oil in a stainless steel or enamelled pan and sauté the onions for 2-3 minutes. Add the cabbage and stir-fry for 4-5 minutes until starting to wilt. Add the wine, apple and sugar and season well.

Cover the pan and cook over a low heat for 30-40 minutes until soft and amalgamated. Stir in the parsley.

Just before serving, grill the mackerel fillets for a few minutes until crisp and bubbling on the surface and hot right through. To serve, pile some red cabbage on each plate and top with a mackerel fillet.

CHARGRILLED WEYMOUTH RED MULLET WITH GARLIC AND ROSEMARY (serves 4)

In the 18th and 19th centuries, the Dorset port of Weymouth was renowned for its mullet, both red and grey. In fact, red mullet is the finer and belongs to quite another family. It is known as the 'woodcock of the sea', because like the woodcock, its liver was considered a delicacy and was left inside the fish after cleaning. The Duke of Portland and his aristocratic friends would travel from London to Weymouth especially to eat red mullet. The medium-sized fish were available for 3d or 4d each, but His Grace was known to pay 2 guineas for red mullet weighing 1½ lbs.

Today, red mullet is a fairly common fish in the South-West, particularly in October and November, although it is usually caught as a by-product of trawling for other fish, so only a few will turn up in the nets at a time.

It has a very good flavour if bought fresh rather than frozen, and can quite happily be partnered with other strong flavours like garlic and rosemary as here. Use red gurnard or grey mullet if you can't buy red mullet.

> 4 medium red mullet, gutted and scaled
> 1 large clove garlic, quartered lengthways
> about 1½ tablespoons fresh rosemary, roughly chopped
> 80ml (3fl oz) olive oil
> juice of 1 large lemon
> 2 medium garlic cloves, chopped
> sea salt and freshly ground black pepper
> 1 unwaxed lemon, quartered

Cut 2 diagonal slashes across the thickest part of each fish on both sides. Slip a quarter of a garlic clove and a little chopped rosemary into each fish. Place in a close-fitting dish. Mix together the olive oil, lemon juice, chopped garlic, and remaining rosemary. Season well, then pour over the fish. Leave to marinate for at least half an hour and up to 4 hours, turning occasionally.

Pre-heat the grill to high.

Take the fish out of the marinade and grill for about 5 minutes on each side, squeezing a lemon quarter over them.

Serve with extra lemon wedges.

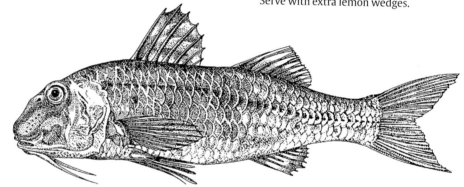

RIVERSIDE MUSSEL AND CRAB CHOWDER

I begged the Riverside Restaurant in the heart of the fishing village of West Bay near Bridport in Dorset to part with this recipe after enjoying it one cold February lunchtime, and the Head Chef, Chris Ansell, agreed. Now a well-known fish restaurant run by Arthur and Janet Watson, the building started life as a hot-water hut for local campers. Outside, it looks not unlike a large, smarter version of the fish and chip sheds lining the road, but inside it is full of fishy paintings and flooded with light from the surrounding water – a wonderfully informal place for a relaxing meal.

There is no commercial fishing off National Trust land around West Bay, but several local angling clubs hold competitions for mackerel and bass from Cogden Beach to the east where the dramatic Chesil Beach starts. To the west, the Trust owns 7½ miles of coastline to the Devon border including the highest cliff in southern England, Golden Cap. From here there are breathtaking views along the coast to Portland Bill.

900g (2lb) mussels, scrubbed and bearded
110g (4oz) white crab meat
50g (2oz) brown crab meat
50g (2oz) butter
½ small onion, finely chopped
1 clove garlic, finely chopped
½ glass dry white wine
sprig fresh thyme
4 rashers green streaky bacon, cut into lardons
olive oil
2 shallots, finely chopped
1 leek, finely chopped
1 waxy potato (Charlotte, Jerseys, Pink Fir Apple, Ratte or Nicola according to availability), peeled, diced and par-cooked
600ml (1pt) whole milk
150ml (5fl oz) double cream
sea salt and freshly ground black pepper
1 tablespoon fresh chives, chopped
420ml (14fl oz) dry cider
600ml (1pt) fish stock (see p.222)

In a pan with a tight-fitting lid, melt the butter and sweat the onion over a high heat until soft, but not coloured. Add the mussels, half the garlic, white wine and thyme, then place the lid on the pan and simmer for about 2 minutes until the mussels have opened. Discard any that remain firmly closed. Strain the mussels through a colander, reserving the liquor in a bowl. Put on one side until the mussels are cool enough to handle.

In a heavy-based pan, cook the bacon in a little olive oil until crispy, then add the shallots, leek and remaining garlic. Cook until soft, but not coloured, then add the potato. Add the reserved mussel liquor and bring to the boil. Add the milk and bring to the boil again, then turn down to a simmer.

Pick the mussels from their shells and add to the chowder together with the crab. Add the double cream, then season to taste with salt and pepper. (Be careful when adding salt because of the natural salt content in the seafood.)

Finally, add the chives, then reheat and serve with crusty bread.

SOUTH-WEST MACKEREL HANDLINE FISHERY

An area kown as the 'mackerel box' is located mainly within 8 nautical miles of the shore from Start Point in South Devon, all around the coast to Hartland Point in the north. The fishery was set up in 1981 to protect juvenile mackerel.

Fishing is by handline only (with hooks) One industrial trawler may take 1,800 tonnes of fish per week – as much as the entire South-West handline fleet removes in a year.

The main handline fishing season runs between September and April although there is a small summer fishery. Approximately 100 boats make up the fleet which comes from small coastal communities. Larger vessels land mainly in Newlyn, Falmouth, Looe, Mevagissey and Plymouth, while smaller boats work from coves and harbours all around the coast.

In July 2001 the fishery was certified by the Marine Stewardship Council as environmentally responsible because the fishing methods allow long-term stability of fish stocks, so look out for the MSC label when buying from supermarkets.

Above: Golden Cap, Dorset

BOSCASTLE BAKED MEGRIM WITH A MUSSEL, CIDER AND CLOTTED CREAM SAUCE
(serves 4)

From the end of the 18th century, Boscastle on the north coast of Cornwall grew in importance as the only harbour on the long length of the coast between Clovelly in North Devon and Padstow. The railway didn't reach here until 1893, so all heavy goods had to be carried by sea: coal, timber and manufactured goods were imported, with return cargoes of slate, china clay and manganese ore from a mine in the Valency Valley, which runs down to Boscastle Harbour. More than a dozen ketches and schooners traded regularly through the little port in the 19th century.

The tortuous harbour entrance, with the island of Meachard as an extra hazard, meant it was never safe for sailing vessels to enter Boscastle unassisted. They were towed or 'hobbled' in by the 'hobbler' boats manned by 8 oarsmen. Hauling goods up Boscastle's steep hills needed strong teams of horses, many of them kept at the Palace Stables, now the youth hostel, and there was constant work for the blacksmith in the forge, now the National Trust's shop and information centre.

The National Trust began to acquire land at Boscastle in 1955. It soon became apparent that the loss of the breakwater, blown up by a drifting sea mine in 1941, was causing damage to the quay and it would have to be replaced. In the winter of 1962, which turned out to be exceptionally cold and stormy, the Trust's building gang from Cotehele began the job, following it with the repair of the quays and slipways at the head of the harbour.

The trading role of the harbour had declined almost to nothing by the 1950s and with the breakwater in ruins, few fishermen would risk mooring their boats inside the jetty. Once the breakwater was rebuilt, fishing revived, since Boscastle is the nearest harbour to the rich shell-fishing grounds off Lundy. Today, there is a regular, if hazardous, fishery and the local fishermen's association runs the harbour in cooperation with the National Trust. Eighteen boats work out of Boscastle in the summer, potting for lobsters and crabs immediately offshore. The larger boats fish 3 or 4 miles out for mackerel, pollack, flat fish and bass, but no netting is carried out.

Just along the coast is the quaint fishing village of Port Isaac and its subsidiary harbours of Port Gaverne and Port Quin, which together had the largest pilchard fishery on the north coast of Cornwall apart from St Ives. The beach at Port Gaverne and two fish cellars where pilchards were cured, belong to the National Trust, as do a series of fish cellars at Port Quin, which have been converted into holiday cottages.

I have used megrim (grey sole) in this recipe because it is commonly caught off the South-West coast, and is of less commercial interest in the UK than other flat fish such as plaice. It has a good flavour and is well worth trying. Catfish would also be suitable.

2 x 175g (6oz) or 4 x 90g (3oz) megrim fillets, skinned
40 small fresh live mussels, scrubbed and bearded
100ml (3½ fl oz) dry farmhouse cider
60g (2oz) clotted cream
sea salt and freshly ground black pepper
1 tablespoon fresh chives, roughly chopped

Place the mussels in a large pan with a little of the cider. Cover with a lid and cook them over a high heat for about 3 minutes until they have opened, shaking them from time to time. Discard any mussels that have not opened, then tip them into a colander with a bowl underneath to catch the cooking liquor. Remove the meat from all the shells except 16, which should be left intact.

Pre-heat the oven to 180°C/350°F/GM4.

If you have bought large fillets, cut each in half lengthways, then arrange the fillets in a shallow buttered ovenproof dish. Strain the mussel cooking liquor through a sieve lined with 2 layers of muslin and pour a little over the fish. Cover with buttered paper and poach in the oven for about 5 minutes until just cooked through. Drain off the cooking liquor and keep the fish warm.

Pour the remainder of the mussel liquor into a small saucepan with the fish cooking liquor, cider and clotted cream. Bring to the boil, then reduce by rapid boiling until the sauce coats the back of a spoon. Add all the mussels (including the unshelled) and the chives. Warm through and season to taste.

Place the fish fillets on 4 warm serving plates. Pour the sauce over, dividing the mussels evenly. Serve immediately.

Left: Boscastle Harbour and Village, a photograph taken before the disastrous storms of August 2004
Right: Boscastle Baked Megrim with a Mussel, Cider and Clotted Cream Sauce

FAL ANGELS ON HORSEBACK
(serves 4)

The main River Fal oyster beds are found inside the Special Area of Conservation in the estuary, which stretches from St Antony Head, owned by the National Trust (a favourite place for anglers to catch black bream), to Manacles Point off The Lizard Peninsula. Only traditional fishing is allowed and the Restronguet Creek Oyster Dredgers, as they were once called, are the world's last oyster boats with only sails or oars. They work the oyster beds using triangular iron dredgers that are dragged along the bottom as the boat is allowed to drift. This might seem inefficient, but years ago the fishermen agreed not to use powered boats because they realised that stocks would last no other way. Indeed, in the Fal today the quality and quantity of the native oysters are as good as they have been for 50 years, despite being wiped out by the disease *bonamia* in the 1980s, probably brought over from Brittany where it was rife.

A working core of about 15 boats regularly dredges, and their distinctive brown sails are a magnificent sight. The Falmouth Oyster Festival takes place annually in October at the beginning of the new season when the fishing fleet can be viewed, tied up outside the National Maritime Museum Cornwall in Falmouth. Four days of fun and entertainment inspired by oysters and seafood with plenty of locally brewed ale, culminate in the Oyster Ball.

8 large Native or Pacific oysters, removed from the shell
4 rashers dry-cured streaky bacon, cut as thinly as possible
2 shallots, peeled and finely chopped
1 tablespoon fresh parsley, chopped
50g (1¾oz) butter
4 slices baguette about 1cm (½in) thick cut diagonally

Cut the rashers of bacon in half and, with the back of a wet knife on a chopping board, stretch the bacon as thinly as possible until almost transparent. Dry the oysters on kitchen paper, then wrap each one in a piece of bacon.

Heat a little sunflower oil in a heavy-bottomed frying pan and quickly fry the oysters on a high heat for a minute or so on each side. Remove from the pan and add the butter and shallots.

Fry on a low heat for a minute or so without colouring, then add the parsley. Remove from the heat.

Meanwhile, toast the bread on both sides, arrange 2 oysters on each and spoon the shallots and parsley over them. Serve immediately.

SPAGHETTI WITH CORNISH SALT PILCHARDS
(serves 4)

For hundreds of years it was Cornish salt pilchards rather than anchovies that provided the distinctive taste in the classic Italian dish *spaghetti alla puttanesca,* said to come from the Trastevere district of Rome. This version of the recipe comes from Nick Howell who runs British Cured Pilchards Ltd., sole producers and exporters of traditional Cornish salt pilchards. Seventy per cent of the output goes across the Channel to Italy and Spain.

Nick sources his fish from small local boats, fishing for a few hours in the evening between June and March. The fishermen use traditional drift and ring nets specifically designed not to catch other species and land the pilchards directly to the factory where they are immediately layered with salt in tanks.

Several weeks later, when they are cured, the fish are slowly pressed to extract the excess water and oil. The blocks of fish are then transferred to wooden boxes still bearing the stencilled trade marks that have been used for nearly a century.

You can of course use anchovy fillets instead, but there's nothing like the real thing.

400g (14oz) dried spaghetti or
   450g (1lb) fresh
450g (1lb) small cherry or
   vine-ripened tomatoes
3 tablespoons olive oil
50g (1¾oz) butter
3 garlic cloves, finely chopped
1 sprig fresh rosemary leaves,
   finely chopped
4 fresh sage leaves, finely shredded
1 small fresh red chilli,
   deseeded and finely chopped
1 tablespoon baby capers, drained
100g (3½oz) large, black olives,
   stoned and sliced
4 Cornish salt pilchard fillets,
   or 2 x 50g (2oz) cans of anchovy fillets
   in oil, drained and chopped
1 tablespoon fresh oregano, chopped
freshly ground black pepper
2 tablespoons fresh flat-leaf
   parsley, chopped

To make the sauce, squeeze the tomatoes to get rid of most of the juice, then cut in half. Heat the oil and butter in a pan with the garlic, rosemary and sage. Cook gently for about 1 minute without browning, then add the tomatoes, chilli, capers, olives, chopped pilchard or anchovy fillets and oregano. Season with black pepper, then simmer gently for 10 minutes, stirring frequently.

Cook the pasta in a large pan of boiling salt water until just tender or *al dente* (about 7 minutes for dried, 2-3 minutes for fresh). Drain well, then tip into a large warmed serving dish. Pour over the sauce, add the chopped parsley and toss together well until the sauce coats the spaghetti. Serve immediately with plenty of red wine.

THE FAIR-MAIDS OF CORNWALL

Of the many types of fish, one species holds a cherished place in Cornwall's maritime history, the pilchard, a mature sardine, and the same species as caught off Brittany, but unlike the canned South African pilchard.

Traditionally, the main shoals appear in mid-July starting south west of Land's End. Some move east up the English Channel, whilst others swim to the Celtic Sea between Cornwall and Ireland. The appearance of shoals has always been very erratic; they appear without warning and only briefly and might disappear for some years, as happened in the 1920s. It was the job of the 'huer' to keep watch from a cliff-top for the characteristic reddish stain that marked a shoal. He would let the waiting fishermen know by furiously waving a 'bush' – wooden hoops covered with white linen – in each of his hands.

The pilchard is a delicate fish that travels badly, so it had to be smoked, salted or, in more modern times, canned as soon as possible. Vast numbers of smoked pilchards were exported to Spain and called 'fumedos', Spanish for 'smoked'. The name corrupted to 'fair-maids' by the Cornish continued to be applied to salted, barrelled pilchards.

Until the early 20th century, almost every port along the Cornish coast had at least one salting cellar where the enormous catches of pilchards were salted down. Women and children sat for hours gutting, salting and packing the fish into barrels, before they were exported to Italy, Spain and France. Today, only one pilchard works remains, in Newlyn, a stone's throw from the harbour. The haul of pilchards has shrunk to a fraction of what it once was and the demand for salted pilchards has dwindled with it.

Left: St Anthony Head looking towards Falmouth, Cornwall
Right: Penzance 'jouster', 1890. Jousters were fish vendors who carried their load in a large basket strapped across the shoulder

NICK'S ORANGE AND SALT PILCHARD SALAD
(serves 2)

This recipe is from a mountain village near Sasso Marconi in Italy, which is twinned with Helston in Cornwall.

Take 1 large orange and peel carefully. Remove as much pith as you can, then divide into segments. Thinly slice 2 salt pilchard fillets. Mix with the orange segments, then add 1 teaspoon each of chopped fresh basil and parsley, and 1½ tablespoons olive oil. Mix well and season with black pepper and a squeeze of lemon juice. Refrigerate for at least an hour and serve on a bed of lettuce or salad leaves decorated with 6 black olives. Use 4 anchovies if you can't find salt pilchards.

CORNISH PILCHARD FILLETS ON TOAST
(serves 1)

In 2003 Newlyn's Pilchard Works (p.227) joined forces with the Eden Project to reintroduce canned Cornish sardines (young pilchards), featuring on the cans one of the Newlyn School's most famous paintings, *Between the Tides*, by Walter Langley.

I make no apology for including this simple recipe, because well-made sardines/Cornish pilchards on toast are delicious, and anything more complicated would mask the flavour of Nick Howell's excellent product.

1 x 100g (3½ oz) pilchard fillets
  or good-quality sardines in olive oil
2 slices wholemeal or granary bread
good-quality horseradish sauce to taste
sea salt and fresh ground black pepper

Heat the grill. Remove the pilchards or sardines from the can, reserving the oil.

Toast the bread lightly, then divide the pilchards between the 2 slices of toast. Mash them lightly with a fork, then dot with horseradish. Drizzle a little of the reserved oil over the fish. Place under the grill and cook until the toast starts to char a little.

Serve at once with a tomato salad.

Above: The sea's rich harvest: fishing for pilchards in a photograph taken *c.* **1900**
Right: Fishing Boats at Polperro, 1924

POLPERRO SCROWLERS WITH TOMATO AND CAPER SAUCE
(serves 6)

When John Wesley visited Polperro on the south coast of Cornwall in the 1760s, he was left in no doubt that fishing was important to the village: 'Here the room over which we were to lodge being filled with pilchards and conger-eels, the perfume was too potent for me; so that I was not sorry when one of our friends invited me to lodge at her house'!

In fact, Polperro was noted as a fishing community as early as 1303 and still has a fairly healthy number of fishing boats in the harbour as well as a good-smelling fish market on the quay and a famous fishermen's choir.

For some years before the end of the pilchard seine fishery a great change had taken place in the method of dealing with the fish. Owing to the invention of curing in tanks, the process of laying the pilchards in bulk was entirely dispensed with and as a result many hundreds of men, women and children were robbed of their former means of support. The new process is said to have been introduced first at Mevagissey and it is certainly a curious fact that shortly afterwards the vast shoals of pilchards disappeared from the Cornish coast. Many of the old fishermen regarded this as a direct judgement of Heaven on the infamous invention of curing in tanks!

Originally a Cornish Scrowler was a fresh pilchard split open, rubbed all over with a mixture of salt, sugar and black pepper, then left overnight. Next day, the fish was 'scrowled' on a gridiron over the fire and eaten with 'mahogany', a powerful mixture of black treacle and gin, a favourite tipple of Cornish fishermen for keeping out the cold!

The old fish-curing tanks, where the fish were salted before being packed in barrels and sent to Italy, can still be seen in Polperro. In the 1980s the National Trust restored the old fishermen's net loft sheltering against the harbour's craggy guardian rock; its tenant still mends and stores nets. The Trust also owns the cliffs on either side of the harbour and most of the glorious stretch of coastline from here to Polruan. From the coastal path, the ruins of fish-drying houses can be seen in the undergrowth.

Fresh pilchards are great for grilling, or barbecuing, accompanied by a zingy tomato sauce. Ask your fishmonger for line-caught mackerel, or herrings, if pilchards are unavailable, but serve 1 or 2 per person depending on size.

12-18 really fresh pilchards or sardines, depending on size, cleaned
coarse sea salt

For the tomato and caper sauce
450g (1lb) ripe plum or baby cherry tomatoes, de-seeded and finely chopped
1½ tablespoons baby capers, drained
4-6 spring onions, finely chopped
2 teaspoons garlic, crushed
2 salt pilchard fillets or 4 anchovies, drained and finely chopped
2 tablespoons olive oil
½ cup fresh chives, garlic chives and parsley, mixed and finely chopped
1 or 2 tablespoons good-quality white wine vinegar or lime juice
sea salt and freshly ground black pepper

Make the sauce first by mixing all the ingredients together. Taste and adjust the seasoning as necessary. Chill before serving.

To cook the fish, roll them in coarse sea salt and place under a hot grill. Turn over when the skin starts to blacken and cook the other side. The skin and scales easily come off together and the meat will fall off the bones.

Serve immediately with the sauce.

PRIEST'S COVE POLLACK PIE WITH CRUSHED POTATO TOPPING
(serves 6)

About 6 small boats still fish out of this tiny cove on magnificent Cape Cornwall, England's only cape, near Land's End. This is the National Trust's further-west fishing connection, where recently it helped rebuild the slipway. The small fisherman's huts, clustered round the top, began as oar and sail stores and several of them retain the long, narrow shape that their early use dictated. The sea is so wild here, it's a salutary reminder of the dangers of fishing and the bravery of generations of Cornish fishermen. They land only line-caught fish – bass (dolphin- and porpoise- friendly), mackerel and pollack, as well as lobsters and spider crabs.

Substitute any other line-caught white fish for pollack.

1.5kg (3lb 5oz) new potatoes
500g (1lb 2oz) line-caught pollack fillet
500g (1lb 2oz) smoked line-caught pollack fillet
150ml (¼pt) dry white wine
600ml (1pt) full-fat milk
½ onion, sliced
1 bay leaf
1 strip lemon peel
2 sprigs fresh parsley
1 sprig fresh dill
100g (3½oz) butter
40g (1½oz) flour
2 free-range eggs, hard-boiled, quartered
1 heaped tablespoon fresh parsley, or 1 level tablespoon fresh dill, finely chopped
50g (1¾oz) Cheddar, grated
sea salt and freshly ground black pepper

Cook the potatoes in salted water until tender, then drain and crush roughly with a fork, seasoning well.

Place the wine, milk, onion, bay leaf, lemon peel, parsley and dill in a large shallow pan. Bring to the boil, then simmer for 5 minutes. Add the fish and poach gently for about 5 minutes until just cooked through. Remove the fish with a fish slice, then strain the pan juices into a bowl, discarding the aromatics.

Make the sauce by melting 50g (1¾oz) butter in a heavy-based pan and stir in the flour. Cook for about 2 minutes, stirring continuously without letting it colour. Remove from the heat and allow to cool slightly, then gradually add the hot poaching liquor, stirring until smooth. Return to the heat and simmer over the lowest possible heat for 10 minutes, stirring frequently.

Meanwhile remove the skin and bones from the fish and break into bite-sized pieces. Place in a buttered shallow ovenproof dish with the eggs, then sprinkle over the parsley or dill.

Remove the sauce from the heat and add the grated cheese, stirring until smooth. Season to taste, then pour over the fish mixture. Cover with the potato and dot with the remaining butter.

Bake for 30 minutes in a pre-heated oven at 200°C/400°F/GM6 until piping hot and the topping beginning to brown. Put under a hot grill to finish if you prefer it browner.

Serve hot with peas.

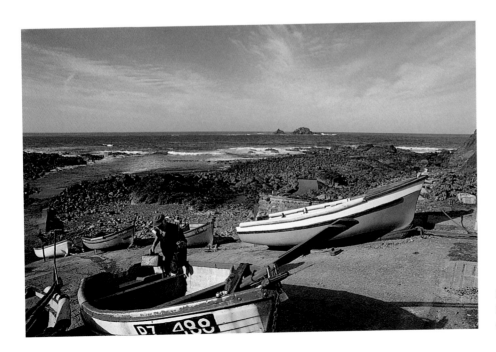

**Far left: Cape Cornwall, near Land's End
Left: A fisherman loading up his boat on Cape Cornwall, ready to go fishing for lobster and crab**

LYN SALMON WITH CHAMPAGNE AND SAFFRON SAUCE
(serves 4)

The National Trust protects the steep wooded valleys of Watersmeet near Lynmouth, North Devon, where the East Lyn River and Hoar Oak Water meet. Watersmeet House, built around 1832 as a fishing lodge, is now a National Trust shop with refreshments and information. The site has been a tea-garden since 1901 and is the focal point for several beautiful walks.

The River Lyn is the most significant salmon river in the West Country and the healthiest. For its size it has a very good number of salmon and fishing can be very good immediately after spates. Sea trout catches are quite small, partly because it is not an easy place to fish at night, but brown trout fishing is good to very good throughout the season.

The Westcountry Rivers Trust, an environmental organisation formed in 1995 to conserve, maintain and restore the natural beauty and ecological integrity of rivers and streams in Devon, Cornwall and West Somerset, uses the Lyn as a benchmark. There are still wetlands and moorlands at its source, very good woodlands on its banks to give shade to fish and wildlife and there is very little intensive farming. Fishing is controlled for the National Trust by the Environment Agency who organise day permits in the trout season (15 March-30 September) and salmon season (1 March-30 September). A catch and release system is mandatory for salmon until 16 June, although it is also encouraged after this.

Salmon with a champagne sauce is typical of the way the fish would be served in Victorian times when Watersmeet House was a fishing lodge. The recipe also works well with sea trout, red gurnard, bass and catfish.

4 x 175g (6oz) wild Pacific or responsibly farmed Atlantic salmon steaks or fillets
1 tablespoon olive oil
25g (1oz) butter
2 shallots, finely chopped
300ml (½pt) champagne
a pinch of saffron strands
150ml (¼pt) double cream or crème fraîche
sea salt and freshly ground black pepper

Heat a frying pan until hot and add the oil and half the butter. Fry the salmon for about 5 minutes on each side. (It should be slightly pink and tender inside.) Remove and keep warm.

Melt the remaining butter and soften the shallots for about 3 minutes. Add the champagne and boil for 5 minutes until reduced, then add the saffron, followed by the cream. Boil for 3-5 minutes, until thickened. Season to taste.

Place the salmon on 4 serving plates and serve with the sauce.

Left: Sir Francis Acland, 14th Bt of Killerton in Devon, c. 1930. He is showing off his catch from the River Exe
Right: Watersmeet, the confluence of the East Lyn and Hoar Oak Water, in North Devon

TAMAR SALMON AND PARSLEY SAUCE
(serves 4)

The River Tamar twists its way through the fertile landscape of the West Country, separating Cornwall both geographically and politically from the rest of Britain. Just beyond Calstock it takes one of its innumerable sharp turns and passes under a densely wooded cliff. Hidden in the oaks and chestnuts, over 200 feet up, stands Cotehele House, the ancestral home of the Edgcumbe family and one of the least altered medieval houses in the county, now owned by the National Trust.

A little further downstream are the warehouses and abandoned lime-kilns of Cotehele Quay, a busy place in the mid-19th century. The river would have been crowded with sailing boats, schooners, ketches, barges and paddle steamers. One of the old sailing barges, *Shamrock*, has been restored by the National Trust and is now moored alongside an outstation of the National Maritime Museum on the Quay.

Today, all is peaceful, with no activity on the river apart from the occasional pleasure boat and passenger ferry, or the salmon fishers working their nets. Although the Tamar offers some of the best salmon fishing in the West Country, like everywhere stocks have decreased considerably in recent years. A local warden told me that only 23 salmon were caught in his section of the river last season, where 20 years ago it would have been at least 250.

The Westcountry Rivers Trust (p.42) launched a millennium project in 1996 working with farmers, landowners and the wider community to improve the condition of the river and its tributaries. In partnership with the Environment Agency and local fishing associations, it is providing salmon-spawning boxes. The gravel areas in the river bed which salmon need for spawning are buried under fine sediment produced by intensive agriculture. This is thought to be one of the principal limiting factors for salmon populations.

This salmon recipe is popular in Cotehele Barn's restaurant. Sea trout or trout could be used instead.

4 x 175g (6oz) wild Pacific or responsibly farmed salmon fillets or steaks, skinned and boned
fish stock for poaching (see p.222)
450ml (16fl oz) full-cream milk
1 tablespoon onion, peeled and grated
6 white peppercorns
1 bay leaf
25g (1oz) butter
25g (1oz) plain flour
1 glass (6fl oz) dry white wine
4 tablespoons fresh parsley, chopped
1 dessertspoon baby capers or chopped baby gherkins, drained
sea salt, freshly ground black pepper, grated nutmeg and lemon juice to season

Make the parsley sauce first by heating the milk until just under boiling point. Add the onion, peppercorns and bay leaf, then leave to infuse for 20 minutes. Strain.

Melt the butter in a small heavy pan, then add the flour. Using a wooden spoon, stir over the heat for a minute or so until you have a smooth paste.

Take the pan off the heat and beat or whisk in the flavoured milk. Make sure it is well blended before adding the wine. Return to the heat and slowly bring to the boil, stirring or whisking all the time. Turn down the heat and simmer gently for 30 minutes, stirring occasionally to prevent a skin forming. This is the secret of success with a white sauce – it needs at least 30 minutes to cook out the raw floury flavour. When the sauce is cooked, stir in the parsley and capers and season to taste with salt, pepper, nutmeg and lemon juice. Keep warm while you poach the salmon.

Fill a frying pan with enough fish stock just to cover the salmon. Once the stock is barely simmering, poach for about 5 minutes until opaque and set. Lift out the fish using a fish slice and keep warm, while you reheat the sauce.

If the sauce is too thick, add some fish stock. Check again for seasoning.

Serve the salmon and parsley sauce with new potatoes.

The traditional Tamar sailing barge, *Shamrock*, moored at Cotehele Quay, Cornwall

KOULIBIAC OF TEIGN SALMON WITH TARRAGON
(serves 8)

Julius Drewe, who commissioned the remarkable early 20th-century Castle Drogo in Devon, was a keen salmon fisherman on the nearby River Teign. There is a huge portrait of him in the house next to an enormous salmon. And he had plenty of time for fishing, as he was a self-made millionaire, who retired at 36 having made his fortune by importing tea and setting up the Home & Colonial Stores.

The Castle is one of the most remarkable works of Sir Edwin Lutyens and is perched on a moorland spur overlooking the wooded Teign Gorge, with spectacular views of Dartmoor. The National Trust now owns Castle Drogo, with its 240-hectare (600-acre) estate, and leases the fishing rights on the upper Teign to the local fishing association who provide day permits for visitors to fish for salmon, sea trout and brown trout. Unfortunately, the salmon, as on all rivers, have seen a sharp decline and the local landowners' association is cooperating with the Environment Agency on a long-term rehabilitation programme involving improvement of spawning/nursery areas through coppicing, gravel improvement and juvenile fish, invertebrate and pH surveys. Sea trout fishing is generally good on the Teign, but brown trout fishing, once very good, has declined sharply. The local fishing association has a programme including habitat improvement, reporting catches to the Environment Agency, a catch-and-release policy and a re-stocking scheme, so hopefully the situation will improve.

This Russian fish pie was an Edwardian favourite and might well have been cooked in the Castle's famous kitchen. It is excellent for dinner parties or a celebration because the filling can be made 2 days in advance and the pie assembled the day before and cooked on the day of the party. Once cooked, don't put it in the fridge or the pastry will spoil.

Sea trout can be used.

900g (2lb) wild Pacific or responsibly
  farmed Atlantic salmon fillet (tailpiece)
25g (1oz) butter
225g (8oz) button mushrooms,
  quartered
100ml (3½fl oz) brandy
300ml (10fl oz) double cream,
  or crème fraîche
2 level tablespoons flour
1 level teaspoon mild French mustard
2 tablespoons fresh tarragon, chopped
sea salt and freshly ground black pepper
225g (8oz) long grain rice
600ml (1pt) fish (see p.222)
  or chicken stock
2 x 350g (12oz) packets frozen puff
  pastry
beaten egg for glazing

Skin, bone and cut the salmon into 1cm (½ in) cubes. Melt the butter in a large pan and when foaming, toss in the mushrooms and fish, and fry over a brisk heat. Drain off and reserve any liquor produced.

Warm the brandy, pour over the mixture and allow to ignite. Mix the cream with the flour and reserved liquor and pour over the mixture to quench the flames. Stir in the mustard and tarragon. Season well and simmer gently for 2-3 minutes only. Allow to cool completely.

Boil the rice in the stock for about 12 minutes, then drain, reserving the stock. Mix the rice and fish mixture together in a large bowl. Season well. The mixture should be softish, but hold its shape – if it's too dry, add a little of the reserved stock. Put in the fridge until you want to make the pie.

When you want to assemble the dish, roll out both packets of pastry to approximately the size of a swiss roll tin, or baking tray, (35cm [14in] x 22.5cm [9in]). Lightly grease the tin and place one sheet of pastry on it. Pile the prepared fish mixture on top and lay the second sheet of pastry over the fish mixture. Press the edges well together, then turn them up and pinch to form a firm edge. Make 2 steam holes, then brush with beaten egg.

Bake in a pre-heated oven at 210°C/425°F/GM7 for about 30 minutes until golden brown.

Serve hot with hollandaise sauce (see p.220) or cold with tarragon mayonnaise (see p.221).

Left: Koulibiac of Teign Salmon with Tarragon
Above: Julius Drewe fishing at Faskally, painted by
C.M.Hardie, *c.* 1900

DARTMOUTH SCALLOP AND CAULIFLOWER SOUP
(serves 4)

The River Dart is a famous beauty spot and the National Trust protects several woods along the estuary as well as coast on either side of the mouth at Little Dartmouth. There is no large-scale commercial fishing, but several restaurants along the river serve excellent seafood caught by local boats. I enjoyed a very posh version of this lovely soup at The Carved Angel on Dartmouth quayside; it was served in tiny espresso cups as a taster before our meal.

Scallops eat particularly well with cauliflower, as they do with Jerusalem artichokes.

> 50g (1¾oz) butter
> 1 medium onion, peeled
> 600ml (1pt) home-made chicken
>   or vegetable stock
> 1 large cauliflower, broken into
>   small florets
> 2 bay leaves
> 1 large potato, peeled and cubed
> about 600ml (1pt) whole milk
> 4 tablespoons double cream or
>   crème fraîche
> sea salt and freshly ground black pepper
> pinch freshly grated nutmeg
> 4 dive-caught scallops or 16 queenies,
>   including corals
> fresh parsley, chopped

Melt the butter in a large pan and fry the onion until soft, but not coloured.

Meanwhile, bring the stock to the boil, drop in the cauliflower florets and poach gently for about 6-8 minutes, until almost tender.

Add the bay leaves to the onion, then the cauliflower and its cooking liquor and the potato. Bring to the boil and season with salt. Simmer for 15 minutes.

Bring the milk to the boil and purée with the cauliflower mixture (remove the bay leaves) in a blender or food processor. Pour back into the pan and stir in the cream.

Season to taste with black pepper and nutmeg and more salt if necessary. Bring back to the boil.

Just before serving, dice the white of the scallops and cut the corals into 2-3 pieces. If using queenies, keep them whole. Add to the soup and scatter lavishly with chopped parsley – the shellfish will cook sufficiently in the hot soup.

Ladle into warm bowls and serve with crusty bread.

LYME BAY SCALLOPS AND DENHAY HAM

The National Trust owns land both sides of Lyme Regis, which has long been famed for its scallops. They are landed on the fish quay at the entrance to the harbour and are driven straight to Brixham for sale. But Lyme Bay is in trouble because the scallop dredgers are damaging the seabed, and catching everything in their path. The scallopers' argument is that by flattening the seabed and breaking up all the rocks, they are improving the habitat for the scallops, which will regenerate, but this is at the expense of all the other marine life. The only sustainable way of catching scallops is by diving, but this has its problems. To make it financially viable, the scallops have to be in large colonies so that they can be collected easily. Their whereabouts has to be kept secret. If you ask about the origin of dive-caught scallops, don't expect an answer! Their quality is of course far superior, as they haven't been damaged on collection and are not full of sand, so enjoy! They need very little cooking; if overcooked, they will become tough.

In this recipe, I have combined scallops with air-dried ham produced by Denhay Farms near Bridport. The combination of scallops and bacon is very traditional and this modern version works well.

> 12 dive-caught scallops, including corals
> enough whole milk just to cover scallops
> 50g (1¾oz) unsalted butter
> sea salt and freshly ground black pepper
> 3 tablespoons sherry vinegar
> 1 tablespoon fresh parsley, chopped
> 8 slices Denhay air-dried ham,
>   or other good-quality air-dried ham
> salad leaves (e.g. frisée lettuce, rocket,
>   dandelion, baby spinach)

Put the scallops in a dish and just cover with milk. Leave in the fridge for at least 2 hours.

To cook the scallops, heat a frying pan or griddle over a high heat until blazing hot. Smear the base with a little of the butter, then lift 4 scallops from the milk using tongs. Flash-fry for 2 minutes on each side, pressing them down on the pan and seasoning with a little salt and pepper as they cook. Transfer them to a warmed baking sheet and keep warm while you cook the others.

To make the dressing, remove the pan from the heat, add the sherry vinegar and stir to scrape up any residue from the bottom. Return to the heat and whisk in the remaining butter a little at a time. Add the parsley and season with a little salt and pepper.

Arrange 2 slices of ham and a pile of salad leaves on 4 plates. Top the ham with 3 scallops, and spoon the dressing over the leaves.

Serve immediately with good crusty bread.

Above: The Cobb at Lyme Regis, Dorset
Right: Lyme Bay Scallops and Denhay Ham

TORBAY SOLE GRILLED WITH CLOTTED CREAM
(serves 2)

Torbay sole was originally a speciality of the Tor Bay area in South Devon, but it has been fished for years all round the South-West coast and today is landed at Newlyn in Cornwall. It is the same species as witch flounder caught off the coast of North Yorkshire and a cousin of the lemon sole, but a beautiful pinkish purple. Its flavour has always been appreciated by the French and Spanish, to whom it is exported from Newlyn. The advantage of the fish is that at the moment it is a sustainable species because it is not being targeted commercially, and can be substituted for lemon or Dover sole in any recipe. Catfish could also be used.

Here the fish is cooked with one of the best-known foods of the West Country, a traditional combination.

2 Torbay sole or megrim, filleted but
    with skin left on
sea salt and freshly ground black pepper
juice of ½ lemon
50-75g (1¾-2¾oz) clotted cream,
    depending on size of fish
1 tablespoon fresh parsley,
    finely chopped
2 teaspoons fresh chives, chopped
25g (1oz) butter, melted

Season the flesh side of each fillet with salt, pepper and lemon juice. Mix the clotted cream with the herbs and spread over the fillets. Put the matching fillets on top to make 2 sandwiches and brush the skin of each with melted butter.

Line your grill pan with kitchen foil and place the fish on top. Cook under a hot grill for about 5 minutes on each side, depending on size.

Serve immediately with new potatoes and salad.

CHARGRILLED SQUID, POTATO AND ONION SALAD WITH LIME DRESSING
(serves 4)

As well as feathering for mackerel, Cornish fishermen from Penberth land line-caught squid.

Small squid are best for frying or char-grilling as they are more tender. If you want to make sure the texture is not at all rubbery, freeze either whole or prepared, overnight or longer, to break down the rigid cell structure and therefore tenderise the flesh. Tina Bricknell-Webb, who with her husband owns Percy's, a country hotel/restaurant in North Devon, gave me this tip, and it works.

Make up this salad at least 2 hours before you want to eat it.

about 450g (1lb) small line-caught
    squid, cleaned and sliced into even-
    sized rings about 1cm (½in) thick
16 small waxy potatoes (Charlotte, Anya,
    Pink Fir Apple, Belle de Fontenay or
    Ratte), washed and halved lengthways
3 tablespoons virgin olive oil
sea salt
2 red onions, peeled and cut into eighths
2 red peppers
2 mild chillis, deseeded and finely
    chopped
a small bunch of fresh coriander leaves,
    finely chopped

For the dressing
    a generous pinch of sea salt
    1½ tablespoons lime juice
    grated rind of 1 unwaxed lime
    2 cloves garlic, crushed
    1 teaspoon Dijon mustard
    1 teaspoon runny honey
    ½ tablespoon fresh dill, coarsely
    chopped
    125ml (4fl oz) groundnut oil

Pre-heat the oven to 200°C/400°F/GM6 for the vegetables.

To make the dressing, whisk the salt, lime juice and rind, garlic, mustard, honey and dill together, then add the oil, whisking continuously to make a smooth emulsion.

Heat a ridged griddle over a high heat until searingly hot. Toss the potatoes in 2 tablespoons of the oil, shaking off any excess and place them on the griddle side down. Leave for 5 minutes, then transfer them to a roasting tin. Season with salt and roast in the oven for 15-20 minutes, or until tender.

Meanwhile, skin the red peppers by placing them under a pre-heated grill, keeping them as close to the heat as possible and cooking until almost burnt. As the peppers colour, turn until completely coloured and tender. Remove from the heat and leave to one side until just warm enough to handle. The skins can now be easily removed. Split the peppers in half lengthwise, remove the stalks and seeds, then cut into strips.

Dip the onion wedges into the oil left from the potatoes, shake off the excess and cook on the hot griddle for about 5 minutes until coloured, turning once or twice. Add them to the potatoes and continue to cook for at least 10 minutes or until the onions are tender. Remove the vegetables from the oven and leave to cool. Combine the potatoes and onions with the red pepper, chillis, and coriander in a large bowl. Pour over the dressing and toss well.

To cook the squid, toss it in the remaining tablespoon of oil and season. Heat up the griddle again until extremely hot. Throw in half the squid and cook for 1½-2 minutes, turning it over. Remove and add to the salad, then repeat with the remaining squid. Toss everything once again, then leave for 2-8 hours before serving for the flavours to develop.

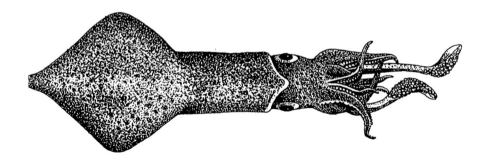

POACHED FOWEY SEA TROUT WITH GREEN MAYONNAISE
(serves 6)

The magnificent River Fowey rises on Bodmin Moor in Cornwall and flows through the National Trust's Lanhydrock Estate for 2 miles on its way to the sea at Fowey. The river used to be a great place for salmon, sea trout and brown trout and the Robartes family who lived at the house were keen anglers. Recently, the number of fish has dropped dramatically, but the Trust's Countryside Manager works closely with all the River Fowey associations; their agreement to voluntary catch limits over the past few years is already showing dividends.

Fowey sea trout with green mayonnaise was on the menu when George VI, Queen Elizabeth and Princess Margaret came to lunch with the Robartes on 5 June 1950. The royal family had been to visit the Royal Cornwall Show, still very popular today. Word was sent later that luncheon had been delicious.

A classic green mayonnaise is made with spinach, but use watercress, or fresh herbs (a mixture of parsley, chives and tarragon) if you prefer.

**6 x 175g (6oz) wild or responsibly farmed sea trout fillets
fish stock to cover (see p.222)**

**For the green mayonnaise
175g (6oz) picked and washed spinach
300ml (½pt) good-quality bought mayonnaise or home-made (see p.221)
sea salt and freshly ground black pepper**

Make the green mayonnaise first. Dry the spinach leaves well on kitchen paper, then blitz in a food processor or blender, add the mayonnaise and blitz again until smooth and creamy. Season to taste.

To poach the fish, place the fillets in a wide frying-pan. Pour over enough stock just to cover, then slowly bring to barely simmering point. Poach for about 5 minutes until opaque and just set, then remove from the stock.

Serve the sea trout with the green mayonnaise handed around separately.

Wild Pacific or responsibly farmed Atlantic salmon, line-caught or responsibly farmed bass, or red gurnard can be used.

The Fish Larder at Lanhydrock House, Cornwall

THE EAST

Here is a largely remote coastline studded with unspoilt fishing villages and famous for the variety and quality of its shellfish and of its fish, both sea and freshwater. The National Trust looks after concentrated pockets of the East Anglian coast: from Brancaster to Blakeney in North Norfolk, Dunwich Heath down to Orford Ness in Suffolk, and the salt-marshes of West Mersea and Northey Island in Essex.

This is an unpredictable sea, with a treacherous coastline. Bars or sandbanks running across harbour mouths have increased the difficulties of navigation, and periodically villages lying behind the saltings have been inundated by scouring tides, or in places entirely lost to the sea, a process that seems to be accelerating. The open unprotected beaches are notoriously dangerous: not only is it difficult to push boats off against an incoming wind, but masterly precision is required to land them up the steep slope of the shelving beaches. Yet despite all these hazards, men have dredged for oysters, set pots for crabs, lobsters and whelks, raked cockles and, in season, gone musselling, trawling for shrimps and flat fish, long-lining for cod and seine-netting for mackerel and herring.

There has always been a strong link between fishing and agriculture along the immediate coastal fringe, but with the expansion of the English herring industry in the 19th century, more labour was required to crew the boats and work in the fish-curing houses. Once the harvest was over, many farmworkers went to work in Yarmouth and Lowestoft for the home herring fishing season. By the end of the century, these country 'joskins' or 'half-breed fishermen', as they were called in North Suffolk, played an important part in the East Anglian fishing industry, trawling as well as drifting. Many of them became full-time fishermen, finding the sea more profitable and secure than the land.

But the tide has turned and the numbers employed in fishing are dwindling. Each year the average age rises, for as the older men retire, their places are no longer being filled. Four or five hundred trawlers used to be based at Lowestoft, but today there are only four or five, with a small inshore market.

The size of the Grimsby fleet has also shrunk from over 500 trawlers in the 1950s to only 12 today. The town's three huge docks stand almost empty where once the 73-acre space could be crossed by leaping from boat to boat. Now, there is a shimmering expanse of water half a mile in length. But it is not all doom and gloom. Grimsby's fish-processing industry has been booming in recent years. Just under 1 million tonnes of fish a year is handled, almost five times the UK's EU fishing quota. Since the North Sea's fish stocks are at crisis point, this fish comes mainly from Iceland and the Faroes.

Although the fishing is on a small scale, gourmets have a wonderful time in East Anglia. Fresh fish and shellfish of excellent quality can be bought regularly straight from the boats, or from fishermen's beach huts, or from improvised stalls outside their cottages. Delicious smoked fish and shellfish can also be purchased directly from local smokehouses, and samphire gathered from the creeks.

Previous pages: Low tide at Blakeney Point, Norfolk
Left: Detail from an Empire Marketing Board poster, *c.* 1930, entitled 'There's All the Health of the Sea in Fish'

STIFFKEY BLUES

The North Norfolk coast has always been famed for its cockles and is now one of the three main fisheries in Britain. The best are said to come from the small village of Stiffkey. They are rich and meaty and are called 'Stewkey' or 'Stookey Blues' (how Stiffkey is actually pronounced), because of their blue colour, ranging from lavender to dark grey-blue, derived from the mud they inhabit.

Cockle gathering was a hard life in the old days, usually done by the women of Stiffkey to supplement their income. With layers of clothing to protect them from the treacherous winds, they would dig for the cockles, carrying them home in sacks and baskets. Today, cockling is men's work and licensed cocklers travel to and from the beds, located several miles from Stiffkey on the seaward side of a salt-marsh, by boat, working the mudflats with their short-handled rakes. Stiffkey Salt-marshes and 2 miles of this coastline are protected by the National Trust and are a stunning sight in the summer when covered with sea lavender and marsh samphire. Salt-marshes are important habitats for birds as well as plants, but so many are disappearing in England due to coastal defence works and to erosion as a result of rising sea levels that it is vital that as many as possible are preserved in good condition.

After harvesting, cockles are washed and packed in sacks for carriage back to sheds on the quayside in the village. There they are cleaned in sea water, opened by steaming and finally boiled. The National Trust owns a group of early 19th-century cockle sheds at Brancaster, which are rented to the local fishermen for boiling their cockles.

Always buy shellfish from managed fisheries harvested by licensed fishermen. Illegal harvesting causes huge problems - both environmental and social.

STEWKEY BLUE AND SAMPHIRE RISOTTO
(serves 4)

Any freshly cooked cockles, clams, mussels or whelks may be used for this recipe and if samphire is not obtainable, use asparagus. If you haven't the time to make your own vegetable broth, use a good-quality vegetable or chicken stock cube and add a small glass of dry white wine.

For the broth
- 1 large onion, roughly chopped
- 1 leek, cleaned and roughly chopped
- 1 large carrot, peeled and roughly chopped
- 2 celery sticks, roughly chopped
- 2 garlic cloves, peeled and roughly chopped
- 2 ripe tomatoes, roughly chopped
- 3 black peppercorns
- 1 bay leaf
- 2 parsley stalks
- 2 thyme stalks
- 1 litre (1¾pts) water
- 1 bottle dry white wine

For the risotto
- 50g (1¾oz) butter
- 2 tablespoons light olive oil
- 2 large shallots, peeled and finely chopped
- 250g (9oz) Arborio or risotto rice
- 350ml (12fl oz) cooking broth
- 300ml (½pt) hot water
- a pinch of saffron strands
- 225g (8oz) samphire, washed, trimmed and cut into 2.5cm (1in) lengths
- 100g (3½oz) freshly cooked cockles or clams, shelled or 1kg (2¼lb) unshelled
- 50g (1¾oz) freshly grated Parmesan cheese
- lots of freshly ground black pepper
- a little lemon juice

To make the broth, place all the ingredients in a large pan and bring to the boil. Skim, then reduce the heat and simmer uncovered for 2 hours. Strain and chill until needed. When ready to make the risotto, melt half the butter and the oil in a heavy-bottomed pan and very gently fry the shallots for about 10 minutes until soft but not coloured.

Reheat the prepared stock in another pan. Add the rice to the shallots and stir well for 2-3 minutes until each grain is coated with buttery juices and has turned translucent. Over a moderate heat, add the hot broth, a ladleful at a time, stirring frequently, until absorbed. Once the broth is used up, add the hot water in the same way, together with the saffron. Continue cooking and stirring until all the liquid has been absorbed, then test the rice. You want it soft, but with a bite in the centre. When the rice is cooked, stir in the samphire, cockles, remaining butter, cheese and black pepper. Taste and add sea salt if necessary – but be careful because the samphire and cockles are salty – and a little lemon juice. Stir well to ensure the samphire and cockles are heated through, then serve at once on heated plates.

Left: Stewkey Blue and Samphire Risotto
Above: Reed beds at Sutton Staithe on the North Norfolk coast

COCKLE AND CROMER CRAB CAKES WITH SAMPHIRE AND CHILLI SALAD
(serves 4 as a starter)

Although the best cockles on the East Coast are said to come from Stiffkey, cockle beds exist in many places. At Leigh-on-Sea in Essex there is almost a miniature village of sheds where the cockles are unloaded and boiled. Cockle cakes are so called because the fishermen's wives used the shells as containers for baking small cakes.

Cockles combine very well with crab, although you could use clams if you wished.

    225g (8oz) freshly cooked cockles
      or clams (shelled weight)
    225g (8oz) mixed brown and
      white crab meat
    1 small bunch fresh coriander leaves,
      chopped
    1 garlic clove, chopped
    juice of ½ lemon
    100g (3½oz) breadcrumbs
    1 free-range egg yolk
    sea salt and freshly ground black pepper
    a little groundnut oil, for frying

For the samphire salad
    200g (7oz) samphire, washed
      and trimmed
    1 fresh red chilli, de-seeded and
      finely chopped
    juice of 1 lime

Mix the cockles and crab meat in a bowl. Add the coriander, garlic, lemon juice, breadcrumbs and egg yolk. Season well, then mould gently with your fingertips into 8 equal-sized cakes. Chill until ready to cook.

To make the salad, blanch the samphire for 2 minutes in boiling water, drain and refresh in cold water. Tip into a bowl and mix in the chilli and lime juice.

To cook the crab cakes, heat a frying pan until very hot, then add a little oil. Carefully fry the crab cakes for about 3 minutes on each side, then drain on kitchen paper.

To serve, place the samphire salad in the centre of 4 serving plates and top with 2 crab cakes. Add a dollop of saffron mayonnaise (see p.221) or drizzle with warm white wine butter sauce or hollandaise (see p.220).

CROMER CRAB TART WITH ORANGE PASTRY
(serves 4-6)

For the pastry
    175g (6oz) plain flour
    a pinch of salt
    grated rind of 1 orange
    75g (2¾oz) cold butter, cubed
    1 free-range egg yolk, beaten with
      2 tablespoons cold water

For the filling
    125g (4½oz) full-fat cream cheese
    1 free-range egg, beaten
    150ml (5fl oz) single cream
    grated rind and juice of ½ unwaxed
      lemon
    2 tablespoons fresh chives, snipped
    sea salt and freshly ground black pepper
    freshly grated nutmeg
    225g (8oz) mixed white and brown
      crab meat
    4 spring onions, finely sliced

To make the pastry, sieve the flour and salt into a bowl, then stir in the orange rind. Rub in the butter until the mixture resembles fine breadcrumbs. Add the egg yolk and water and mix to a smooth dough. Knead gently, then roll out to line a 23cm (9in) loose-bottomed flan ring. Prick the base, then refrigerate for 20 minutes.

Pre-heat the oven to 200°C/400°F/GM6. Line the pastry case with greaseproof paper and fill with baking beans, rice or pulses. Bake for 10 minutes, then remove the greaseproof paper and beans. Return to the oven for about 5 minutes to dry out the base, then remove.

Reduce the oven temperature to 190°C/375°F/GM5. Mix together the cream cheese, egg, cream, lemon rind and juice and chives. Season well with salt, pepper and nutmeg.

Mix the crab with the spring onions and spread in the pastry case. Pour over the cream cheese mixture. Bake in the oven for 25-30 minutes until set and golden. Serve warm or cold with a mixed leaf salad.

CROMER CRAB
Brown and edible crabs are a North Norfolk speciality and those from around Cromer and nearby Sheringham are the most special and justly famous. 'A Cromer crab is small, stocky and well-filled – just like our Norfolk men,' says Julie Davies, who sells all the crabs her husband and son can catch from their shop in Cromer. Locals claim that crabs caught off this coast are noticeably sweeter and should be cooked in a minimum of salt to bring out this sweet flavour. John Griffin of Gurney's in Burnham Market recommends 1 tablespoon of salt to a large pan of water.

Cromer became a fashionable seaside resort in Victorian times with the coming of the railway. Holiday-makers still flock to the town, attracted by its pier, fine beach, deck-chairs and beach huts, probably unaware of its long and important maritime history and the hazardous lives led by its fishermen. The first half mile off the coast is the most treacherous, with the breakers hitting the beach and in the past, the most common fatalities among fishermen occurred within 200 yards of the shore. Further out to sea this stretch of coast is notorious for its submerged rocks, unpredictable tides and fierce winter weather.

Sadly, the fishing here has declined rapidly, but the reputation of the traditional Norfolk crabbing boat is still considerable. It is small, about 20 feet in length, light, clinker-built and double-ended. The ribs of the boat are always of oak, while the planking is larch and there is a metal rim around the boat to stop the edge wearing as the crab pots are dragged up from the bottom of the seabed.

Crab pots were not used in North Norfolk until 1863, when a man called Sandford saw one in use on the south coast of England and introduced them. Before this, hoop nets – a net bag attached to a circular metal ring – scooped up crabs and lobsters.

Cromer lighthouse, Norfolk

CROMER CRAB AND ASPARAGUS SALAD WITH LEMON AND CORIANDER DRESSING
(serves 6 as a starter)

Originally a seashore plant, asparagus grows extremely well in East Anglia's light sandy soil and relatively dry and warm climate. If you visit any time from the end of April to mid-June, you can see fields striped with raised asparagus beds, the spears poking through. Several growers will sell direct to the public from the farm.

Asparagus is very good with most types of shellfish, but exceptionally good with crab.

> 350g (12oz) fresh white crab meat
> 450g (1lb) asparagus (medium-sized spears)
> about 125g (4½oz) mixed salad leaves
> 2 vine-ripened, or good flavoured tomatoes, skinned, de-seeded and chopped

For the dressing
> 150ml (¼pt) mild olive oil
> 1 garlic clove, peeled and sliced
> 1 dessertspoon freshly ground coriander seeds
> 2 tablespoons fish stock (see p.222) or water
> juice of ½ lemon
> 1 good-flavoured tomato, skinned and de-seeded
> sea salt and freshly ground black pepper

Wash the asparagus and cut off the tough ends of the spears. Steam for a few minutes until tender then leave to cool. Reserving the tips for decoration, cut the stalks into small pieces.

To make the dressing, gently heat the olive oil in a small pan and add the garlic and coriander seeds. Gently heat for about 2 minutes until they start to sizzle, then blend in a liquidiser with the remaining ingredients. Season to taste.

Fold the pieces of asparagus into the crab meat with 1 tablespoon of the dressing (use 2 forks so that you shred and pull the crab meat apart rather than mixing it). To serve, arrange a few salad leaves round the edge of 6 serving plates. Scatter the chopped tomato on top of them, then spoon the crab and asparagus mixture in the centre. Carefully pour over a little dressing and arrange the reserved asparagus tips to decorate.

SEA LAVENDER HONEY
On the North Norfolk coast, sea lavender, a plant of the *statice* family, is a dominant species. Man's attempts over the centuries to control the water level have created a larger area of suitable habitat. Sea lavender flowers in August and is a useful source of nectar for bees when the flowering season of most other species is over, so sea lavender honey has probably been collected for as long as bees have been present in East Anglia. The honey is not widely known, as the crop is small and almost all the production is consumed locally. You can find pots of sea lavender honey in good delis in North Norfolk; it is pale yellow-green with a mild delicate flavour.

Right: Fishermen mending lobster pots at Sheringham, Norfolk, photographed in 1906
Far right: The church of St Nicholas at Salthouse, Norfolk, looking out towards the North Sea. In the Middle Ages, Salthouse was a port

SMOKED EEL, FENNEL AND APPLE SOUP
(serves 4)

Eels have been on the East Anglian menu for centuries, moving in and out of fashion. Indeed the Venerable Bede maintained that the city of Ely's name derived from the vast numbers of eels caught in the surrounding marshes. Much of the region had been drained and turned over to corn-growing during the Roman occupation, but a fall in the land level before the middle of the 5th century had led to flooding and so for many centuries after, the principal products were fish and waterfowl. Some manors paid many thousands of eels each year in rents to the Abbot of Ely. Eels were cheaper than most fish and probably the only fresh variety, other than shellfish, bought by everyone. Tubs of jellied eels are still sold in local East Anglian markets as snacks.

There is a lovely story from the National Trust's Oxburgh Hall, near King's Lynn, the 15th–century moated manor house built by the Bedingfelds who still live there. In the 1920s, one of the Bedingfeld girls had been sent to her room for bad behaviour. She tied her bed sheets together and dropped them down into the moat to catch eels. When the maid came up later with some food, there were several eels on her bedroom floor.

Fresh eel soup was an 18th-century favourite, but smoked it makes a 21st-century gourmet feast.

125g (4½oz) smoked eel fillet, chopped
25g (1oz) butter
1 fennel bulb, finely chopped
4 dessert apples, peeled, cored
  and finely chopped
juice of ½ lemon
300ml (½pt) fish stock (see p.222)
300ml (½pt) farm-pressed apple juice
sea salt and cayenne pepper
a pinch of ground ginger
200ml (7fl oz) single cream

Melt the butter in a large pan, then add the fennel. Cover with greaseproof paper and sweat for about 5 minutes without colouring. Add the chopped apple and lemon juice and season with salt, cayenne and ginger, then cover again with the greaseproof paper and sweat for a further 2-3 minutes. Add the smoked eel and sweat again for 2-3 minutes, again without colouring. Pour in the fish stock and apple juice and bring to the boil. Add the single cream, then liquidise or process. Pass through a fine sieve into a clean pan, then heat up gently before serving. Serve with warm crusty bread and a glass of farmhouse cider.

SMOKED EEL AND ROCKET SALAD WITH GREEN CREAM DRESSING
(serves 4-6 as a starter or lunch)

350g (12oz) smoked eel fillets
150ml (5fl oz) sour cream
2 tablespoons fresh chives snipped,
  or ½ shallot, finely chopped
2 tablespoons fresh flat-leaf
  parsley, chopped
1 tablespoon fresh dill, chopped
sea salt and freshly ground black pepper
a few drops of lemon juice
100g (3½oz) rocket or watercress,
  washed and trimmed

Mix the sour cream with the fresh herbs. Season to taste and sharpen with lemon juice – it should be fairly sharp.

Place the rocket in a serving bowl. Snip the eel into large chunks and place on top. Spoon over the cream dressing and serve with rye or wholemeal bread and butter.

Left: The gatehouse front at Oxburgh Hall, Norfolk. Are there eels still lurking in the moat?
Right: An eel catcher, from a photograph taken
c. **1900**

BLAKENEY FRIED DABS WITH SAMPHIRE
(serves 4)

Blakeney Point, a 3½ mile-long sand and shingle spit on the North Norfolk coast, is one of Britain's foremost bird sanctuaries, protected by the National Trust since 1912. The spit is noted in particular for its colonies of breeding terns and for the rare migrants that pass through in spring and autumn. Until the 17th century, Blakeney was a port which at times exceeded King's Lynn and Great Yarmouth in importance, but the constant growth of the spit and of the marshes gradually rendered it useless for all but the smallest vessels.

The shallow water of Blakeney channels has been the fishing ground for dabs, a separate species of flatfish, although they look like the young of a larger fish. They are rather like rough-skinned plaice or flounder, but very sweet and the delight of inshore anglers. They were traditionally caught in creeks by spearing with 'butt' forks - all flatfish used to be called butts here - but these are now illegal.

If your dabs are large, they may be skinned and filleted before cooking, but smaller fish should be cooked whole. The skin can be removed after cooking if you wish, but it crisps up well. Flounders, lemon, Dover or Torbay sole, or megrim as well as catfish may be used instead.

> **4-8 dabs, cleaned and heads removed**
> **if you wish**
> **1 tablespoon seasoned flour**
> **50g (1¾oz) unsalted butter**
> **2 tablespoons sunflower oil**
> **150ml (5fl oz) dry white wine**
> **2 tablespoons full fat crème fraîche**
> **110g (4oz) samphire, trimmed weight**
> **sea salt and freshly ground black pepper**

Lightly dust the fish with seasoned flour and wash the samphire.

Fry the dabs for 3-4 minutes on each side, then remove to 4 serving plates. Meanwhile, cook the samphire for 3-4 minutes in a pan of boiling water, drain and dry off over heat.

Pour the wine into the frying pan and stir with a wooden spoon, scraping up any bits of fish that have stuck to the bottom. Stir in the crème fraîche, season with salt and pepper to taste, then simmer for 1-2 minutes, or until slightly thickened.

Serve the fish with the sauce spooned over it and garnish with the hot samphire dressed with a little melted butter and black pepper. Accompany with new potatoes and a green vegetable or salad.

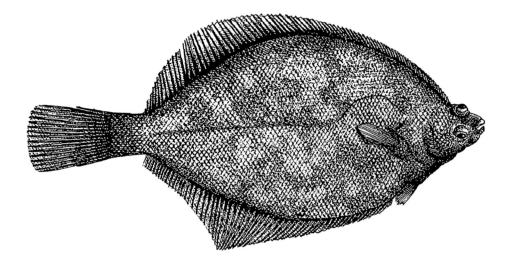

Above right: Barrels of herring piled up on the harbour at Wick, Caithness, in Scotland, _c._ 1880, photographed by George Washington Wilson

KING HERRING

The herring was the great fish of the Middle Ages, when the eating of meat was forbidden on at least two days of the week. The fat oily herrings caught off the coast of East Anglia in huge numbers were salted and packed into barrels or smoked, then transported inland or exported overseas as part of the massive trade in salt fish to the Mediterranean.

By the 12th century, Great Yarmouth had become the centre of the herring trade and indeed remained so right up until the end of the fishing in the 1960s. It was ideally sited; there were salt workings nearby, which were vital for the curing of the fish; it was convenient, near to the shoals; and even before the town was built, it was a meeting place for fishermen and buyers every autumn. This continued as the Free Fair from Michaelmas to Martinmas, 29 September to 11 November, which went on well into the 18th century.

Once the drifter fleet had returned safely the whole of Yarmouth and Lowestoft came to life. According to George Ewart Evans in his fascinating book about fishing in East Anglia *The Days That We Have Seen*, the whole place would be alight with flares on carts and boats, the horses would be stamping, men shouting, loose herrings flying all over the place. There were no hours of work; boats came in and were unloaded and the fish carted away to the fish-houses for curing. People worked until it was done.

One of the features of the Yarmouth and Lowestoft scene during the herring season was the Scots 'girls' who came down to do the salting of the herring and some splitting of the kippers in the fish-houses. They were referred to as 'girls' despite the fact that some of them were grandmothers. They used to arrive on special trains from Scotland, bringing all their belongings in great wooden boxes. Local people would give them lodgings to make extra money, but they always stripped the rooms bare, because the girls' working clothes, covered in herring scales, smelt pretty awful. They always dressed in shawls and long skirts covered with oil-skins, or 'balm-skins', which made them creak as they walked. The work was very hard, but these girls displayed awesome skill as they gutted and packed the herring in sheds open to the wind blowing off the North Sea.

The herring fishery is, and always has been, unpredictable. The size of catch can fluctuate enormously from year to year and in East Anglia, this happened after the Second World War, when over-fishing reduced the great shoals to a pitiful remnant. The drifter fleet dwindled season by season until it was non-existent and the once great ports of Lowestoft and Yarmouth were taken over by the big processors of frozen fish and vegetables, although Lowestoft does still have a small fish market selling locally landed fish.

North Sea herring stocks completely collapsed in the 1970s, resulting in a total fishing ban between 1977 and 1981 and again in the 1990s when levels of spawning stock fell. Today stocks are at sustainable levels and the fishery has recently been certified by the Marine Stewardship Council. Herrings are probably the cheapest and most highly nutritious food available to us.

BEETROOT AND SOUSED HERRING SALAD WITH A SOUR CREAM DRESSING
(serves 6 as a starter)

A traditional way of preserving herring in East Anglia, this recipe, using cider vinegar and herbs, makes the herrings sweeter than the more familiar rollmops.

> 6 herrings, about 225g (8oz) each, heads and tails removed, cleaned and boned
> freshly ground black pepper
> 300ml (½pt) local cider vinegar
> 300ml (½pt) cold water
> 1 level teaspoon salt
> 10 black peppercorns
> 2 bay leaves
> 2 sprigs fresh marjoram
> 4 sprigs fresh parsley
> 1 large onion, peeled and thinly sliced
> 1 large carrot, peeled and thinly sliced

> For the beetroot salad
> 350g (12oz) beetroot, cooked, skinned and thickly sliced
> 2 tablespoons vinaigrette dressing
> 350g (12oz) waxy salad potatoes, cooked and thickly sliced
> ½ small red onion, thinly sliced and separated into rings
> 150ml (5fl oz) sour cream
> 2 tablespoons fresh chives, snipped

Pre-heat the oven to 180°C/350°F/GM4. Wipe the fish with a damp cloth, then lay them out flat with the flesh sides uppermost. Season well with the pepper, then roll each one up from the head end and secure with a cocktail stick. Arrange the herrings in an ovenproof dish.

Put all the remaining ingredients into a stainless steel pan and bring to the boil. Reduce the heat, cover and simmer gently for 10 minutes. Pour over the herrings, cover with foil and bake in the oven for 15 minutes. Remove from the oven and allow to cool in the cooking liquor and refrigerate for 1-2 hours before serving.

To serve, mix the sliced beetroot with the vinaigrette dressing, arrange randomly on individual serving plates with the sliced potato. Remove the herrings from the sousing liquor and take out the cocktail sticks. Place a herring on top of each beetroot and potato salad then scatter with onion rings. Add a generous dollop of sour cream and sprinkle with snipped chives. Serve with warm crusty bread and a glass of cider.

Beetroot and Soused Herring Salad with a Sour Cream Dressing

GRILLED SILVER DARLINGS WITH GARLIC AND CORIANDER
(serves 4)

Like mackerel and sprats, herring are an ideal fish for grilling because they are so rich in oil. Ask your fishmonger to remove the heads, backbones and bones for you but keep the herrings whole.

> 4 very fresh herrings, boned, but left whole
> sea salt and freshly ground black pepper
> a little melted butter
> 2 tablespoons fresh coriander leaves, finely chopped
> 2 small garlic cloves, very finely chopped
> juice of 1 lemon

Pre-heat the grill. Place the herrings, butterflied out and skin side up, on the grill rack and scatter over a good sprinkling of sea salt and pepper. Put the grill pan as close as you can under the grill and cook for about 3 minutes. Turn over the herrings, which should be almost tender when pierced with a skewer, and brush the flesh side with butter. Season with salt and pepper and place back under the grill for about 1 minute.

Remove the herrings and place on warm serving plates. Scatter a little coriander and garlic over each one and squeeze over some lemon juice. Serve with brown bread and butter.

HERRINGS MARINATED IN LIME AND LEMON JUICE WITH AVOCADO
(serves 6)

For this simple lunch dish or starter you must have spanking fresh herring. It is also good made with small mackerel, sprats or sardines, or smoked eel. Prepare at least a couple of hours in advance.

> 6 very fresh herring, filleted but unskinned
> juice of 3 lemons
> juice of 3 limes
> 2 small red onions, peeled and very finely chopped
> 1 fresh red chilli
> 2 tablespoons fresh coriander leaves, finely chopped
> sea salt
> 3 very ripe avocados
> a few slices of red chilli, red onion and coriander leaves, to garnish

Cut each herring fillet into 3 pieces and lay them skin-side down in a large shallow glass or china dish. Pour over the lemon and lime juice and scatter over the red onion. Split the chilli lengthways, remove half its seeds and finely chop. Add to the fish with the coriander. Liberally season with sea salt and mix together thoroughly. Cover the dish and refrigerate for at least 2 hours. When ready to serve, halve and peel the avocados and cut the flesh into thick wedges. Divide between 6 serving plates and pile the herring on top. Garnish with a few slices of chilli, red onion and coriander leaves. Serve with crusty bread.

> **THAMES BLACKWATER HERRING DRIFT NET FISHERY**
> This driftnet (a small floating gillnet) fishery for spring spawning herring is located in the Greater Thames Estuary within the 6-mile limit in the UK. It was awarded accreditation by the Marine Stewardship Council in 2000 as an environmentally responsible fishery – look out for the MSC label when you buy herring in supermarkets and at fishmongers.

SOFT HERRING ROES ON TOAST WITH CAPER AND ANCHOVY BUTTER
(serves 2 as a starter, light lunch or supper)

The creamy texture of soft herring roes (the male melt) lends itself to some delectable but cheap and easy dishes, providing you can buy them in good condition. It is difficult these days to buy unfrozen roes unless you catch the herrings yourself, but try to get hold of roes that are still whole after thawing. Damaged roes are fine for sauces or pâtés.

250g (9oz) whole soft herring roes
a little seasoned flour
75g (2¾oz) butter
2 slices hot wholemeal or sourdough toast, or fried bread
3 anchovy fillets, finely chopped
1 generous tablespoon, baby capers, drained
freshly ground black pepper
grated rind of ½ unwaxed lemon
1 tablespoon fresh parsley, chopped
lemon wedges, to serve

Pat the roes dry with kitchen paper, then coat in seasoned flour. Melt 25g (1oz) butter in a frying pan and fry the roes for 2-3 minutes until pale golden and crisp. Place on the slices of toast and keep warm.

Tip the fat out of the frying pan, then add the remaining fresh butter. When foaming, add the anchovy fillets and cook for a few minutes, mashing down the pieces. Add the capers, stir briefly and spoon over the roes. Season with pepper and scatter over the lemon rind and parsley. Serve immediately with lemon wedges.

BAKED SOFT HERRING ROES
(serves 2 as a starter or light lunch)

250g (9oz) whole soft herring roes
sea salt and freshly ground black pepper
40g (1½oz) butter
about 50g (1¾oz) fresh white breadcrumbs
2 tablespoons fresh flat-leaf parsley, chopped
1 garlic clove, crushed
lemon wedges, to serve

Pre-heat the oven to 220°C/425°F/GM7. Pat the roes dry with kitchen paper, then place in a shallow buttered ovenproof dish in a thin layer. Season well, then dot with half the butter.

Mix the breadcrumbs with the parsley and garlic and sprinkle over the roes to cover completely. Dot with the remaining butter. Bake for 15-20 minutes until the topping is golden brown and crisp. Serve immediately with lemon wedges.

SOFT HERRING ROES WITH CREAM AND TARRAGON
(serves 3-4 as a starter)

350g (12oz) whole soft herring roes
a little seasoned flour
40g (1½oz) unsalted butter
225ml (8fl oz) dry white wine
grated rind and juice of 1 unwaxed lemon
225ml (8fl oz) single cream
about 1 tablespoon fresh tarragon, chopped
triangles of wholemeal toast, to serve

Pat the herring roes dry with kitchen paper, then lightly coat in seasoned flour.

Melt the butter in a frying pan and fry the roes briefly. When they are just beginning to cook, add the wine, lemon juice and rind. Cook for a few minutes until the wine reduces by half, then add the cream. Stir to make a sauce and adjust the seasoning if necessary. Sprinkle with tarragon, and serve immediately with triangles of toast.

SOFT HERRING ROE PÂTÉ

This makes a good starter, or aperitif before a meal. Serve with raw vegetables or lightly toasted French bread.

15g (½oz) butter
100g (3½oz) soft herring roes
sea salt and freshly milled black pepper
75g (2¾oz) cream cheese
1 tablespoon double cream
a small piece of garlic clove
a little lemon juice
cayenne pepper (optional)

Melt 15g (½oz) butter in a frying pan and briefly fry the roes until just cooked. Season well, then place in a food processor with all the other ingredients. Blitz until blended together, then check and adjust seasoning as necessary. Chill until ready to serve.

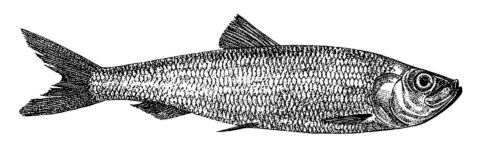

Yarmouth Fish Market just after the First World War, with baskets and barrels for herring

RED HERRINGS

These were the great mass-produced food of the Middle Ages. Legend has it that a Yarmouth man discovered red herring accidentally when he hung his excess catch from the rafters where, in the smoke of the fire, they turned from white to red. The curing was done in the numerous fish-houses, particularly in Great Yarmouth and Lowestoft. Each fish-house was a working unit with its own stables, horses, carts, cooper's shop for making barrels, salt stores, smokehouse and stacks of oak shavings for smoking. It would open on 1 September and work through until the end of the herring season on 30 November. Many farm-labourers worked in fish-houses after the harvest, then went back to work on the land at the end of the herring season.

Fish landed in October-November with a fat content of about 15 per cent were required to make red herring – not enough and they dried out, too much and they went rancid. The fish were heavily salted without splitting or gutting, then hung up in specially constructed chimneys and smoked for several weeks until completely dried out and coloured a bright tandoori-red. In Yarmouth they were also called 'militiamen', with their red coats.

The development of refrigeration in the 19th century meant that the heavy cures used for red herrings were unnecessary and most of the curing houses fell into disuse. Today, only a few are produced for the British market, but exports to hot countries like Africa and Asia continue. Red herrings will keep for a year.

HOW TO COOK RED HERRINGS

In Florence White's *Good Things in England*, published in 1932, she includes an 1823 recipe for cooking red herrings from Great Yarmouth, which involves soaking the fish in beer or milk for 30 minutes, before toasting in front of the fire and serving with butter. Another East Anglian recipe suggests soaking in whisky and then setting alight. When the flames go out, the fish is ready to eat. Traditional accompaniments were egg sauce, buttered eggs and mashed potatoes.

Certainly, red herrings do need to be split open and soaked, because they have a very hard, dry texture and concentrated flavour. I think they are best soaked in milk for at least 2 hours, then grilled briefly, or cut into strips and used like anchovies.

ORFORD BLOATER MARINATED IN CIDER AND MUSTARD
(serves 4 as a lunch, 8 as a starter)

There are no fishing boats working off the beach of Orford Ness in Suffolk, the largest vegetated shingle spit in Europe. The Ness was a secret military site from 1913 until the mid–1980s, but is now a National Nature Reserve protected by the National Trust and an important location for breeding and passage birds, as well as rare species of shingle flora.

However, several inshore trawlers and long-liners work from the village of Orford itself, landing mainly flat fish but some cod, dog fish and herring, which is sold locally or sent to Lowestoft Market.

The combination of bloaters and mustard is an old East Anglian tradition. The most famous name in English mustard, Colman's, was established in 1814 when a young Norfolk miller named Jeremiah Colman moved into the water-mill at Stoke Holy Cross near Norwich. At this time mustard fields surrounded the city and his factory thundered to the sound of whole batteries of pestles and mortars grinding and pulverising the mustard seed into fine mustard flour which was then sieved through specially woven silk to remove the coarse bran. Today, Colman's still dominates the market, although there has been a shift of fashion since the 1970s with the rise of small enterprises producing a whole range of English coarse-grained mustards.

In this recipe the bloater is placed in a marinade and eaten raw.

4 bloaters, skinned, gutted, boned and filleted or 4 undyed kipper fillets
1 teaspoon Colman's English mustard powder
2 tablespoons wholegrain Dijon mustard
2 teaspoons mixed black and white peppercorns
1 teaspoon sea salt
2 teaspoons dark brown sugar
300ml (½ pt) dry cider
apple slices to garnish
a few salad leaves, to serve

Place the bloater fillets in a shallow glass or china dish. Mix the rest of the ingredients together in a jug, adding the cider last.

Pour over the fish and refrigerate for at least 12 hours. Drain the fish and place on serving plates. Garnish with apple slices and salad leaves and serve with brown bread and butter.

BLOATER PASTE

This was a favourite Victorian spread for breakfast toast, made by skinning, cleaning and mincing the cooked bloaters, mixing with lard and spices and pressing into small china pots, patent jars or tins. Because the mild bloater cure results in fish that will not keep for very long, paste was a convenient way of extending the range of the bloater trade before refrigeration.

A well-respected Great Yarmouth fish merchant, W. Masterson Ltd, gave me the following traditional recipe. To make bloater paste, grill the fish for a few minutes until the skin is crisp. Remove the skin, guts and bones, then weigh the flaked fish. In a food processor, blitz the flesh with an equal amount of softened unsalted butter. Season with a little cayenne pepper and lemon juice to taste then pack into a suitable pot. Serve with hot wholemeal toast for breakfast or tea or with melba toast as a starter. Scrambled eggs on toast spread generously with bloater paste makes a scrummy breakfast or supper treat.

YARMOUTH BLOATERS

The best bloaters come from Yarmouth and the East Coast; the name indicates a specific type of light cure used for herring. Yarmouth legend has it that the process was discovered in 1835 by Mr Bishop, a fish curer in the town, who found that his workers had gone home one day leaving a batch of fresh herring unattended. He therefore threw salt over the fish and left them to smoke overnight, ungutted as they were, to preserve them temporarily. Next morning, the results were very pleasing and far less salty and dry than the traditional red herring, so he began marketing them.

The word bloater is said to come from the Old Norse *blautr*, meaning fish that are soft and swollen or plump, which is a good description of this lightly salted and smoked herring. Bloaters have a silvery gold skin with dark pink translucent flesh and a mild, delicate, but unmistakable gamey flavour, as they are cured whole and ungutted.

Bloaters are only made in the autumn when the herring have the correct oil content, and fish landed at East Anglian ports are preferred. The whole ungutted herring are dry-salted for about 6 hours, then suspended on spits of wood pushed through their gills over cool smoke from hardwood sawdust for 8-12 hours to achieve the light cure which makes a bloater. The fish will not keep for more than a few days because of this light cure.

HOW TO COOK BLOATERS

The old East Anglian method of cooking bloaters was to boil or grill them on a gridiron rubbed with a piece of mutton fat over a gentle fire for a few minutes. Simple grilling is still the best way of eating a bloater in my opinion.

Remove the head and split open, then remove the guts and the backbone, or ask your fishmonger to do it for you.

Place under a hot grill for 3-4 minutes on each side, then rub over with a good knob of butter and serve on its own, or with creamy scrambled eggs, brown bread and butter and, if liked, a little mustard.

Bloaters can also be fried in a little butter or oil for 3-4 minutes, or baked in foil or buttered greaseproof paper in a slow oven for about 20 minutes and served with a home-made potato salad.

Orford Bloater Marinated in Cider and Mustard

BETTY'S SPECIAL BLOATERS
(serves 6)

Betty Nice used to run the Guildhall Tea-Rooms at Lavenham in Suffolk for the National Trust some years ago and was an excellent cook. She sent me this recipe for bloaters, which is so rich and delicious. It reminds me of the traditional West Country combination of pilchards and clotted cream.

**6 bloaters, with heads, guts
   and backbones removed
300ml (10fl oz) double cream
1 tablespoon fresh dill, chopped**

Pre-heat the oven to 200°C/400°F/GM6. Fold the cleaned and boned bloaters back into shape again, then arrange in an ovenproof dish. Cover with the cream and sprinkle over the dill. Bake for 10-15 minutes then serve with warm crusty bread.

BUCKLING PÂTÉ

Buckling makes an excellent pâté or fish paste, which is really a Danish speciality. Smoked trout or mackerel can be used instead.

**3 buckling, filleted, gutted and skinned
grated rind and juice of 1 unwaxed
   lemon
1 tablespoon good-quality horseradish
   sauce
150ml (5fl oz) sour cream
freshly ground black pepper**

Put the fish into a food processor or liquidiser with all the other ingredients. Blend to a smooth purée. Season to taste, then pack into a suitable pot. Cover and refrigerate until needed. Serve with hot wholemeal bread or raw vegetables.

BUCKLING

This is the luxury fish of the herring trade. Like bloaters, buckling are cured unsplit and ungutted, but are lightly hot-smoked, which means that the fish is cooked as well as flavoured in the curing process. They have the slightly gamey flavour of a bloater, but in a milder form. Buckling, like bloaters, will not keep for long, even in the fridge.

Eat buckling cold as you would smoked trout, with lemon juice, horseradish sauce and brown bread and butter. If you want to serve hot, warm them through in the oven or under the grill and serve with a knob of herb butter melted on the flesh.

Above: The mysterious pagodas that remain from the testing of nuclear warhead detonators at Orford Ness, Suffolk

Right: Orford, looking from the Ness. In the Middle Ages, this was a major port for the North Sea coast, but over the centuries the river has silted up, causing the shingle spit to form

BAKED BRANCASTER
STAITHE MUSSELS
(serves 4)

It was the exquisite, slightly sweet flesh of mussels that first attracted prehistoric man to the shores and estuaries of East Anglia. They remained extremely popular right up to Victorian times as a welcome addition to the diet of salt and dried fish. Then over-fishing suddenly made them more expensive and scarce, like oysters.

Fortunately, mussels have again become cheap and plentiful especially in North Norfolk, where there are vast areas of mussel lays of excellent quality at Brancaster Staithe. The National Trust protects an extensive area of salt-marsh, mud and sand flats and beach here, including the site of the Roman fort of Brandodunum. A boat can be hired at the Staithe to take visitors to the National Nature Reserve on nearby Scolt Head Island, which is an important breeding site for terns, oyster-catchers and ringed plovers.

The areas covered by the mussel lays belong to the National Trust, but are rented out to the local fisherman's society, whose members work the beds. The mussel seed is collected in the summer from The Wash when it is 2.5cm (1in) long and transferred to lays in Brancaster Harbour mouth, where it stays for 2 years to grow. When of marketable size, the mussels are harvested between September and April. The fishermen work with the tides, often from dawn to dusk, either alone or in pairs, using a 45cm (18in) fork to load the mussels into a boat, 6kg (14lbs) at a time. In 1 hour, they can load 1-1½ tonnes. Brancaster fishermen also pot for lobsters and crabs and net sea trout, bass, mullet and mackerel during the summer months.

If visiting North Norfolk between September and April you can buy sacks of mussels from fishermen's cottages on the roadside – winter's cheapest gourmet treat. The traditional Norfolk ways of cooking were to boil them in water and eat the meat with vinegar accompanied by bread and butter, or to boil, then leave in the half shell and grill with cheese and bacon. This recipe is an adaptation of the latter; omit the bacon if you prefer and sauté the garlic in 50g (1¾oz) butter.

1.5kg (3lb 5oz) live mussels, scrubbed and bearded
100ml (3½fl oz) dry white wine, or water
4-6 rashers dry-cured smoked streaky bacon
2 fat garlic cloves, crushed
50g (1¾oz) dry breadcrumbs
4 tablespoons fresh parsley, finely chopped
sea salt and freshly ground black pepper
2 tablespoons Parmesan cheese, freshly grated
1 unwaxed lime cut into 4 wedges, to serve

Pre-heat the oven to 230°C/450°F/GM8.

Place the mussels in a large pan with the wine or water. Bring to the boil, cover and cook over a high heat for about 3 minutes or until the shells open, shaking the pan occasionally. Remove the mussels from the pan, discarding any that remain closed and drain the cooking liquor through a fine sieve. Reserve for later. Cook in several batches if you haven't a very large pan.

Allow the mussels to cool a little, then remove and discard the top half of each shell, leaving the mussels on the remaining halves.

Fry or grill the bacon until very crisp and crumble into small pieces. Keep warm while you cook the garlic for about 2 minutes in the bacon fat. Stir in the breadcrumbs and cook, stirring until lightly browned. Remove the pan from the heat and stir in the herbs and reserved bacon. Moisten with a little of the reserved mussel liquor, then season to taste with salt and pepper.

Press the breadcrumb mixture, quite firmly, on each mussel, ensuring the flesh is well covered. Arrange them on 2 baking sheets, then sprinkle the tops with grated Parmesan. Bake for just 10 minutes, then serve hot with the lime wedges and crusty bread.

Left: Fresh mussels on the salt-marshes at Brancaster Staithe, Norfolk
Above: Scolt Head Island

MUSSEL AND TOMATO SOUP WITH SEVILLE ROUILLE FRIED BREAD
(serves 4)

This substantial soup would be good for a winter lunch or supper.

- 1kg (2lb 4oz) live mussels, scrubbed and bearded
- 2 shallots, peeled and finely chopped
- 1 fennel bulb, trimmed and finely chopped, reserving any feathery leaves for decoration
- 50ml (2fl oz) olive oil
- 200ml (7fl oz) strong still cider, or dry white wine
- 2 bay leaves
- 2 x 400g (14oz) cans of chopped tomatoes
- grated rind and juice of 1 unwaxed orange
- sea salt and freshly ground black pepper
- a little freshly ground coriander seed

For the Seville rouille
- 1 free-range egg yolk, at room temperature
- 2 garlic cloves, crushed
- 50ml (2fl oz) best virgin olive oil
- 75ml (3fl oz) peanut or sunflower oil
- juice of 1 Seville orange, or sweet orange
- sea salt, freshly ground black pepper and cayenne
- 8 slices French bread, preferably a day old
- a few fine strips of orange rind, to garnish

In a large lidded pan, fry the shallots and fennel briefly in the olive oil over a moderate heat. When they are sizzling, add the cider or wine and bay leaves. Bring to the boil, then throw in the mussels. Cover with the lid and cook over high heat for 3-4 minutes, shaking the pan once or twice. Transfer the mussels to a colander over a bowl using a draining spoon, discarding any that haven't opened. Reserve the cooking liquor. Add the tomatoes to the pan and simmer for about 20 minutes while you remove the mussel meat from the shells, leaving some unshelled for decoration. Return the reserved cooking liquor to the pan and as much of the shallot and fennel mixture from the shells as you can. Set the mussels aside.

Add the orange juice to the pan, reserving the rind for the rouille. Season the soup to taste with salt, pepper and coriander.

To make the rouille, beat the garlic into the egg yolk. Mix the olive oil with 50ml (2floz) peanut or sunflower oil in a jug. Whisk this into the yolk, starting a drop at a time and whisking constantly until it has the consistency of mayonnaise, then add in a thin stream, whisking all the time. Beat in the Seville juice and reserved orange rind and season to taste with salt, pepper and cayenne. Fry the bread in the remaining peanut or sunflower oil until golden brown. Drain on kitchen paper and keep warm.

Return the mussel meat and whole mussels to the soup and reheat. Serve in warm soup plates, garnished with strips of orange rind and sprigs of reserved fennel frond.

Spoon the rouille on to the fried bread and float in the soup.

TAGLIATELLE WITH SAFFRON MUSSELS
(serves 4)

- 1.75kg (4lb) live mussels, scrubbed and bearded
- 150ml ($\frac{1}{4}$pt) dry white wine
- 2 shallots, chopped
- 350g (12oz) dried tagliatelle or 450g (1lb) fresh
- 25g (1oz) butter
- 2 garlic cloves, crushed
- 250ml (9fl oz) double cream
- a generous pinch of saffron strands
- 1 free-range egg yolk
- sea salt and freshly ground black pepper
- 2 tablespoons fresh flat-leaf parsley, chopped
- freshly grated Parmesan cheese, to serve

Discard any mussels that are open and place the rest in a large pan with the wine and shallots. Cover with a tight-fitting lid and cook over a high heat, shaking the pan occasionally, for 3-4 minutes until the mussels have opened. Drain the mussels into a colander, reserving the liquor. Discard any that remain closed. Remove the meat from most of the shells, reserving a few whole mussels for garnishing. Keep these warm.

Bring the reserved cooking liquor to the boil, then continue boiling to reduce by half. Strain into a jug to remove any grit.

Cook the tagliatelle in a large pan of boiling salted water for about 10 minutes (2-3 minutes if fresh), or until *al dente*.

Meanwhile, melt the butter in a pan and fry the garlic for 1 minute. Pour in the mussel liquor, cream and saffron, then heat gently until the sauce thickens slightly. Remove from the heat and stir in the egg yolk, and mussel meat. Season to taste.

Drain the pasta and transfer to 4 warm serving bowls. Spoon the sauce over and sprinkle with parsley and freshly grated Parmesan. Garnish with the reserved whole mussels and serve immediately.

Ladybirds clinging to grasses at Brancaster, Norfolk

BRANCASTER STAITHE OYSTERS ROCKEFELLER
(serves 6 as a starter)

The first people to exploit the British Native oyster on a large scale were the Romans, who were oyster farming in Norfolk almost two millennia ago. The oyster fishery, established at Brancaster Staithe on the North Norfolk coast, was flourishing right up until 1900. The oysters were dredged in Brancaster Bay and Burnham Flats and were known as 'Burnham Grounders'. In 1908 whelk fishing took over and, together with nearby Wells-next-the-Sea, Brancaster became famous for its whelks. Today, there is no whelking from Brancaster, but both Native and Pacific oysters were reintroduced into the staithe 30 years ago and supply local restaurants, pubs and markets.

The land is owned by the National Trust, but is leased to the Brancaster Staithe Fisherman's Society, whose members cultivate the lays. One of the oyster fishermen, Cyril Southerland, walks students, who have enrolled for a short fish cookery course at the Trust's Brancaster Millennium Activity Centre, across the marshes to the oyster beds and mussel lays where he picks oysters straight out of the sea and opens them for everyone to enjoy. On the last day of the course, the students are taken to The Fish Shed, in Brancaster, where they can buy sparklingly fresh fish to take home with them.

This is a famous oyster dish said to have been invented at Antoine's, the well-known New Orleans restaurant, in the late 1800s. Some inspired customer is supposed to have remarked that oysters prepared this way were 'as rich as Rockefeller'.

36 Native or Pacific oysters, opened with deep shells reserved
450g (1lb) fresh spinach, finely chopped
225ml (8fl oz) sour cream
2 garlic cloves, crushed
4 rashers locally smoked streaky bacon, cooked until crisp, then crushed into crumbs (optional)
freshly ground black pepper
3 tablespoons good mature Cheddar cheese, finely grated
25g (1oz) stale breadcrumbs
36 lemon slices, for supporting oysters during cooking

Steam the spinach until cooked, then drain well and place in a sieve. Using the back of a spoon, press the spinach to remove as much moisture as possible. Place in a bowl and mix with the sour cream, garlic and bacon if using. Season to taste with black pepper.

Place a teaspoon of the spinach mixture in each oyster shell and set on a slice of lemon on a baking sheet. Top with the oysters and then another teaspoon of spinach mixture. Place the cheese and breadcrumbs in a small bowl and mix to combine. Sprinkle over the oysters and cook under a pre-heated grill for 3-4 minutes, or until the cheese has melted and the topping is brown.

Serve immediately.

Left: Boats on the salt-marshes at Brancaster Staithe
Right: The windmill at Burnham Overy, looking across Burnham Norton Marshes

COLCHESTER POACHED OYSTERS WITH SCRAMBLED EGGS AND CAVIAR
(serves 4)

In the past the most important oyster production in the East of England was concentrated on the Thames Estuary, with Colchester on the north side and Whitstable in Kent on the south. Oysters were an important food to Londoners; the Lord Mayor regulated the price from at least the 15th century and an early reference to 'Colchesters' from 1625 confirms the identification of the town with the product. The Colchester Fishery had been granted a charter in 1189.

Oysters were apparently plentiful until the 1860s when disease and bad weather seem to have caused a shortage. The oyster ceased to be the food of the masses and became a costly delicacy and the native oyster beds have suffered acute decline ever since.

In 1966 the Colchester Oyster Fishery was established to restore the oyster beds. Colchester oysters are fattened in the Pyefleet, a creek in the estuary of the River Colne, just south of the town of Colchester, but silt had accumulated on the derelict beds. This was cleared in the 1960s and natural restocking followed. New storage tanks were built: water for these is pumped from settlement ponds into a storage pond and filtered into temperature-controlled, oxygenated tanks. The water for holding oysters is circulated through an ultra-violet treatment plant and the water composition is monitored daily. Unfortunately the restocked oyster beds were hit badly by the disease *bonamia* in 1982. The good news is that once again the native beds are slowly recovering and 'Colchesters' are available to enjoy. The company now supplies 250,000 oysters worldwide each year to customers. The famous 'Oyster Feast' at Colchester Town Hall is still held annually, when many famous people from far and wide celebrate the renowned shellfish.

Eight miles south of Colchester, the National Trust protects Copt Hall Marshes near Little Wigborough on the Blackwater Estuary, a salt-marsh extremely important for overwintering birds. Visitors can park their car and follow a footpath encircling the marsh.

This recipe makes a very luxurious starter, or special breakfast or supper. Splash out on black caviar or use lumpfish roe or Avruga smoked herring roe, which is available from some supermarkets and has a good flavour.

6 organic or free-range large eggs
30ml (1fl oz) double cream
25g (1oz) butter
16 Native or Pacific oysters, opened juices and deep shells reserved
100ml (3½ fl oz) beurre blanc (see p.221)
25g (1oz) caviar, lumpfish roe or Avruga smoked herring roe, thoroughly washed and blanched seaweed, to serve

Warm the reserved oyster shells in the oven. Meanwhile, beat the eggs and stir in half the cream. Melt the butter in a non-stick pan, then add the egg mixture. Cook until set, then keep warm.

At the same time, lightly poach the oysters in their own juices for 1 or 2 minutes, then keep warm.

Arrange the warmed oyster shells on a serving plate, decorated with blanched seaweed. Stir the rest of the cream into the scrambled eggs and place a little in each shell. Top with a poached oyster, then the beurre blanc sauce and finish with caviar.

CREAMED LENTIL SOUP WITH OYSTERS
(serves 4-6)

This thick rich soup is filling enough to serve for lunch or supper. By all means up the number of oysters!

12 Native or Pacific oysters, opened and juices reserved
40g (1½ oz) butter
1 red onion, peeled and finely chopped
1 large carrot, peeled and finely chopped
3 garlic cloves, peeled and crushed
225g (8oz) green lentils
700ml (1¼ pts) cold water
200ml (7fl oz) full-cream milk
200ml (7fl oz) whipping cream
sea salt and freshly ground black pepper
2 tablespoons fresh chives, snipped

Melt the butter in a large pan and sweat the onion, carrot and garlic for about 5 minutes without colouring. Add the lentils and cover with the cold water. Bring to the boil, then turn the heat down and simmer very gently for 30-40 minutes until the lentils are soft, but not breaking up. Add the milk and cream and bring to the boil. Liquidise about one third of the soup, then pour back into the pan with the rest of the lentils. Season to taste with salt and pepper. When ready to serve the soup, put the oysters and their juices into a small pan and heat through for just a few seconds to firm them slightly.

Serve the soup in warm bowls. Top with the oysters and sprinkle with chives. Serve with warm crusty bread.

MALDON SEA SALT

The long Essex coast is flat with salt-marshes and tidal inlets well suited to salt extraction and the industry has flourished for many centuries. Salt is known to have been extracted from the Maldon area since the Iron Age and in the Domesday Book of 1086, 45 salt pans were listed. The present company grew from a salt works established in 1823 and became the Maldon Crystal Salt Company in the 1880s.

To make Maldon sea salt, sea water is collected from salt-marshes when the salt content is at its maximum, after a period of dry weather at the spring tides. It is kept in holding tanks and allowed to settle before being filtered and pumped into storage tanks, then drawn off into pans about 3 metres (9 feet) square, mounted on a system of brick flues. The water is brought to a rapid boil and skimmed, then the heat is reduced and the water allowed to evaporate, concentrating the salt in minute, pyramid-shaped crystals, which are unique to this process. The pans are cooled and the salt harvested by raking it to one side with wooden hoes. It is then drained in special bins for 2 days, and drying is completed in a salt store. The resultant salt is white, with a soft flaky texture and a good clean flavour, which is wonderful for cooking and the table. Good supermarkets and specialist food shops stock Maldon sea salt.

The causeway leading to Northey Island, near Maldon in Essex

FISH HLAF FROM SUTTON HOO
(serves 4)

Sophisticated fish cookery disappeared from Britain with the withdrawal of the Romans at the beginning of the 5th century AD and fish became unpopular. In the Celtic parts of Britain, it was looked upon with disfavour by the early Christian Church; fish was sacred to Venus, a pagan goddess whom the Church particularly disliked, and in eastern Britain the Anglo-Saxons, who were gradually occupying the area, were farmers and not fishermen, although they made use of fish that they could easily catch inland or on the coast.

The situation began to change when the rites of the Roman Church were brought to England at the end of the 6th century AD and the heathen Anglo-Saxons were gradually converted to Christianity. Unlike the Celtic Church, that of Rome did not look askance at fish; its policy was to replace a pagan observance with a Christian one. If fish had formerly been eaten on Friday by the devotees of Venus, it was now to be eaten on the same day by good Christians in memory of the events of Good Friday. These religious feast days gave a new impetus to fish eating and the fishing industry expanded to meet it. Basket weirs were put across rivers to catch salmon as they swam up to spawn. In Anglo-Saxon cooking the fish was often blended with oats and flour to form a loaf or 'hlaf'. This recipe is Sutton Hoo's interpretation of that loaf which they serve in the National Trust's bistro-style restaurant, although, of course, potatoes didn't arrive in this country until many centuries later.

> 450g (1lb) responsibly farmed
>   salmon fillet
> 1.25kg (2lb 12oz) floury potatoes,
>   cooked and mashed
> fresh dill, chopped
> fresh chives, snipped
> sea salt and freshly ground black pepper
> a little plain flour
> 2 free-range eggs, beaten (to coat)
> fresh granary breadcrumbs
> sunflower oil for frying

Poach the fish gently in water for about 5 minutes then remove. When cool enough to handle, take off the skin and remove any bones. Flake carefully with a fork without breaking it up too much. Leave to get cold.

Fold the cold salmon carefully into the mashed potato and add as many herbs as you like. Season to taste. Divide the mixture into four and mould gently into 4 large fish cakes. Put them on a plate and leave in the fridge for about 1 hour to firm up.

Pre-heat the oven to 200°C/400°F/GM6. Lightly dust each fish cake with flour, then dip into the beaten egg. Coat well in the breadcrumbs. Heat a little oil in a frying pan and fry the fish cakes lightly to give them a good colour, then place on a baking tray and bake in the oven for 20-25 minutes. Serve immediately with a dressed leaf salad.

SUTTON HOO GRAVADLAX WITH A SWEET MUSTARD DRESSING
(serves 8-10 as a starter)

At Sutton Hoo you can get close to one of the most fascinating archaeological finds in Britain's history – the Anglo-Saxon royal burial site where priceless treasure was discovered in a huge ship grave in 1939. An exhibition hall houses a full-sized reconstruction of the burial chamber and tells the story of the site. You can also enjoy walks over rare lowland heath on the estuary of the River Deben.

Sutton Hoo's catering manager tells me that the restaurant chose this dish as part of their function menu to celebrate the Anglo-Saxon links with Scandinavia and Germany. Gravadlax is very suitable for a dinner party as it has to be prepared well in advance; 4-5 days' curing is needed for the best flavour. Make sure you use very fresh salmon.

> 1.35kg (3lb) piece wild Pacific or
>   responsibly farmed Atlantic
>   salmon, filleted and unskinned
>   (i.e. 2 equal-sized fillets that will
>   fit together)
> 2 tablespoons whole black peppercorns,
>   coarsely crushed
> 3 tablespoons fresh dill, finely chopped
> 2 tablespoons caster sugar
> juice of 1 large lemon
> 2 tablespoons or other
>   coarse sea salt
> 1 lemon to squeeze over

> For the sweet mustard dressing
> 200g (7oz) crème fraîche
> juice of 1 large lemon
> 2 tablespoons caster sugar
> sea salt and freshly ground black pepper
> 2 tablespoons wholegrain mustard
> 1 tablespoon extra virgin olive oil

Remove any bones from the salmon fillets and wash well under cold running water. Dry well with kitchen paper. Mix the peppercorns, dill, sugar, lemon juice and salt into a paste and spread evenly over the fish, both sides. Fit the salmon fillets flesh sides together and place in a large container that will hold the fish and the excess liquid that will collect during marinating. Put a large dinner plate on top of the fish and add several heavy weights, or tins from your store cupboard, to weigh down the fish.

Leave to cure for 4 or 5 days, turning the fish and draining off the excess liquid at least twice during the curing time. Keep the fillets weighed down well. To make the dressing, beat all the ingredients together vigorously until well blended.

To serve the fish, thinly slice it and remove the skin. Arrange on serving plates. Squeeze over extra lemon juice and drizzle with the prepared dressing.

Right: Burial mounds at Sutton Hoo, Suffolk

SAMPHIRE

There are two forms of samphire, often referred to as poor man's asparagus. The first, and original, is rock samphire, which still grows abundantly on rocky cliffs on the coasts of south and west Britain. The second is marsh samphire, once more commonly known as glasswort because it was used as a source of soda for glassmaking. Marsh samphire is found on many tidal marshes around the British coasts, but is very common and better known in Norfolk, where there are seven varieties covering the lower levels of the salt-marshes and mudflats. The plant is one of the first colonisers of a mudbank and sprouts from the bare mud like a forest of miniature trees trapping yet more silt, especially in the autumn and building up mud at a rate of as much as 3.8cm (1$\frac{1}{2}$in) a year. The fleshy stems and branches, which are well adapted to retain the plant's moisture, are smoothly curved to offer the least resistance to the currents which will try to shift the seedlings from their shallow-rooted anchorages. In some creeks, the plants are pushed tight together and come up with just one straight stem, but the best to eat are the bushy plants.

Rock samphire was highly esteemed, unlike marsh samphire which was historically a food for the poor. However, marsh became a substitute for the increasingly rare rock samphire in the late 19th century and is now the better known. Recently, it has become extremely fashionable amongst chefs,

and if gathered commercially on a large scale it will have a terrible effect on saltwater wild life. Most commercial gathering takes place around The Wash and if you are a holder of rights to gather, this over-rules the Wildlife and Countryside Act, which states that it is illegal to uproot any wild plant. Marsh samphire is collected by hand and should be cut from the plant just above the base with a sharp knife, leaving the root system intact. After cutting, it should be washed and used while very fresh or frozen, as it freezes well.

Sold from fishmongers, markets and roadside stalls in North Norfolk, samphire was traditionally eaten hot with lamb or mutton, but its aromatic salty taste combines so well with fish and shellfish that it features on many local hotel and restaurant menus in the early summer.

HOW TO COOK SAMPHIRE

In June and July when the plant is young and tender, the tips can be eaten raw or lightly blanched for 2 minutes. Later on in the year, in August and September, pick off only the very tender side shoots and about 3.8cm (1$\frac{1}{2}$in) from the main stalk. Boil briskly in a large pan of unsalted water for 4-5 minutes, or until just tender. Drain well, then eat with melted butter and black pepper. Samphire is full of iron and very good for you.

DOVER SOLE WITH SEA SPINACH
(serves 2)

Dover sole is one of the flat fish caught by the two or three small boats selling their catch off Dunwich Beach in Suffolk. The beach was once common land attached to an important medieval city that has since disappeared into the sea, leaving just the village. Fishing has been very important to this area; as far back as King John's reign, the then borough of Dunwich paid annual charges of 5,000 eels and 8,000 herrings and by the 16th century, boats were fishing as far away as Iceland for cod and other white fish. But, by 1947 there were no boats working from here.

Today, the fishermen may catch a little cod and whiting in the winter by long-lining and sprats are netted in December. From May until September/October the boats trawl for Dover soles, plaice and dabs and pot for lobsters and crabs.

Behind the beach is Dunwich Heath, all that remains of the once extensive Sandling heaths, with open tracts of heather and gorse, shady woods and sandy cliffs. This is an important nature conservation area now protected by the National Trust, with a network of footpaths giving access to the beach and coastal path. The Trust's Neptune Coastline Campaign has recently raised funds, with the help of Pizza Express customers who munched their way through 400,000 Neptune pizzas, to acquire farmland at Dunwich, which will be allowed to return to heather heath. It is certainly a breathtakingly beautiful place when the heather and gorse are flowering.

Sea spinach, or sea beet, which grows on the seaward side of sea walls around the high spring tide mark of the East Anglian coast, is the direct ancestor of many of our cultivated beetroots and chards, and indeed of sugar beet. It looks like old-fashioned spinach, dark green with waxy leaves, but has a much fuller flavour and is packed with vitamin C. Pick the young tender leaves only between May and October.

If Dover sole is not available, use lemon or megrim sole, plaice, dabs or flounders for this recipe.

> 2 large Dover sole, filleted and
>   skinned (4 fillets)
> 700g (1lb 9oz) wild sea spinach,
>   or cultivated spinach, washed
>   and trimmed
> sea salt, freshly ground pepper and
>   freshly ground nutmeg
> a little seasoned flour
> butter and oil for frying
> a squeeze of lemon juice, to serve

> For the sauce
> 125g (4½oz) butter
> 4 shallots, finely chopped
> 100ml (3½fl oz) double cream
> sea salt and freshly ground pepper

Heat a large frying pan, then add the butter and oil.

Dip the sole fillets into seasoned flour and shake off the excess. Make the sauce by heating a small piece of the butter in a pan. Add the shallots and sauté very gently for about 10 minutes until soft, but without colouring. Add the cream and continue to simmer gently. Cut the remaining butter into small knobs, adding a few pieces at a time to the simmering cream and mixing well with a balloon whisk. When all the butter is added, you should have a glossy sauce. Season to taste. Keep warm over hot water while you fry the fish.

Melt a little butter and oil in a frying pan and gently fry the fish for a few minutes each side until golden brown. Remove and keep warm. Meanwhile, cook the spinach. Heat a knob of butter in a large pan until sizzling, then add the spinach. Cook over a high heat until wilted, but still retaining its shape and texture. Drain well and season with salt, pepper and nutmeg.

Divide the spinach among 4 warm serving plates and arrange the fish on top. Pour the sauce over the top and finish with a squeeze of lemon, or serve the sauce separately.

Left: Victorian coastguard cottages and look-out tower at Dunwich Heath, Suffolk. Three of the cottages are now National Trust holiday homes Right: Dover Sole with Sea Spinach

ALDEBURGH SPRATS
(allow about 5 sprats per person)

Aldeburgh in Suffolk was a prosperous port in the 16th century, but is now widely known for its music festival started in 1948 by Benjamin Britten and held annually in June. Aldeburgh and Southwold sprats have been famous for centuries. The first catch of the season used to be smoked and sent to London for the Lord Mayor's Banquet. Their season is October to March and they are some of the best fish in East Anglia.

The sprat is one of the smaller members of the herring family, is very cheap and highly nutritious. They are best bought on the beach straight from the fishermen's boats.

Local fishermen don't cut the heads or tails off the sprats so that they can eat them in their fingers. There is also no need to gut them as they are such small fish, but if you wish, clean them through their gills so that the body is not damaged. Put the fish in a very hot frying pan without fat, but just a sprinkling of salt, which draws out the oil. Fry quickly, 2 or 3 minutes each side.

Another traditional way of cooking sprats is to grill or barbecue them whole for a few minutes on each side. As with whitebait, their flavour is improved by a little lemon juice and cayenne or mustard. Sprats are also excellent baked in the oven.

COUPLED SPRATS
(serves 1 as a starter)

This is another traditional East Anglian way of serving fresh sprats; allow 2 or 3 pairs of fish for each person. They may be shallow-fried instead if you wish.

> **4-6 fresh sprats, cleaned and butterflied**
> **by a fishmonger if possible**
> **1½-2 tablespoons fresh parsley,**
> **chopped**
> **1½-2 tablespoons fresh chives, snipped**
> **sea salt and cayenne pepper**
> **1 large free-range egg, beaten**
> **seasoned flour**
> **sunflower oil, for frying**
> **lemon wedges, to serve**

If you are not lucky enough to have a tame fishmonger, prepare the sprats yourself. Cut off their heads and tails, split them down one side of the backbone and open them out flat like miniature kippers. Remove the backbone by holding the flesh down with the first and second fingers of your left hand and pulling the bone up between them, starting from the head end.

Heat the oil in a deep-fat fryer with a basket to 190°C/375°F. Mix the herbs together and season with salt and cayenne. Sprinkle this mixture generously over the flesh side of the split sprats. Make the fish into pairs by putting them face to face, dip in beaten egg and then in seasoned flour. Deep-fry for 3-4 minutes until golden brown and crisp. Serve immediately with lemon wedges, thin brown bread and butter and a glass of the local Adnams bitter.

CRISPY BACON &
GARLIC SPRATS
(serves 4)

> **450g (1lb) fresh or frozen sprats, cleaned**
> **25g (1oz) butter**
> **4 rashers local dry-cured smoked back**
> **bacon, chopped**
> **2 garlic cloves, finely chopped**
> **4 tablespoons fresh brown breadcrumbs**
> **2 tablespoons fresh flat-leaf parsley,**
> **chopped**
> **1 lemon cut into quarters, to serve**

Using scissors, snip off the heads of the sprats. Melt the butter in a large frying pan and fry the bacon until crisp. Add the garlic and sprats and cook for 3-5 minutes until pale golden brown. Sprinkle over the breadcrumbs and parsley and cook for a further 2-3 minutes, until the breadcrumbs are crisp.

Serve immediately with a crisp green salad, thin brown bread and butter and lemon quarters.

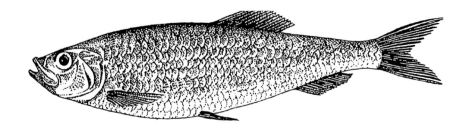

NORFOLK SEASIDE PLATTER

Use any combination of shellfish available, but do make sure it is all very fresh.

Make a mound of crushed ice on a very large serving platter or tray. Cover it with fresh washed seaweed, or fresh dill and parsley. Place a bowl of home-made or good-squality lemon, garlic or mustard mayonnaise (see pp.221-3), slightly off-centre on top of the ice. Arrange a few small lettuce leaves round the bowl. Carefully open some fresh oysters and place them on the platter sitting in their deep shells. Arrange cooked shell-on prawns, brown shrimps, cockles, whelks, winkles, mussels and clams around the oysters. Include Cromer crab and lobster if available.

Garnish the seafood with lemon wedges and fresh dill. Serve the platter with warm crusty bread and butter, a crisp green salad and ice-cold Norfolk cider. (You will also need pins to extract the winkle and whelk meat.)

HOW TO COOK WHELKS

Most whelks are sold ready cooked, but a few fish shops sell them alive. When you get home, steep your whelks in cold fresh salted water for at least 12 hours, changing the water occasionally to get rid of any sand they may be harbouring. (Use a lidded container or you will find the whelks all over the kitchen!)

When ready to cook, drain the shellfish, then place in a large pan of boiling salted water. The RSPCA recommends that they should be cooked in small batches, so the water temperature is maintained and the shellfish die in seconds. As soon as the water comes back to the boil, lower the heat to a simmer and continue cooking for 4 minutes. Drain through a colander, then, when cool enough to handle, 'winkle' or twist the whelks out of their shells with a long pin or small fork. Cut off the small hard disc at the mouth of the shell.

Traditionally, whelks are served sprinkled with lemon juice or vinegar, black pepper and plain or garlic-flavoured melted butter and accompanied by a glass of local beer, but they make a delicious addition to seafood salads, or can be coated in batter and fried to make fritters. Sliced they can be added to pasta sauces, soups and chowders.

Eat whelks fresh or they will be tough. Even when fresh they can be chewy, but they are flavoursome and high in protein.

Blakeney Point, Norfolk

WELLS WHELKS

Whelks from Wells-next-the-Sea in North Norfolk are almost as famous as Cromer crabs; in fact, about 80 per cent of those used for the English market are caught within a few miles of this shore. They are also exported to Asia in large quantities. Other areas of production in eastern England are the Thames Estuary and Whitstable in Kent. Total landings amount to several tonnes per annum.

In the past, whelks were much used in British fish cookery; the Romans carried them to various inland sites and they are mentioned in the accounts of 15th-century fishmongers and many medieval households. At the enthronement of the Archbishop of Canterbury in 1504, 4,000 whelks were offered to the more distinguished of the guests as a garnish for salted sturgeon. They were also put into stews, soups and salads, or plainly boiled and eaten with vinegar and parsley. Later, they became part of the diet of the London poor. Ready-cooked whelks are still sold from seaside stalls alongside cockles and winkles to be eaten splashed with vinegar, but the uncooked meat has found a new market in Chinese and Japanese restaurants.

Whelks live offshore and are caught in plastic or iron pots baited with dead shore crabs, fish offal or salt herring. In Norfolk, a number of these pots are tied to one rope to form a shank with a buoy at each end. Weather permitting, the pots are emptied and re-baited daily. Once landed, the shellfish are boiled in sea water in their shells, then cooled and the meat extracted. If the whelks are to be sold raw, the shells are crushed and removed before packaging.

THE NORTH EAST

Some of the most magnificent, wild and rugged coastline in England's far north-eastern counties of Northumberland, Durham, Tyne & Wear and North Yorkshire is in the care of the National Trust, including two castles, Dunstanburgh and Lindisfarne, a complete fishing village, Low Newton-by-the-Sea, and a group of islands, The Farnes.

The Berwickshire and North Northumberland Coast has been designated a Special Area of Conservation, stretching over 90 miles of coast and 250 square miles of sea. The National Trust is one of the bodies involved in the management of the area, discussing how its conservation can be married with fishing and recreational demands. As a result, the Northumberland Sea Fisheries Committee has recently banned all pair-trawling and pair-seining off the coast as far out as 6 nautical miles. Both these fishing practices are very damaging to the seabed and marine life, as well as to seabirds.

Forty-five miles of the North Yorkshire Heritage Coast have been identified as worthy of protection. Currently the National Trust owns about twelve, so additional funds are urgently needed to buy more coast when the opportunities arise.

The harvest of the sea has been one of the chief concerns of the inhabitants of this coast since time immemorial. Athough most of the villages have generally been too poor to provide themselves with man-made harbours, the innumerable creeks and bays have given enough protection for the launching and landing of small boats, or cobles, unique to this area. From Seahouses to Amble in Northumberland, and Staithes to Bridlington in North Yorkshire, these sturdy little cobles still fish the inshore waters.

Larger boats, known as keels, work from the bigger fishing ports of Whitby, Scarborough and Bridlington. Using trawls, seine and drift nets, or lines, keels have traditionally caught cod, haddock, flat fish, whiting and skate, with some concentrating on crab and lobster. Although these boats now carry a mass of modern equipment, they still bear a close resemblance to the old Humber keels from which they sprang.

Today, the entire North East coast is suffering from the effects of over-fishing and pollution. A relatively small number of businesses are now involved in commercial fishing, but they remain important to the economy. Because of this, European funds have been made available to modernise the industry in North and East Yorkshire. To overcome a built-in resistance to change, plans are being developed to employ for a short period specialist business advice on the benefits of quality control, consistency of supply, the use of technology and marketing.

Hull's new high-tech Fishgate Market is poised to join the Electronic Fish Information Centre Europe (EFICE) network of electronic fish auctions that was set up in 2000 by the Dutch. This network allows fish traders to buy at connected markets and to create a more transparent basis with fewer price fluctuations and higher average prices for the fishermen. As a result, the Fishgate Market will be linked to eight auctions in The Netherlands and Belgium and 600 local and 65 remote buyers, who have access to the 150,000 tonnes of fresh fish landed each year.

Previous pages: Staple Island on the Farne Islands, with the Longstone lighthouse in the distance on the left
Left: A little girl with a fisherman mending a lobster pot. This photograph, taken in the 1920s, is part of a collection created as the result of an appeal by the
Daily Express in the 1970s for images from family albums that reflected life in 20th-century Britain

STAITHES COD, SMOKED BACON AND PARSLEY PIE

Just north of Port Mulgrave, on the Yorkshire coast, where the National Trust protects the cliffs and undercliff surrounding the harbour, is the quaint storm-battered village of Staithes, birthplace of Captain Cook. In the 19th century it was a very busy fishing port with 400 men directly employed in the industry. The fishing fleet was one of the most important on the whole Yorkshire coast for the capture of ling, cod, haddock and mackerel and at the height of the herring season it went, with other vessels from northern ports, as far as Great Yarmouth. Today, there are just a very small number of cobles.

Ling, the largest member of the cod family, has been overfished in the North Sea for so many years that, together with cod and haddock, it is now considered to be outside safe biological limits, but in the past ling pie was a speciality of all the northern fishing villages on the Yorkshire coast. Its cooking was particularly important in Staithes where no girl was considered a good wife unless she could make a really good ling pie – 'A dish fit for anny King is yan o'them ling pies; Steeas women – an they're wise Knows what ti deea wi ling'. The 'Steeas women' also had to be tough to help push out, or haul in, the coble boats in rough weather, mend nets and bait hundreds of hooks with mussels and limpets. Today, the women still wear the traditional fishergirls' white cotton bonnets on special village occasions.

This northern coast of Yorkshire and Northumberland has a predominantly Viking heritage. Staithes' speech is full of old Viking words and many traditional fishing recipes like ling pie include bacon. Baked traditionally at Lent, in more recent times the pie became associated with Good Friday.

Ask for line-caught cod, coley, pollack or haddock from Icelandic waters.

1kg (2½ lbs) Icelandic line-caught cod fillet, at least 2.5cm (1in) thick, skinned and boned
2-3 rashers dry-cured smoked bacon
3 medium-sized leeks, trimmed
225g (8oz) medium-sized brown mushrooms, wiped
50g (1¾oz) butter
50g (1¾oz) flour
600ml (1 pt) full-fat milk
2 tablespoons fresh flat-leaf parsley, chopped
2 tablespoons fresh chives, chopped
4 tablespoons crème fraîche or double cream
sea salt and freshly milled black pepper
450g (1lb) ready-made puff pastry, chilled
1 free-range egg, beaten, or milk for glazing

Pre-heat the oven to 210°C/425°F/GM7.

Cut the fish into 2.5 cm (1 in) chunks and place in a deep ovenproof pie dish with a rim. Season well. Snip the bacon into fine strips and fry in a small pan until brown. Drain and add to the dish.

Slice the leeks into rounds about as thick as your finger, then rinse thoroughly under running water. Drain well. Melt the butter in a pan and cook the leeks until soft.

Meanwhile, slice the mushrooms and when the leeks are soft, add to the pan. Cook for about 5 minutes, then sprinkle over the flour and continue to cook for 1-2 minutes. Gradually stir in the milk and gently bring to the boil, stirring all the time. When the consistency is that of a thick sauce, leave to simmer gently for about 15 minutes. Stir in the herbs and the cream and season to taste. Pour over the fish (the filling should come almost to the top of the dish). Put a pie funnel, cup or egg-cup in the middle to hold up the pastry, then let the mixture cool before putting on the pastry topping.

Roll out the chilled pastry 2.5cm (1in) larger than the pie dish, then cut out a 2.5cm (1 in) strip to fit the edge of the dish. Wet the rim with water or milk and press the strip of pastry firmly in place. Wet this edge of pastry and lay the remaining pastry on top to form a lid. Press firmly down on the rim and pinch the edges together to seal, and make a steam hole in the centre.

Brush with a little beaten egg or milk and place on a baking sheet. Bake on a high shelf in the oven for 30-40 minutes until golden brown and crisp at the edges.

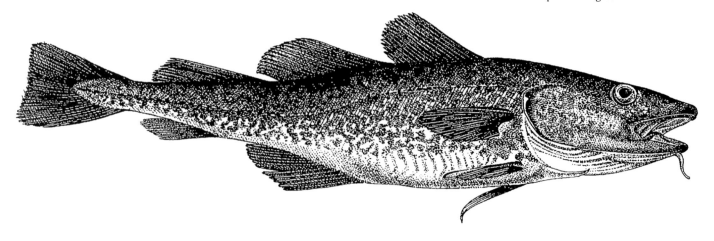

The village of Staithes in North Yorkshire, with Cowbar Nab rearing above the cottages on the left. Staithes was the birthplace of Captain Cook in 1728

BAY TOWN HOT SPICED CRAB
(serves 2)

The village of Robin Hood's Bay, known locally as Bay Town, is a picturesque place, with narrow streets leading down to the sea and an attractive collection of red-roofed cottages huddled around the slipway at the foot of a steep ravine. The National Trust owns the Old Coastguard Station and is running it as an exhibition and education centre in partnership with the North York Moor National Park Authority.

Bay Town was once a thriving fishing centre; in the mid-19th century there were still 35 cobles working from the village. The coble has changed little since the 16th century and is descended from the Viking longboat that brought the Norsemen, first to plunder, then to settle in this region. Its distinguishing features are a deep bow, high shoulders, and a low, sloping, square stern with a long detachable rudder ideal for launching into the waves. From the beach it heads into the sea, but is landed stern-first, with rudder unslipped. In the days before the petrol engine, the coble's brown, square sail must have made a fine sight, as it sped out to sea with a stiff westerly behind.

There is no harbour at Bay Town, so only boats that could be beached on sand could fish from here. Today there are just three very conservation-minded fishermen netting for bass and pollack, a few flatfish, a bit of cod and haddock in winter and potting for lobster and crab in the summer.

This recipe is a modern version of a famous Georgian and Victorian dish particularly popular in Yorkshire.

225g (8oz) mixed brown and white crab meat (from 2 small freshly cooked crabs if possible)
1 small onion, finely chopped
2 tablespoons melted butter
3 tablespoons fresh white breadcrumbs
3 tablespoons double cream, or crème fraîche
2 tablespoons wholegrain mustard
1 tablespoon soft green peppercorns in brine, drained
2.5cm (1in) piece of fresh ginger
sea salt and freshly milled black pepper

For the topping
2 tablespoons fresh white breadcrumbs
1 tablespoon Wensleydale or Cheddar cheese, grated
2 tablespoons double cream or crème fraîche

Pre-heat the oven to 200°C/400°F/GM6.

Melt the butter in a small pan and sauté the onion for about 10 minutes until softened and translucent, but not browned. Place in a bowl with the crab meat, breadcrumbs and cream. Stir in the mustards and peppercorns. Peel and grate in the ginger. Season with salt and pepper. Spoon the mixture into 2 crab shells if available, or into 2 ovenproof dishes.

For the topping, mix the breadcrumbs and cheese together and sprinkle over the crab. Spoon over the cream and bake for about 15 minutes until brown and bubbling.

Serve with slices of warm wholemeal toast.

Left: The cliffs and foreshore at Ravenscar in Robin Hood's Bay, North Yorkshire
Above and above right: Bay Town

POTTED CRAB
(serves 6 as a starter)

The fishing cobles at Seahouses in Northumberland mostly pot for crabs, lobster and langoustines. In the early 19th century, these crustaceans were caught all over Britain using bag-nets, or 'trunks', fixed to iron hoops about 50cm (20in) in diameter. From around the 1850s they were replaced in many areas by round woven wicker pots, baited and dropped on to the seabed, with lines and floats enabling them to be drawn up to remove a catch. In turn, the wicker was replaced by plastic. In Northumberland, the lobster pots are quite unlike the round pots of the south and west, being rectangular and partly of metal, more like huge rat-traps. Interestingly, I have noticed that the latest pots in the West Country are large, rectangular and D-shaped, made of steel and plastic, so maybe the round pots will disappear completely.

Traditionally in Northumberland, as in Scotland, only the legs and claws of crabs were eaten, the rest being thought unwholesome, but to me it is the brown body meat which has all the flavour, so I have used both in this recipe for potted crab. On the east coast there is a long tradition of potting crab and no high tea 'up north' was complete without a white jar of crab paste, or potted crab, to eat with oatcakes, or hot buttered toast. It is very rich so a little goes a long way.

> **110g (4oz) freshly boiled brown crab meat**
> **110g (4oz) freshly boiled white crab meat**
> **125g (4½oz) butter, diced**
> **freshly grated nutmeg**
> **a small pinch of curry powder**
> **freshly ground black pepper**
> **50g (1¾oz) clarified unsalted butter, to finish**
> **segments of lemon, to serve**

Put 100g (3½oz) butter into a small pan and place over a very low heat. When the bottom of the pan is filmed with butter, stir in the spices and plenty of black pepper. When the butter is completely melted, but still cool, stir in the shredded white crab meat. Add the remaining 25g (1oz) diced butter and cook over a very low heat for 3-4 minutes, stirring frequently. Add the brown crab meat and continue cooking very gently for another 3-4 minutes. Remove the pan from the heat, season to taste, then pack the mixture into small pots. Pour the clarified butter over the top to seal and leave to get cold.

Cover and store in the fridge, where it will keep well for about a week, but bring it back to room temperature at least 1 hour before serving.

Serve as a starter for dinner, or a special tea-time treat, with oatcakes or fingers of hot wholemeal toast and lemon segments. It is also good with chunks of crusty wholemeal bread and a large green salad for lunch.

Left: Crab and lobster pots on the Northumbrian shore with Lindisfarne Castle in the background
Right: Fishing boats in the harbour at Seahouses, Northumberland. This photograph was taken in 1989, when there were twice as many boats as today

BEADNELL CRAB AU GRATIN
(serves 6 as a starter)

The picturesque fishing village of Beadnell just south of Seahouses in Northumberland also has an agricultural history. To provide lime for the fields at the end of the 18th century, a huge kiln was built on the pier by Richard Pringle. Later three more kilns, stoutly built of sandstone, were added. When lime-burning decreased, the kilns were used for herring curing. Now the kilns have another use; they are owned by the National Trust and local fishermen store their lobster pots in them.

Special fast potters work out of Whitby, Scarborough and Bridlington, setting pots as far as 50 miles from their home. Potting is now crucial to most of the small fishing ports along this coast.

25g (1oz) butter
1 small onion, peeled and chopped
2 teaspoons cornflour
2 tablespoons Dry Vermouth
150ml (5fl oz) single cream
450g (1lb) fresh white crab meat
110g (4oz) white seedless grapes
sea salt and freshly ground white pepper
450g (1lb) floury potatoes, cooked and
  mashed well with cream and butter
1 tablespoon good-quality Cheddar
  cheese, grated
1 tablespoon fresh white breadcrumbs
1 tablespoon flaked almonds (optional)

Melt the butter in a pan and cook the onion gently for about 10 minutes until soft and transparent, but not coloured. Mix the cornflour, mustard and Vermouth together, then stir in the cream. Add this mixture to the onion and simmer gently, stirring all the time. (Don't let the mixture boil.)

Stir in the crab meat and cook very gently for about 3 minutes, then stir in the grapes. Season to taste, then spoon into 6 individual heatproof dishes (or small crab shells if available). Pipe a border of potato around the outside edge, then place under a grill until lightly golden on top. Remove from the heat.

Mix the grated cheese and fresh breadcrumbs together and sprinkle a little over the top of each dish or shell. Scatter the flaked almonds over the top, then return to the grill until golden brown. (Be careful not to burn the almonds.) Serve at once.

Dunstanburgh Castle, Northumberland

MADGE'S SPECIAL FISH BATTER
(serves 4)

Madge is my sister's late mother-in-law and, like a true Yorkshire woman, was an excellent cook. As a young woman, she worked in her mother's fish-and-chip shop in Leeds until selling out to Bryan's; the shop has since become famous for its wonderful fish-and-chips traditionally fried in beef dripping.

This is the batter recipe that Madge and her mother used, light and really crisp. Some recipes suggest using beer, yeast, lemon juice and eggs, but this is the best fish batter I have ever eaten.

Ask for line-caught haddock from Icelandic and Faroese waters.

4 very fresh haddock fillets, skinned
a little flour
sea salt and freshly ground black pepper
beef dripping, good-quality lard
**   or sunflower oil for frying**

For the batter
110g (4oz) plain or self-raising flour
a pinch of sea salt
3 teaspoons malt vinegar
about 150ml (¼ pt) cold water

To make the batter, sieve the flour and salt together into a bowl, make a well in the centre, then gradually beat in the vinegar and enough water to make a smooth batter that will coat the back of a spoon.

Heat the fat in a deep-fryer with a basket to 180°C/350°F.

Wipe the fish with a damp cloth, then dry well with kitchen paper. When the fat is hot enough, cut off a tiny piece of fish, dip in batter and deep fry. Taste, when cooked, to check the seasoning of the batter; if necessary, add more salt. Sieve a little flour onto a large plate and season well, then dip the fish in this before dipping into the batter. Allow the excess to drip off, then lower gently into the fat, one piece at a time. Cook until puffed, crisp and golden, then drain on kitchen paper and keep warm while you cook the rest of the fish.

Serve immediately with freshly fried chips, and vinegar if you want to have really traditional fish-and-chips, or offer wedges of lemon, bread and butter and a pot of tea. Mushy peas are also a favourite accompaniment in Yorkshire.

THE PERFECT CHIPS
(serves 4)

Chips are Britain's favourite food; we get through over 22,000 tonnes every week. To cook the perfect chips you must start with the right potato; Maris Piper, King Edward and Desirée work best. Thick chips absorb less fat than thin ones because of their proportionately lower surface area, but they take longer to cook.

As ever, the quality of the frying fat is crucially important to the flavour of the chips. Use beef dripping like all the best fish-and-chip shops in Yorkshire, or lard from organically reared pigs; both produce particularly delicious chips for serving with fish. If you want to use oil, choose a good-quality sunflower or arachide.

8 floury potatoes, depending on size,
**   scrubbed and unpeeled**
fat or oil for deep-frying
sea salt and freshly ground black pepper

Half-fill the deep-fryer with fat or oil, then heat to 180°C/350°F.

Cut the potatoes into even-sized chips, so that they all cook evenly. Dry well on kitchen paper.

Fry the chips in batches, not too many at a time, until soft, but not coloured (8-10 minutes depending on size of batch). Shake the basket and drain well. Grind over some sea salt.

Increase the heat to 190°C/375°F, then put the chips back in and cook for a minute or two until really crisp and golden. Drain again, then season with more salt and pepper. Tip onto kitchen paper for a final draining before serving.

YORKSHIRE FISH-AND-CHIPS

Fish-and-chips is a British institution whose roots lie in our industrialised past. Jewish traders in London used to fry fish because it tasted good and extended the life of fish on the turn, and sell it with baked potatoes or bread. Meanwhile, a trade in fried potatoes grew in the industrialised northern towns of the Pennines. Nobody is quite sure who first put fried fish-and-chips together, but their spread throughout the country was very much a product of the mass market. Their growth in popularity centred on London and the northern cotton towns where wives and mothers continued to work, cooking facilities were limited and budgets were tight, but the organisation of the trade as we know it began in Yorkshire, the first co-operative on record being in Hull in 1893.

Fishing had been a small-scale, even cottage industry until the advent of steam trawlers opened up fishing grounds further away, particularly in Icelandic waters with their great catches of cod. It was the network of fish-and-chip shops, with their growing need for plenty of fish, which provided a market for these hauls. In Edwardian times, there were local preferences for the particular fish that landed on the nearby stretches of shore, but in the 1920s and '30s, cod became prominent overall, although Yorkshire tends to eat haddock before cod, and Lancashire the other way round. At the height of their popularity in the 1930s, there were at least 35,000 fish-and-chip shops in Britain; in some working-class areas their density was as high as one per street. Even in the 1970s, Holbeck, in Leeds, had eight chippies in an area the size of a small village.

Fish-and-chips still play an integral part in Yorkshire life, but whether haddock or cod, the fish comes from Icelandic or Norwegian waters.

TRADITIONAL WHITBY FISH CAKES WITH LIME CHILLI RELISH
(serves 6)

One mile east of Whitby is the very well-known local landmark of Saltwick Nab, jutting out into the North Sea. The low rocky nab and cliffs, home to a wide variety of wild flowers and insects, are protected by the National Trust.

In Whitby itself, perched on a high cliff overlooking the sea, are the ruins of the Abbey, founded in AD 657 by St Hilda and run as a mixed community until the Synod of Whitby 7 years later. The monastery collected dues from the fishing boats when Whitby first became a port in 1088 and the ruins still dominate the town, clustered on both banks of the River Esk linked by a bridge between the west and east cliffs. The most spectacular way to approach the town is from the Abbey ruins; the colourful scene with the quaint red-roofed houses, brightly painted fishing boats, yachts and sea is quite delightful.

Whitby has had a spectacular history as a seaport since the 17th century when vast quantities of alum were shipped from here; by 1828 it ranked seventh in England. Captain Cook grew up in Whitby and the harbour witnessed his departure as an apprentice on his first ship and later was to provide for his great voyages of discovery. The Captain's ships, *HMS Endeavour*, *Resolution* and *Adventure* were built here.

From 1753 to 1837, Whitby was an important whaling port and the blubber was unloaded into boiler houses on the quays; the jawbone of a whale still forms an unusual arch on the west cliff. Captain William Scoresby, who caught 533 whales and invented the 'crow's nest', was also a famous Whitby man.

Much of the other fish landed on the North Yorkshire coast was handled by Whitby market and, before the railway arrived, great quantities were carried inland by teams of pack ponies with panniers, first to Pickering, Malton and York, then across to the towns of the industrial West Riding.

The present fish quay was built in 1957 and although there is still a small fishing fleet of motor cobles and keel boats, commercial fishing is very low key today. Even the few commercial salmon fishermen have recently been bought out. A small selection of white fish, flat fish and bass is caught in nets for the local market during the winter, while, in the summer, most of the cobles concentrate on crab and lobster potting for the Continental market.

Fish cakes have always been very popular in Yorkshire for high tea. Many recipes use equal quantities of fish and mashed potato, but they have much more flavour if the quantity of fish is higher. Kipper, smoked trout fillets, or hot-roasted salmon could be used in this recipe instead of smoked haddock. Ask for line-caught fresh haddock, coley or pollack from Icelandic and Faroese waters.

700g (1 lb 9 oz) fresh haddock fillet, unskinned
350g (12 oz) undyed smoked haddock fillet, unskinned
150ml ($^1/_4$ pt) full-cream milk
25g (1oz) butter
sea salt and freshly ground black pepper
3 medium floury potatoes, peeled, cooked and mashed
$^1/_2$ teaspoon celery salt
a pinch of cayenne
2 heaped tablespoons fresh flat-leaf parsley, chopped
1 free-range egg, beaten
sieved flour for coating
olive oil, for frying

For the lime chilli relish
4 tablespoons extra virgin olive oil
2 medium red onions, skinned and very finely chopped
about 5cm (2 in) fresh ginger, peeled and grated
2 garlic cloves, skinned and finely chopped
2 organic red peppers, halved, seeded and diced small
1 green chilli, seeded and finely chopped
3 teaspoons sesame oil
$^1/_2$ teaspoon sea salt
50g (1$^3/_4$oz) sesame seeds
grated rind and juice of 3 unwaxed limes

Heat the oven to 180°C/350°F/GM4.

Butter a gratin dish and place the fish in it. Pour over the milk, dot with little pieces of butter and season with black pepper. Cook in the oven for about 15 minutes until the fish is tender.

Drain the fish and remove all the skin and any bones, then flake into large chunks. Pile the fish on top of the mashed potatoes and add the celery salt, cayenne and parsley. Season (remember smoked haddock is quite salty), then mash together lightly without breaking the fish up too much. Flour your hands, then form the mixture into 12 cakes. Chill until firmed up.

Meanwhile make the relish. Heat the olive oil in a frying-pan and add the onions. Cook for 3-4 minutes, stirring occasionally, then add the ginger, garlic and peppers. Continue to cook for about 10 minutes until the peppers are soft, then stir in the chilli.

While this is cooking, heat the sesame oil in a small pan, then add the salt and sesame seeds. Cook over a moderate heat until they turn light brown, then stir into the peppers with the lime juice and rind. When ready to cook the fish cakes, put the beaten egg into a large plate or baking tray and some flour into a second plate, or tray. Dip each fish cake thoroughly into the egg, then coat in flour, shaking off the excess.

Heat about 6 tablespoons olive oil in a frying-pan, fry the fish cakes for about 5-6 minutes on each side until well-browned and warmed through. Serve immediately with the warmed relish or with tartare sauce (see page 222).

Saltwick Bay and Nab, North Yorkshire

YORKSHIRE FISH SCALLOPS
(serves 4)

These 'fish cakes' can be bought in many of the fish-and-chip shops in Yorkshire, but they are also very popular as a home-made dish. I think they are quite delicious and look forward to my first Yorkshire fish scallop when visiting my sister.

> **4 small pieces of line-caught haddock fillet, skinned**
> **sea salt and freshly ground black pepper**
> **8 potato slices, the same size as the fish, cut about 5mm (¼ in) thick**
> **Madge's Special Fish Batter (see p.103)**
> **beef dripping, lard or oil for deep-frying**

Heat the fat in a deep-fryer with a basket to 180°C/350°F.

Season the fish well and sandwich each piece between 2 potato slices. Dip each sandwich into the prepared batter and deep-fry two at a time for 8-10 minutes, or until the potato is tender. Keep warm while you fry the remainder, then serve with vinegar, bread and butter and a pot of tea.

LYNN'S HADDOCK, SEAWEED AND VEGETABLE TERRINE
(serves 10–12 as a starter)

Boldly painted in red and white hoops, Souter Lighthouse stands on the coast road between Sunderland and South Shields. Now owned by the National Trust, it opened in 1871 and was the first lighthouse to use alternating electric current, the most advanced lighthouse technology of its day. The engine room, light tower and keepers' living quarters are all on view and there is a model and information display.

A rockpool fish tank by the National Trust shop (also the entrance to the lighthouse), is proving a great success with visitors. Monitored daily, it is filled with creatures that the children find when they go out on Rockpool Rambles with the Wardens – squat lobsters, shore crabs, anemones, star fish, urchins and various tiny fish. However, there are no plans to supply the tea-room!

Lynn Bay, who cooks for the tea-room, gave me this haddock recipe, which looks beautiful and tastes even better. Sometimes she serves it with a dressing made with single cream or yoghurt flavoured with crushed green peppercorns. Ask for line-caught inshore, or Icelandic, haddock. Any sustainable white fish can be used, but it must be very fresh.

> **450g (1lb) very fresh haddock fillet, skinned and chopped into small pieces**
> **1 packet sushi-type dried seaweed sheets**
> **700g (1lb 9 oz) carrots, peeled and sliced**
> **about 100g (3½oz) butter**
> **3 free-range eggs**
> **200ml (7fl oz) whipping cream**
> **¼ teaspoon ground coriander**
> **½ medium onion, minced**
> **1 tablespoon plain flour**
> **200ml (7fl oz) full-cream milk**
> **sea salt and freshly ground black pepper**

Pre-heat the oven to 150°C/300°F/GM2.

Use a little of the butter to grease a 900g (2lb) loaf tin, then line it with sheets of the dried seaweed. Cook the carrots in a small amount of water and 40g (1½ oz) butter until tender, then purée in a blender. Add 1 egg, 125 ml (4 fl oz) whipping cream, and the ground coriander to the carrot purée and mix well.

Melt the remaining 40g (1½ oz) butter in a pan, add the minced onion and cook for about 2 minutes. Stir in the flour and cook for a further 2 minutes, then remove from the heat and stir in the milk gradually. Put back onto the heat and bring slowly to the boil, stirring until thick and smooth. Blend the sauce, raw chopped fish, remaining whipping cream and the 2 eggs together and season to taste. Put the carrot mixture into the loaf tin and smooth over. Top with 2 layers of seaweed, then add the fish mixture. Cover with buttered greaseproof paper and foil, then cook in the oven, in a roasting tin half-filled with hot water, for about 1½ hours, or until firm to the touch. Remove from the oven and leave to cool completely. Refrigerate until needed, turn out and slice thinly. Serve on chilled plates with a few salad leaves mixed with a few sprigs of fresh coriander.

Lynn's Haddock, Seaweed and Vegetable Terrine

EYEMOUTH PALES
(serves 4)

Although the attractive village of Eyemouth lies just over the border in Scotland, there has always been an association with Northumberland. As early as the 11th century, a colony of monks from nearby Berwick decided that the bay of Eyemouth was the only safe landing place in the area, so the village developed into a busy port with a steady trade, particularly in grain, until the 18th century, when fishing became the main livelihood.

Eyemouth, still a fishing port with a picturesque sheltered harbour, has given its name to a special method of curing fish. The name 'Pales' is an apt description for a haddock smoked over sawdust to a pale golden colour quite distinct from the darker colour of the better-known Finnan haddock. The fish is split with the bone on the right-hand side, dry-salted overnight and smoked for only 30 minutes to 2 hours, to give a delicate smoky flavour. A similar cure produces the Glasgow Pale.

Pales are best left whole and slowly grilled with butter and black pepper, or poached in milk or water for a few minutes. The cooked fish can also be used to make the most delicious breakfast, lunch or supper dishes. Finnan haddock or any undyed smoked haddock may be used.

2 large Eyemouth Pales
1 bay leaf
300ml (10fl oz) double cream or
    crème fraîche
freshly ground black pepper
triangles of hot wholemeal toast,
    to serve

Pre-heat the oven to 180°C/350°F/GM4

Put the fish in a large pan with the bay leaf and cover with water. Bring to simmering point, cover with a lid and poach gently for about 2 minutes. Drain and discard the bay leaf. Dry well with kitchen paper, then remove the skin and all the bones. Break the fish up with a fork into large flakes.

Butter an ovenproof gratin dish and arrange the fish on it. Pour over the cream, completely covering the fish, and grind black pepper on top.

Bake in the oven for 10 minutes, then brown under the grill. Serve immediately with hot brown toast.

Souter Lighthouse, Tyne and Wear

EYEMOUTH FISH PUDDING
(serves 4)

Fish pudding recipes made with breadcrumbs or potatoes are many and varied in this area. Again, Finnan haddock or any undyed smoked haddock can be used to make this delicious pudding, which is as light as a soufflé, to serve at lunch or supper.

2 large Eyemouth Pales
50g (1³⁄₄oz) fresh white breadcrumbs
2 large free-range eggs, separated
1 tablespoon fresh flat-leaf parsley,
    chopped
sea salt
a small pinch cayenne pepper
25g (1oz) butter, melted
150ml (5fl oz) single cream

Pre-heat the oven to 180°C/350°C/GM4.

Poach the fish as in the previous recipe, remove all the skin and bones and flake into a bowl. Add 40g (1¹⁄₂oz) breadcrumbs, the egg yolks, parsley, salt, cayenne pepper and butter. Stir in the cream and mix together well. Beat the egg whites until stiff and fold gently into the fish mixture. Turn into a buttered ovenproof dish and sprinkle with the remaining breadcrumbs. Stand in a roasting tin half-filled with hot water. Bake for 35-40 minutes, or until the top is lightly browned. Serve immediately with a leaf and herb salad.

SOUTER LIGHTHOUSE MARINATED HALIBUT AND TOMATO CHILLI SAUCE
(serves 4– 6 as a starter)

I based this recipe on one for monkfish given to me by Barbara Matheson, catering manager at Souter Lighthouse tea-room. Monkfish is particularly vulnerable to over-fishing because of its life-history characteristics. There is general consensus amongst scientists that there is only one stock and that this spawns in deep water to the west of Scotland. Levels of fishing in these waters is too high and it is estimated that an average 55% of males and 92% of females are immature when caught.

North Atlantic halibut used to be one of the great fish of the North Sea. It is the largest of the flat fish and can grow as long as 10 feet. Halibut is highly nutritious, full of vitamin D and has a valuable liver oil, so has been subject to over-fishing. Stocks are now very low, so ask your fishmonger for farmed Norwegian halibut, but make sure it is sparklingly fresh.

You need to start 'cooking' the fish at least 5 hours before you want to eat it.

450g (1lb) very fresh halibut, Dover sole
    or lemon sole fillets, or dive-caught
    scallops
1 large unwaxed lemon
2 unwaxed limes
sea salt and freshly ground black pepper
1 garlic clove, finely chopped
¹⁄₂ medium onion, finely sliced
1 tablespoon fresh coriander leaves,
    chopped
1 fresh chilli, finely diced
¹⁄₂ green pepper, finely diced
¹⁄₂ red pepper, finely diced
a few crisp lettuce leaves to serve
    (e.g. Cos or Little Gem)
extra finely diced red and green pepper
    to serve
a few sprigs fresh coriander to garnish

For the tomato chilli sauce
1 small red onion, finely chopped
¹⁄₂ red pepper, finely chopped
¹⁄₂ yellow pepper, finely chopped
2 red chillies, finely chopped
2 green chillies, finely chopped
6 ripe good-flavoured tomatoes,
    skinned, seeded and diced
¹⁄₂ teaspoon garlic, finely chopped
2 tablespoons fresh coriander leaves,
    chopped
olive oil
a dash Tabasco and Worcestershire sauce
sea salt and freshly ground black pepper

Skin the fish and cut into 1 cm (¹⁄₂ in) cubes. Scallops can also be cut into pieces. If you are using sole, slice into thin strips. Put into a china bowl. Squeeze over the lemon and lime juice, sprinkle with salt and garlic and grind over some pepper. Cover with clingfilm and leave to marinate for 2-3 hours in the fridge.

Meanwhile, make the tomato chilli sauce by mixing the ingredients together with enough olive oil to loosen the mixture slightly. Season to taste.

Add the onion, coriander, chilli and peppers to the fish. Cover again and leave for at least another 2¹⁄₂ hours in the fridge (preferably overnight).

To serve, arrange a few crisp lettuce leaves on individual plates and place a tablespoon of the fish, including the vegetables, in the centre. Garnish with a little diced pepper and a sprig of coriander, then serve with warm stottie bread and the tomato chilli sauce.

It is also good with a sweet fruit chutney.

NORTHUMBRIAN HERRINGS IN OATMEAL WITH MUSTARD SAUCE
(serves 4)

In the 19th and early 20th centuries the herring fishing industry was very important to Northumberland. The memory of the local fishergirls who gutted and salted the fish still lingers on. They were a hardy breed, usually recruited in February, travelling the whole of the east coast during the herring season. They all knew the cry 'Get up and tie your fingers' – old cloths or 'clooties' were used as bandages to protect their fingers against the sharp knives and coarse salt. The work was cold and very hard, and in the early 1900s the girls were paid 8d a barrel, or 3d an hour, shared amongst three of them. They worked a 12-hour day and had certainly earned every penny by the end of the season. In spite of the messy work, the fishergirls took a pride in keeping clean and were proud of their jerseys made to traditional patterns. Many of them wed fishermen whom they met on their travels.

Until the 18th century when more corn was produced, the chief grains grown in Northumberland were oatmeal and rye. There are still many local savoury and sweet recipes using oatmeal, like this one for frying herrings with an oatmeal coating. Mackerel may be used.

2-4 fresh herrings (depending on size), cleaned and filleted
a little flour for dusting
sea salt and freshly ground black pepper
$^1/_2$ teaspoon dry English mustard
110g (4oz) porridge oats
1 free-range egg, beaten
a little butter or bacon fat for frying

For the mustard sauce
110g (4oz) butter, chilled and cubed
1 shallot, finely chopped
1 bay leaf
sea salt and freshly ground black pepper
2 tablespoons white wine vinegar
4 tablespoons dry white wine
6 tablespoons fish stock (see p.222)
2 tablespoons single cream
$^1/_2$ -1 tablespoon wholegrain mustard

Make the sauce first. Melt a small knob of the butter in a small pan and add the shallot, bay leaf and a little black pepper. Cook for a few minutes until softened, but not coloured. Add the vinegar and reduce over rapid heat by about three-quarters. Add the wine and reduce again by three-quarters. Pour in the fish stock and reduce by half. Add the single cream, then bring to a simmer. Whisk in the remaining butter, a few pieces at a time, and season to taste. Strain through a sieve, then stir in mustard to taste. Keep warm over a pan of hot water or stand in a roasting tin of hot water while frying the fish.

Wipe the herrings with a damp cloth and pat dry. Season the flour with salt and pepper, then dust the herrings with the seasoned flour. Mix the mustard powder and porridge oats together on a baking tray or plate. Pour the beaten egg into a baking tray or plate, dip the fillets in and coat with the oat mixture. Heat the butter or bacon fat in a frying-pan and cook the fish for 3-4 minutes on each side, until the fish is cooked and the oat coating is crisp and golden. (Be careful not to burn the coating.) Serve at once with a dollop of mustard sauce.

Left: Whitby fishergirl, a photograph taken in 1891
Right: Fishermen's cottages in Cullercoats, Tyne and Wear, a photograph taken *c.* 1955

NORTHUMBERLAND KIPPER SAVOURY
(serves 4 as a starter)

This spicy pâté is ideal as a starter or light lunch. If you want to keep it for a few days before serving, cover with a film of clarified butter. Keep in the fridge for up to 1 week.

1 jugged traditionally cured, undyed kipper
110g (4oz) cream cheese
¹/₂ teaspoon wholegrain mustard
¹/₂ teaspoon lemon juice
¹/₂ teaspoon ground allspice
¹/₂ teaspoon freshly ground white pepper
¹/₂ teaspoon paprika
¹/₄ teaspoon ground ginger

Jug the kipper for 6 minutes (see box below).

Dry well with kitchen paper, then remove all the skin and bones. Flake, then mash the flesh.

Beat the mustard, lemon juice and spices into the cream cheese. Add the mashed kipper flesh and beat again or blitz briefly in a processor (don't make it too smooth, it should have texture). Pack into small pots, cover and chill for several hours.

Before serving, remove from the fridge in plenty of time for the flavour to develop. Serve with oatcakes, or hot brown toast and a glass of Newcastle Brown Ale for lunch.

LOBSTER IN CREAM WITH LINDISFARNE MEAD
(serves 2–3)

Holy Island, lying 6 miles north of Bamburgh in Northumberland, is linked to the mainland by a 3-mile causeway, which is under water for several hours at high tide. A small hut on stilts has been provided by the south of the causeway for travellers unfortunate enough to be caught by the incoming sea.

In a 1561 survey the island is described as a poor place, the main houses in ruins and a population largely composed of poor fishermen, but by the 19th century fishing had become a really well-established industry. There were 37 herring boats and 17 white fish boats working from the island in 1863. The wives and daughters of the fishermen worked hard at packing and gutting the fish and they were so busy at times that help was brought from the mainland.

Lindisfarne Castle was built in Tudor times to protect the harbour from attack. It was converted into a private house by the young Edwin Lutyens in 1903 for his friend Edward Hudson, the owner and founder of *Country Life*. Both the men were romantics at heart and the opportunity to rebuild a castle on a splendid and historic site caught their imaginations.

The great event in the life of the Castle during Hudson's ownership (he sold up in 1921 and it was given to the National Trust in 1944) was the visit of the Prince and Princess of Wales in 1908, but Hudson entertained a great deal, especially in the summer. His guests must often have enjoyed the local lobsters, especially cooked in the typically extravagant Escoffier way with cream, truffles and brandy. I have used Lindisfarne mead instead, which is still produced by the Lindisfarne Liqueur Company, who have a small distillery on the island.

Lobsters are caught all along the Northumbrian and North Yorkshire coast. Their numbers have been greatly improved by a tagging system where the fishermen cut a V-shaped notch in the tail of female lobster and return them to the sea, so that they can be identified easily, even when they don't have eggs. A minimum size, which takes 7 years for a lobster to achieve, has also been introduced and many fishermen think there should also be a maximum size, so that really old lobsters are left in the sea (they are not worth eating anyway). The majority caught weigh about 450g (1lb). So, when buying lobster, don't buy under-sized or female specimens and don't accept female lobster in a restaurant.

2 small (about 450g [1lb]) freshly cooked lobsters
25g (1oz) butter
2 tablespoons mead or brandy
sea salt and freshly ground black pepper
2 large free-range egg yolks
300ml (10fl oz) double cream
¹/₂ teaspoon paprika

Remove all the meat from the lobsters and cut into neat pieces. Heat the butter in a shallow pan and add the lobster meat. Season and heat gently for 3-4 minutes. Pour over the mead and set alight. When the flames have died down, take the pan off the heat. Beat the egg yolks in a small bowl, stir in the cream and season well with salt, pepper and paprika. Stir quickly into the lobster and shake the pan above the heat, stirring gently all the time until the sauce is thick and creamy: be very careful that it doesn't boil or it will curdle.

Serve immediately with rice.

KIPPERS

Kippers were invented in the small harbour town of Seahouses, once a thriving fishing port on the northern end of the grand, empty stretch of the Northumbrian coast that leads up to Scotland. There was already an established smoked salmon trade in the area to make second-rate salmon, thin after releasing its eggs, more attractive by brining and smoking. These fish were called 'kippered' salmon (the word deriving from the Dutch word 'kuppen' meaning to spawn) and were sold on to London. In 1843, a man called John Woodger started to experiment using the same techniques on herring, but, unlike the salmon, the herring were in their plump prime before spawning as they passed this part of the coast, so the rich-flavoured, glistening kipper was born. It is delicious grilled and served with lemon and butter.

If you find the kippers very salty, you can jug them in the traditional way. Using scissors, remove the head of the kipper, then place it head first in a large heat-proof jug, or place in a large, shallow dish. Pour in enough boiling water to submerge the fish completely, apart from the tail. Leave for 6 minutes, then lift out of the water, drain well and dry on kitchen paper. Your kipper will be cooked to perfection.

Lindisfarne Castle on Holy Island, Northumberland

ROMAN SEAFOOD TART
(serves 4–6)

The Romans had an amazing enthusiasm for eating fish, despite being inland farmers for centuries before military expansion brought them into contact with the Greek way of life. Seafish, always an important part of the Greek diet, became immensely popular, so the Romans who came to Britain must have been very happy to enjoy the local delicacies. The shells of oysters, whelks, cockles, mussels and limpets are found extensively on the sites of Roman towns, villas and forts at least as far north as Hadrian's Wall, not only near the coast, but also at great distances from the sea. The shellfish must have been transported alive in water-tanks, but as yet, no archaeological evidence has been found to show how the trade was organised.

It is now possible to walk the whole 80 miles of Hadrian's Wall along a footpath, which was completed in 2003. The National Trust owns about 5 miles, running west from Housesteads Fort to Cowfields Quarry. The Fort is one of the best-preserved of 13 permanent bases along the Wall and conjures up an evocative picture of Roman military life.

For the pastry
 175g (6oz) plain white flour
 a pinch of salt
 40g (1½ oz) butter, softened
 40g (1½ oz) lard, softened
 40g (1½ oz) Parmesan
  (Parmigiano Reggiano), finely grated
 about 1½ tablespoons cold water

For the filling
 500g (1lb 2oz) prepared mixed
  seafood (mussel and cockle meat,
  white crab meat, prawns and
  dive-caught scallops)
 50g (1¾ oz) butter
 3 garlic cloves, finely chopped
 a large pinch ground ginger
 a large pinch freshly grated nutmeg
 1 teaspoon anchovy essence,
  or Thai fish sauce
 2 tablespoons fresh coriander leaves,
  chopped
 1 tablespoon fresh flat-leaf parsley,
  chopped
 juice of ½ lemon
 1 large free-range egg
 1 free-range egg yolk
 300ml (10fl oz) double cream or
  crème fraîche
 sea salt and freshly ground black pepper
 lemon wedges, to serve

Make the pastry in the usual way, adding the Parmesan after the fat has been rubbed in. Bake blind.

Pre-heat the oven to 190°C/375°F/GM5.

Heat the butter in a frying-pan and cook the garlic for a few seconds without browning. Stir in all the seafood and fry for 2 or 3 minutes, stirring occasionally, until the fish is buttery and the garlic is mixed in well. Stir in the spice, anchovy essence, herbs and lemon juice, then place in the pre-baked pastry case.

Lightly beat the egg and egg yolk together in a bowl. Stir in the cream and season to taste. Pour the egg mixture evenly over the seafood.

Bake in the oven for 25 minutes, or until lightly set and golden brown. Serve warm or cold with a watercress or rocket salad and a wedge of lemon.

Left: Roman Seafood Tart
Right: Hadrian's Wall stretching across the Northumbrian landscape

TWEED SALMON, SMOKED HADDOCK AND LANGOUSTINE PIE WITH CHEESE AND MUSTARD MASH
(serves 6)

As far back as the 14th century, the salmon fisheries of the Berwick area were of note; on the north side of the River Tweed was Crown land with the 'King's Fisheries'; on the south side was Church land with the 'Bishop's Fisheries'. Thousands of barrels of salmon were exported annually from Berwick. By the early 1500s the guilds of Berwick had been set up and laws were laid down regarding the salmon trade; only guild members could rent a fishery, or salt the fish, or export it. Perhaps this is why there was so much poaching. The famous 'Newcastle salmon', so well known in London at the time, was in fact poached Berwick salmon.

By 1800 there were about 300 men employed in the salmon trade and the rental of the fisheries was worth about £10,000 a year, with July as the best month for catches. By then, the idea of packing fish in ice had been adopted and ice-houses built, thus doing away with the old method of boiling in salty water and pickling.

The Berwick Salmon and Fisheries Company was one of the oldest in Britain and began life in the 18th century when a group of local men took shares in a small fleet of sailing ships. These Berwick 'smacks' were fast and could travel from Scotland to London in 3 days, carrying large quantities of boiled and salted salmon. With the coming of the railway, the shipping trade declined, so the directors of the company decided to concentrate instead on improving their salmon fisheries. With 7 to a crew, the fishermen worked on a share basis during the season from 14 February to 14 September, using a coble-type boat only partly decked, so that 40-50 fathoms of net could be easily let out. The fish was taken to the Company's premises in Berwick, where it was washed, graded, packed and then sent by rail, or road, to markets all over the country.

Sadly, the situation has changed drastically since then and a way of life is threatened. In 2002 drift netsmen off the North East coast caught 42,000 salmon and sea trout, the equivalent of half of all salmon caught by rod and line in England and Wales. The majority of these commercial salmon fishermen were bought out in 2003 in a £3.4 million deal described by the Environment Agency as the most important conservation measure for salmon and sea trout for 30 years. Only 16 of the 68 drift netsmen along this coast still have a licence, and for how long?

Langoustines and other crustaceans are, however, plentiful along the Northumbrian coast, caught mainly for the Continental market. They add a touch of luxury to this fish pie, which is delicious enough for a dinner party.

450g (1lb) wild Pacific or responsibly farmed Atlantic salmon fillet, unskinned
450g (1lb) undyed smoked haddock, unskinned
350g (12oz) raw pot– or creel-caught langoustine, peeled and intestine removed (or peeled North Atlantic prawns)
600ml (1pt) full-cream milk
150ml (5fl oz) double cream
1 medium onion, sliced
2 bay leaves
3 whole black peppercorns
2 whole cloves
75g (2¾oz) unsalted butter
75g (2¾oz) plain flour
4 tablespoons fresh flat-leaf parsley, chopped
freshly grated nutmeg
freshly grated black pepper

For the cheese and mustard mash
1.3 kg (3lb) floury potatoes, peeled (King Edward or Maris Piper)
75g (2¾oz) butter
250ml (9fl oz) full-cream milk
3 tablespoons wholegrain mustard
110g (4oz) Wensleydale, Swaledale or Cheddar cheese, grated

Arrange the salmon and smoked haddock in a roasting tin, or large frying-pan, skin-side up. Pour over the milk and double cream, then add the onion, bay leaves, peppercorns and cloves. Bring just to the boil, then simmer gently for 5-7 minutes until just opaque. Lift the fish out on to a plate, reserving the cooking liquor. When the fish is cold enough to handle, pull off the skin, then flake into large pieces, removing any bones as you go. Sprinkle it over the base of a 1.75 litre (3pt) ovenproof dish. Add the peeled langoustines.

Melt the butter in a pan and stir in the flour. Cook for 1 minute, then take off the heat and gradually stir in the reserved, strained cooking liquor. Return to the heat and bring slowly to the boil, stirring all the time. Leave to simmer gently for about 10 minutes to cook out the flour, then stir in the parsley. Season to taste with pepper and nutmeg (it will probably be salty enough because of the smoked haddock, but add a little if necessary). Pour the sauce over the fish and leave to cool. Chill in the fridge for 1 hour.

Boil the potatoes in salted water for 15-20 minutes until tender. Drain well and dry over heat, then mash. Beat in the butter, milk, mustard and grated cheese.

Pre-heat the oven to 200°C/400°F/GM6.

When the fish mixture is set, spoon over the mash and fluff with a fork. Bake for 35– 40 minutes or until piping hot and golden brown.

Serve immediately with buttered garden peas, or fresh spinach.

Tweed Salmon, Smoked Haddock and Langoustine Pie with Cheese and Mustard Mash

SALMON IN NEWCASTLE BEER BATTER AND GREEN MAYONNAISE
(serves 4)

Before the coming of the railways and steam ships in the 19th century, it was impossible to deliver salmon fresh from the North to the London markets, so it was usually pickled. Beer was the secret of the famous 18th-century Newcastle pickled salmon, which came not from Newcastle, but from the River Tweed. The fish was carried 60 miles by pack-horse to the salt pans of South Shields where it was simmered in beer, salt and water, then potted with spices. It was claimed that salmon treated in this way would keep for a year.

Newcastle Brown Ale is used in this recipe to make a dark crispy batter, but any beer or lager can be used. If you can buy 2 x 350g (12oz) tail-end salmon fillets, they will divide neatly in half lengthways to give 4 perfect portions for deep-frying, but any pieces of salmon will do.

> **4 x 175g (6oz) wild Pacific or responsibly**
> **farmed Atlantic tail-end salmon fillets,**
> **skinned**
> **sea salt and freshly ground black pepper**
> **a little self-raising flour for coating**

For the beer batter
> **110g (4oz) self-raising flour**
> **a pinch of salt**
> **150ml (¼pt) Newcastle Brown Ale**
> **freshly ground black pepper**
> **beef dripping or oil for deep frying**
> **green mayonnaise to serve (see p.221)**

Make the batter first. Sieve the flour and salt into a bowl, make a well in the centre, then gradually whisk in the beer until you have a smooth batter which will coat the back of a spoon. Season with pepper, then leave to stand for about one hour before using.

Heat the fat in a deep-fryer with a basket to 180°C/350°F. Season the salmon with salt and pepper, then dip in flour to coat each piece, shaking off the excess. Cut off a tiny morsel of fish, dip in batter, then fry until crisp. Taste to see if the batter is seasoned enough; adjust if necessary. Dip the fish in the batter allowing the excess to drip off and fry one at a time for about 5 minutes until brown and crisp, then lift onto crumpled kitchen paper in a roasting tin to absorb any excess fat and keep warm in a low oven while you cook the remaining fish.

Serve the crispy battered salmon with freshly fried chips (see p.103) and green mayonnaise.

COQUET RIVERSIDE KEDGEREE TART
(serves 4-6)

The River Coquet is famous for its salmon, sea and river trout. It was here that the 1st Lord Armstrong, inventor, engineer and gunmaker, was brought as 'a baby in arms'. His earliest recollections were of paddling in the river, gathering pebbles from the river gravel beds and climbing amongst the rocks. Here too, as an older and somewhat delicate boy, during his parent's annual visits from Newcastle to stay with friends, the young William Armstrong explored Upper Coquetdale, learned to fish and became familiar with the secluded glen through which the Debdon Burn forces its way to the Coquet.

In 1863, some 40 years later, Armstrong made a nostalgic return visit and determined to buy as much as he could of the Debdon Valley, including building what he termed 'a small house in the neighbourhood for occasional visits in the summer time'. This small house grew into the Victorian mansion of Cragside, one of the most modern houses for its time: in the 1880s the house had hot and cold running water, central heating, fire alarms, telephones, a Turkish bath suite and a passenger lift. Most remarkable of all, it was the first house in the world to be lit and powered by hydroelectricity.

This recipe is a variation of the Victorian/Edwardian house-party favourite, which might have found its way onto the breakfast table in the bay window of Cragside's splendid dining room.

Sea, rainbow or brown trout can be used instead.

> **150g (5½oz) shortcrust pastry with**
> **25g (1oz) grated Cheddar cheese,**
> **added to the dry ingredients**

For the filling
> **175g (6oz) cooked responsibly farmed**
> **Atlantic salmon and shelled North**
> **Atlantic prawns**
> **450ml (16 fl oz) full-cream milk**
> **2 bay leaves**
> **50g (1¾oz) butter**
> **1 medium onion, finely chopped**
> **1 dessertspoon mild curry powder**
> **50g (1¾oz) plain white flour**
> **30ml (1fl oz) double cream**
> **sea salt and freshly ground black pepper**
> **3 free-range eggs, boiled for 6 minutes**
> **and quartered**
> **75g (2¾oz) long grain white rice,**
> **cooked with ½ teaspoon turmeric**
> **to colour it**
> **a little paprika for sprinkling**
> **1 tablespoon fresh flat-leaf parsley,**
> **to serve**

Pre-heat the oven to 200°C/400°F/GM6.

Roll out the pastry to fit a 20cm (8 in) loose-bottomed flan ring. Prick the base and chill for 30 minutes. Bake blind until crisp.

Meanwhile, in a pan bring the milk and bay leaves to the boil. Remove from the heat and leave on one side to infuse. To make the sauce, melt the butter in a pan and gently cook the onion for at least 10 minutes until very soft, but not coloured. Stir in the curry powder and cook for another 3 minutes, then stir in the flour. Cook for a further 2 minutes, then remove from the heat.

Gradually stir in the strained infused milk, then put back on the heat and bring slowly to the boil, stirring all the time. Simmer gently for at least 10 minutes, then remove from the heat again and stir in the cream. Season to taste. Fill the pastry case with layers of flaked salmon and prawns, hard-boiled eggs, rice and sauce, piling the mixture up well. Dust with paprika and sprinkle over the parsley. Serve any remaining sauce separately and accompany with a leaf salad.

The west front, Cragside House, Northumberland

THE NORTH WEST

The National Trust's familiar sign of an oak leaf set in an 'omega' appears relatively rarely on the North-West coast of England – on the great wide sands of Formby in Merseyside and at Sandscale Haws in Cumbria. However, the Lake District positively bristles with oak leaves as the Trust protects approximately one quarter of the National Park. There are still healthy numbers of fish here, although the char, which loves the deep waters of the lakes, is now under serious threat and is therefore being successfully farmed along with trout.

The most characteristic seawater fish in the local spring and early summer markets of the North West used to be hake, which matures late and grows slowly and is therefore very vulnerable to over-fishing. Stocks of hake are posing a serious risk of collapse according to the International Council for the Exploration of the Sea (ICES). In 2001 recovery plans were developed for hake in waters managed by the EU. The same sad story applies to fish that appear in markets later in the year: halibut, like hake, is slow to mature and grow, resulting in low stocks; Atlantic cod has suffered from decades of relentless over-fishing and it is now on the endangered list; large plaice are also very rare, although stocks in the Irish Sea generally remain within what are termed by ICES as 'safe biological limits'. This has led to a decline in all the traditional fishing ports – Fleetwood, Whitehaven, Southport and Maryport – not helped by publicity arising from radio-active discharges into the sea.

Shrimping is traditional to Morecambe Bay and, to a lesser extent, the Solway Firth – two of the few parts of the British coastline where the succulent brown shrimp is found. Again, the industry is in decline due to over-fishing and the relatively low value of the species. Although fishermen prefer to concentrate on higher value fish like mullet, this too is vulnerable to over-fishing, so that many angling clubs now promote a 'catch and release' policy. Mullet also feeds off organic muds in the estuaries and bays which can be polluted with pesticides, sewage and heavy metals.

The North West fishing industry has therefore had to diversify. Mussel and oyster fisheries are now widely located in sheltered estuaries and bays like the Solway Firth and Morecambe Bay. A Cumbrian hatchery sends Pacific oyster spat (fingernail-sized shells) to Isle of Mull Oysters, one of Scotland's bigger producers with an annual harvest of 300,000 marketable shells. Best known for its delicious kippers, the Isle of Man still has active fisheries. King and the smaller queen scallops, along with crabs and lobsters, are fished extensively around the island. Scotland, of course, is close by and the fish shops of the North West are full of herrings, kippers, and regional delicacies like Arbroath smokies and Finnan haddocks.

Salmon and salmon trout used to be plentiful in the estuaries and rivers of the North West. A strange method of salmon fishing still survives where an enormous net called a 'haaf' is used (see page 149). It is an efficient method of netting salmon in the estuaries, contributing to the decline in the population, which has halved in the last 20 years.

Previous pages: Crummock Water looking towards the Buttermere Valley, Cumbria
Left: Maryport harbour, Cumbria

BAKED WINDERMERE CHAR WITH BUTTERED ALMONDS
(serves 4)

Visitors to the Lake District may have been puzzled by the strange sight of boats with long poles arching out to the left and right from their stern, being meticulously rowed the length and breadth of Windermere. These are the char fishermen trolling England's largest expanse of water and searching depths of up to 30 metres (100 feet) or more for their quarry, using beautifully sculpted lures of highly polished pure gold and silver.

In colder northern latitudes the char, a relative of the salmon, leads a salmon-style existence, commuting between river and sea. But in Britain and equivalent European latitudes, the fish survives only as a pre-Ice-Age relic and is confined to deep, land-locked lakes. Over the years the char has adapted to its new freshwater life and its wandering instincts have been dulled except at spawning times. The largest concentration of char in the United Kingdom occurs in the Lake District and it is here that most of the commercial fishing took place.

Commercial fisheries existed on Windermere for many centuries. The fishermen mainly used seine nets worked from the shore. Pike, perch, trout and char were all caught by this method, although the char was the most important, as it had a ready market during the 18th and 19th centuries – particularly when cooked and sold potted. By 1860, the fishery was in decline due to over-fishing. Stocks recovered slightly as a result of official restrictions, but ultimately all netting was forbidden; the last occurred in 1921, since when all fishing for char has been by rod and line.

Experts believe that Windermere uniquely boasts two distinct populations. One spawns in November, most fish favouring shallow water on the lake shore, but with a small group migrating to the River Brathey. The other spawns in February and March in deep water, in the lake only.

The National Trust protects some 90 per cent of the land around Windermere, from which the public has free access to the shore. On the west side is Low Wray Campsite and Claife Woods, where visitors can fish for char, trout, perch and pike in the north basin of Windermere. At the southern tip of the lake, near Newby Bridge, is Fell Foot Park with picnic areas, boats for hire and a boathouse café.

Char are similar to trout, but more beautiful, with reddish skin on the underside – their name refers to their rosy belly in old Norse. The fish average around 225g (½lb), but occasionally a really large 900g (2lb) is hooked. Whatever the size, the taste of fresh-caught char is heavenly. Grilled with herbs or baked with almonds as in this recipe, it is far superior to wild brown trout or salmon.

> **4 whole char or trout, cleaned**
> **sea salt and freshly ground black pepper**
> **110g (4oz) butter**
> **110g (4oz) flaked almonds**
> **sprigs of fresh dill**
> **1 lemon cut into wedges**

Pre-heat the oven to 160°C/325°F/GM3.

Wipe the fish with a damp cloth, and season lightly inside and out. Place in an ovenproof dish that fits snugly.

In a small pan melt half the butter and add the almonds. Stir until nice and buttery, remove from the heat and pour over the fish. Dot the fish with the remaining butter then cover the dish with foil and cook in the centre of the oven for about 20 minutes.

Remove the foil, baste the fish and continue cooking for another 10-15 minutes depending on the size of the fish. Test the flesh with a knife to see that it is cooked – it should come away easily from the bone and be opaque. Remove from the oven and leave to rest for 5 minutes, then transfer to warm serving plates. Garnish with dill and lemon wedges.

Serve with new potatoes and a green vegetable, or with salad leaves and some crusty bread.

Early morning on Lake Windermere

POTTED LAKELAND CHAR

Today, gourmets delight in fresh char, but past ages had different tastes. Barrels of salted char were frequently sent to Henry VIII at Hampton Court and massive char pies, weighing up to 4 stone (over 25 kilos) were regularly despatched to the Restoration Court. About the same time pottery was substituted for the pastry; the intrepid 17th-century traveller, Celia Fiennes, certainly appreciated char potted with sweet spices in 1698 at a Kendal Inn.

The tourist explosion to the Lakes in the 1770s produced the char pot. All the early examples were made from Liverpool tin-glazed earthenware (delftware) with beautifully hand-painted char swimming around the outside of the pot. As the Liverpool factories declined and Wedgwood's successful and practical creamware made delftware obsolete, char pots were made from a commoner, white earthenware.

The fish were cleaned, spiced and packed in the attractive pots, then heavily encased in butter and cooked. In this form they kept well and were exported to the rest of Britain, particularly to the luxury end of the market; sent down to London by overnight train to Fortnum and Mason, for example.

BUTTERMERE CHAR WITH A SALMON MOUSSELINE
(serves 6)

There are tiny populations of cousins of the Windermere char in Buttermere, Coniston and Crummock Water, all lakes protected by the National Trust. The species needs clear, pure, well-oxygenated cold water to thrive. From the top of the high fells, Windermere may look beautiful, but beneath the surface all is not well. Pollution from agricultural waste and 12 million tourists who flood into the Lake District every year is putting the char at risk: oxygen is disappearing over a substantial area of the lake, although the Water Authority is spending millions on water improvements.

The char is also affected by global warming as it likes very cold water and is suffering from competition with the roach, introduced into Windermere by anglers as live bait in the 1920s. The roach has a huge number of eggs, so very easily overruns other fish. There is very little the authorities can do to control either the roach, or other competitors, except tell people what is happening and persuade anglers not to put these species into the lake. The National Trust insists that no live bait is used on any of their waters in Britain. It would be a sin if Lakeland char, like so many other great delicacies, were to be allowed to slip away into the mists of culinary memory.

6 char or small trout, cleaned
350g (12oz) responsibly farmed Atlantic salmon or sea trout fillet, skinned
250ml (7fl oz) double cream
2 free-range egg whites
a large pinch of ground coriander
a large pinch of ground mace or nutmeg
sea salt and freshly ground black pepper
sprigs of watercress to garnish

For the orange hollandaise sauce
2 tablespoons white wine vinegar
4 tablespoons water
1 slice onion
1 blade of mace
$^1/_2$ small bay leaf
6 black peppercorns, lightly crushed
sea salt and freshly ground black pepper
3 free-range egg yolks
175g (6oz) unsalted butter
grated rind of 1 orange
orange juice to taste

To make the mousseline, cut the salmon into chunks, removing any bones. Put the fish chunks, your blender, goblet or processor bowl and the cream into the freezer for about 20 minutes to chill thoroughly.

Process the chilled fish to the finest possible paste, add the egg whites one by one with the motor running. Add the coriander and mace, then check to see that the fish mixture is very cold. Put back in the freezer for another 10 minutes if necessary. When cold, add the cream very slowly, again with the motor running. Season to taste. Pre-heat the oven to 100°C/350°F/GM4.

Cut off the heads, tails and fins of the char or trout and remove the bones. Spoon the salmon mousseline into the prepared fish and fold over. Arrange on a baking sheet covered with foil, cover with more buttered foil and bake in the centre of the oven for about 20 minutes or until cooked, depending on size. The flesh should give easily when pressed gently with the finger tips.

Prepare the sauce while the fish is cooking. Place the vinegar, 3 tablespoons of water, onion slice, mace, bay leaf and peppercorns in a small pan. Simmer gently until the mixture is reduced to about 1 tablespoon, then strain into a bowl. Add the remaining tablespoon of water and season. Whisk in the egg yolks.

Set the bowl over a pan of barely simmering water and whisk in 12g ($^1/_2$oz) of the butter, whisking until it has melted. Continue adding the butter, cut into small pieces, allowing each piece to melt completely before adding the next.

When all the butter has been added, continue to whisk the sauce and cook gently for a further few minutes until thick. Remove the bowl from the pan of water and add the orange rind and orange juice. Taste and correct seasoning if necessary. Arrange the fish on 6 warm plates and garnish with the watercress. Serve with the sauce.

Left: Looking from Fleetwith Moor towards Buttermere, with Crummock Water in the far distance
Above: Crummock Water in Buttermere

FRIED FLOOKBURGH FLUKE

These flat fish with longish tails are a speciality of Flookburgh, a small fishing community in Morecambe Bay. They are really flounders with a flavour like that of plaice, although thought to be finer by enthusiasts. Flukes and other flat fish are caught by being driven into stake nets on the sands, and local fishmongers sell them fresh, but the majority of them are frozen immediately after landing.

There is really no better way of serving this fish than fried in butter, which is the local way. Allow 1 fish per person. Clean it and cut off its head, wipe and dry well. Season with black pepper and fry gently in butter each side.

Serve on a hot dish with melted butter and sprinkle with fresh chopped parsley or serve with a pot of herb butter.

FLOOKBURGH FLUKES SERVED WITH SHRIMPS
(serves 2)

The village of Flookburgh is the centre of shrimp fishing from tractors, which replaced the old horse and carts in the 1950s and has been blamed for the decline in the quality of the catch because of over-fishing. About 10 tractor fishermen work from here today. They set out as the tide ebbs, as soon as the water becomes shallow enough to ford the channels and creeks across the sands. Shrimping nets attached by a long line to the tractor are drawn very slowly along the waterline. Periodically the net is emptied, the catch riddled or sieved, small and immature fish being returned to the sea. On return to the shore, shrimps or prawns which are also caught in this area, are boiled in seawater on the sand, then hand or machine picked so that they are ready to eat. Plaice from the Irish Sea, which is still relatively plentiful, or any flat fish, can be used instead.

2 fresh flukes, cleaned
25g (1oz) butter
sea salt and freshly ground black pepper
2 small pots of potted shrimps
1 free-range egg
300ml (10fl oz) double cream
1 tablespoon fresh parsley, chopped

Dry the fish well with kitchen paper and slash them down with the backbone on one side with a sharp knife. Season the fish and arrange them in a well-buttered dish. Top each fish with the potted shrimps and cover with buttered greaseproof paper. Bake in a moderate oven (180°C/350F°/GM4) for 15-20 minutes, depending on the thickness of the fish.

Beat the egg with the cream and season well. Heat the sauce very gently in a small saucepan. Do not let it boil, or it will curdle. When the fish is cooked, add the buttery cooking juices to the hot cream and pour over the fish. Brown under a very hot grill for 2 or 3 minutes and serve sprinkled with chopped parsley.

Left: A shrimper with his equipment, photograph from the early part of the 20th century
Above: Morecambe Bay from Jack Scout, Silverdale, Lancashire

ARBROATH SMOKIES

A few miles north of Arbroath, on the east coast of Scotland, the picturesque village of Auchmithie perches on the edge of a cliff several hundred feet above the harbour. This is where the Arbroath smokie originated, first known as Auchmithie lucken, close fish, or pinwiddie. In the early 1800s, a number of Auchmithie fisher-folk settled in nearby Arbroath, continuing to make the smokie cure. By the end of the century, output from Arbroath greatly exceeded that from Auchmithie so the name of the smokie was changed.

Today the people of Arbroath continue to smoke in their back-yards using brick 'smoke-pits' covered with layers of hessian sacking to regulate the heat. More commercial operations have been developed, but no-one has managed to reproduce the genuine smokie in computer-operated, high-tech kilns.

Originally, all kinds of surplus fish were smoked, but haddock became the most popular. The fish are gutted, beheaded and dry-salted for about 2 hours depending on size, to draw excess moisture from the skin and impart a mild salty flavour. They are tied in pairs and hung over wooden rods; the salt is washed off and they are left to dry for about 5 hours to harden the skins. The rods are placed in the smoke-pit and hot-smoked over oak or beech for approximately 45 minutes. The result is a delicious copper-coloured, mildly smoked fish with a creamy texture; no artificial dyes or preservatives are added.

Since the fish is hot-smoked and therefore cooked, it can be eaten cold with brown bread and butter and lemon, but strangely, smokies are traditionally served hot. They are at their very best straight from the smoke-pit; otherwise split open the fish and remove the bone, then fill the centre with butter and grill or bake in a hot oven for a few minutes until hot. Wrap in foil if you wish.

In the North West, smokies are often eaten with a baked or boiled jacket potato as a favourite high-tea dish.

FINNAN HADDIE

A heavily salt-cured haddock can be traced back for centuries on the east coast of Scotland. As communications improved in the 18th century there was a move towards a lightly salted, smoked fish. The fish-wives of Findon, a village a few miles from Aberdeen, produced a superior cured haddock, which became known as a Finnan. Its reputation is said to have spread quickly through the country at the beginning of the 19th century because the fish was transported to a dealer in Edinburgh by a relation who was a guard on the Aberdeen to Edinburgh stage-coach.

The original Finnans had their heads removed and were split with the bone on the left-hand side, looking at the cut surface, with the tail downwards. They were dry-salted overnight and smoked over soft 'grey' peat for 8-9 hours, cooled and washed in warm salted water. Methods today vary from commercially produced large-scale smoking in Torry kilns to small independent smokers using simpler equipment. A genuine Finnan haddock is pale gold with a lightly salted, delicately smoked flavour.

HAM AND HADDIE
(serves 4)

Finnan haddocks were hawked about the country by fish-wives during the heyday of the east coast fisheries of Scotland and became common fare, cooked simply in milk and butter and served with or without a poached egg, or fried with bacon. They made a special supper or high tea in many parts of the North West of England.

Any undyed smoked haddock can be used in this recipe, although Finnan haddock does have a very delicate and special flavour.

    400g (14oz) Finnan haddock,
        boned but skin left on
    400ml (14fl oz) full-fat milk
    25g (1oz) unsalted butter
    25g (1oz) plain flour
    1 cup fresh parsley, finely chopped
    sea salt and freshly ground black pepper
    a pinch of freshly grated nutmeg
    4 very fresh free-range eggs,
        preferably organic
    4 thick slices of good-quality ham
    4 white muffins

Pre-heat the oven to 190°C/375°F/GM5.

Put the fish in an ovenproof dish, skin side up and pour over the milk. Bake in the oven for 15 minutes, then carefully remove to a separate plate and take off the skin. Reserve the milk. Cover the fish with foil and keep warm in a low oven until ready to eat. Melt the butter in a small saucepan and add the flour. Stir for a minute or two over a low heat, remove from the heat and add a little of the reserved milk, stirring continuously. Add a little more milk and stir again, repeating until the sauce is smooth and creamy. Return to the heat and add the rest of the milk, stirring until the sauce thickens. Continue to cook on a very low heat while you prepare the rest of the dish.

Bring a large saucepan of water to a rapid simmer. Whisk vigorously in a circular motion and crack an egg into the centre. As the liquid spins, it pulls and sets the white around the yolk, before the egg reaches the base of the pan. Add the other eggs quickly and poach for 3– 3½ minutes.

Meanwhile, fry the ham in a little butter for a few minutes and toast and butter the muffins. Keep warm in the oven.

Stir the parsley into the sauce and season to taste with salt, pepper and nutmeg.

When the eggs are cooked, assemble the dish by placing the muffins on 4 warm plates, top with ham, haddock and a poached egg. Pour over the parsley sauce and serve immediately.

CULLEN SKINK
(serves 4– 6)

Although originating from Cullen, a small fishing village in the Moray Firth area of Scotland, this soup-stew, or skink (an old Scots word), became more widely popular. It is typical of fisher food all around the coast of the north of England.

If using Finnan haddock, you will need twice the quantity. Jug the fish in boiling water for 5 minutes, then remove all skin and bones. Flake into large pieces, then continue as follows.

    350g (12oz) undyed smoked haddock,
        skinned and boned
    15g (½oz) unsalted butter
    250g (9oz) onion, peeled and finely
        chopped
    250g (9oz) white part of leek, washed
        and finely chopped
    100g (3½oz) potato, peeled and finely
        chopped
    1 sprig fresh thyme
    1 bay leaf
    2 garlic cloves, peeled and chopped
    700ml (1¼pts) fish stock (see p.222)
    300ml (10fl oz) double cream
    sea salt and freshly ground white pepper
    a small pinch mild curry powder

Heat the butter in a heavy-based pan, cover and sweat the onion and leek with the thyme, bay leaf and garlic for about 5 minutes. Add the potato and continue to sweat for about 15 minutes until the potato is soft. (Cover the surface of the vegetables with buttered greaseproof, or a saved butter paper.)

Meanwhile, cut the fish into chunks checking that there are no bones.

When the vegetables are soft, stir in the stock and bring to the boil. Add the fish and cream, bring back to the boil gently. Simmer for 2-3 minutes to cook the fish, then blitz in a food processor. Pass through a sieve, season to taste with salt, pepper and curry powder. Reheat if necessary, then serve in bowls with some good crusty bread for dunking and mopping up.

For lunch or supper, add a poached quail's egg to the finished soup to make it more filling.

Left: Fishermen's cottages in Newhaven, Lothian in Scotland, photographed in 1897

HOT MANX KIPPER SOUFFLÉ
(serves 4)

There was a small, but significant fishery in the Isle of Man in the 18th and 19th centuries. The original Manx boats, the square-sailed 'scowties' whose design had been influenced by their Viking ancestors, were replaced in the early 19th century by the more modern and larger cutter-rigged boats. Larger smacks cruised around the fleet taking the catch back to the island, to Liverpool or as far as the Mediterranean. By the 1820s, the Manx fleet comprised about 260 cutter or smack-rigged boats, crewed by 2,500 men, many of whom were also crofters.

The coming of the Cornish boats to the Manx summer fishing grounds for herring and mackerel in the 1820s also resulted in more efficient boats, called 'nickeys' because so many of the Cornish vessels being copied were called Nicholas, after the patron saint of fishermen. Local elm and Irish oak were used to build these boats, which were quite speedy. In the 1880s a smaller and more lightly rigged version, the 'nobby', was also developed; so many young men had departed from the island that there was the need for a boat which could be handled by an older, less numerous crew.

The island is best known for its delicious kippers which are world famous and superb. They are cooked from small herrings, about 22cm (9in) including head and tail, caught off the coast and landed at Peel. The cure is similar to that used elsewhere, but several differences make Manx kippers unique. First, they are always undyed and secondly, the herrings are caught early in the season, when they are at their best – the Manx season is from June to August. Fish from Irish boats that work in pairs with 1 net between 2 boats are preferred, as they are always in excellent condition with no bruising. The resultant kippers are a pale lemony fawn fading to silver on the belly, with a mild lightly smoked flavour.

Some of the boarding houses and small hotels in Douglas make this dish as a speciality. It must be served straight from the oven either as a starter, or for lunch.

3 Manx kippers
50g (1³⁄₄oz) butter
50g (1³⁄₄oz) plain flour
300ml (¹⁄₂pt) full-fat milk,
    or single cream
a pinch of cayenne
a pinch of freshly grated nutmeg
4 large free-range egg yolks, well beaten
5 large free-range egg whites
12g (¹⁄₂oz) butter for greasing

Use the jug method to cook the kippers (see p.112). Once cooked, carefully remove all the bones and skin, then mash the flesh.

Melt the butter in a large pan and stir in the flour. Cook over a moderate heat for 2 minutes, but don't brown, then gradually stir in the milk or cream and cook gently for a few minutes until the sauce is thick and smooth. Season with cayenne and nutmeg and stir in the kipper flesh. Remove from the heat and leave to cool a little, stir in the beaten egg yolks. Whisk the egg whites until very stiff and stir a tablespoonful into the sauce. Fold the rest in very carefully.

Butter a 1.5 litre (2¹⁄₂pt) soufflé dish and pour in the mixture. Bake in a fairly hot oven 200°C/400°F/GM6 for about 30 minutes until well-risen and golden.

SOLWAY MUSSEL AND CRAB STEW
(serves 4 as a starter)

The Solway Firth has been designated a Special Area of Conservation, from Caulkerbush in the north across to Mawbray in the south and up the estuary to Gretna, so any fisheries have to be sustainable and non-invasive.

Large numbers of mussels are farmed, which all go down to Poole Harbour in Dorset to be cleaned and processed. Oysters are also farmed and shrimps netted. Solway potted shrimps are not as well known as Morecambe Bay, but are equally delicious. Crabs are caught all along the west coast and landed at Maryport, Whitehaven and further south at Flookburgh.

The National Trust protects 1¹⁄₂ miles of coastline and 69 hectares (170 acres) of common land on the south side of the Solway with magnificent views over the estuary and the mountains of Galloway. Known as Solway Commons, the area has a solitary and breathtaking beauty.

900g (2lb) fresh mussels, scrubbed and
    bearded
110g (4oz) fresh white crab meat
65g (2¹⁄₂oz) butter
1 small onion, sliced
150ml (¹⁄₄pt) dry white wine
2 tablespoons shallot, or onion,
    finely chopped
110g (4oz) chestnut, or button
    mushrooms, wiped and roughly
    chopped
1 level tablespoon plain flour
150ml (5fl oz) single cream
1 level tablespoon fresh parsley,
    roughly chopped
1 heaped teaspoon tarragon leaves,
    torn into pieces
sea salt and freshly ground black pepper
a large pinch of freshly grated nutmeg
a squeeze of lemon juice

Melt 15g (¹⁄₂oz) butter in a large pan and add the sliced onion. Cook for a few minutes, then add the mussels and white wine. Cover with a lid and cook over a high heat for about 3 minutes, shaking the pan occasionally until the mussels have all opened. Drain in a colander, discarding any that are not open and saving all the juices. Strain the reserved liquor through a fine sieve into a clean pan. Bring to the boil and boil rapidly until the liquid is reduced to about 2 tablespoons. Remove from the heat and set aside.

Melt the remaining butter in a pan and add the shallot or onion. Cook on a fairly high heat for further 2-3 minutes, then add the mushrooms. Continue to cook for a further few minutes, then stir in the flour. Cook for about 2 minutes without browning, remove from the heat and gradually stir in the cream and the reserved mussel liquor. Return to the heat and bring to the boil, stirring all the time. Cook gently for another 5 minutes, stir in the mussels, crab and herbs. Season to taste with salt, pepper, nutmeg and lemon juice. Heat through very gently until the fish is warm, serve in 4 warm soup bowls, or individual dishes, with lots of warm crusty bread and a glass of chilled dry white wine.

DERWENTWATER PERCH STUFFED WITH MUSHROOMS AND HERBS (serves 4–6)

The National Trust bought Brandelhow Woods, its first property in the Lake District, in 1902 to guarantee public access to the shore of Derwentwater, near Keswick. Since then it has acquired many areas of land in the Borrowdale Valley including Friar's Crag on the north shore of the Lake from where John Ruskin described the view as one of the finest in Europe.

Perch can be fished on many of the National Trust's waters in the Lake District. It is one of the great freshwater fish honoured in Ancient Greece and Rome and still eaten with great pleasure in Italy and France. China also reveres the fish and perhaps the best opportunity of tasting perch is at a reliable Chinese restaurant, unless you are an angler. It is in season all the year round and has a dusky coloured body with vivid orange and red fins and tail. If you are lucky enough to acquire a fresh perch, it should be scaled immediately after being caught, otherwise it's very difficult to do. (The spines can be painful, so wear gloves.) If the scaling has *not* been done, the whole fish should be plunged into boiling water with vinegar for a few seconds, then the thick skin, complete with scales, can be removed.

Small perch can be filleted and grilled or fried in butter and oil for 2 minutes, whilst large perch are best stuffed with a mixture of herbs, shallots and lemon and braised in red or white wine. Many trout recipes are also suitable.

1 x 900g-1.35kg (2-3lb) whole perch or trout, scaled and cleaned
50g (2oz) butter
1 heaped tablespoon shallot, or onion, finely chopped
75g (2¾oz) mushrooms, roughly chopped
about 4 tablespoons white breadcrumbs, depending on size of fish
sea salt and freshly ground black pepper
grated rind of ½ unwaxed lemon
a little freshly grated nutmeg
2 tablespoons fresh mixed herbs, finely chopped (parsley, chives, fennel and thyme)
a little beaten egg or cream to mix
about 25g (1oz) melted butter for brushing
1 teaspoon lemon juice
150ml (¼pt) dry white wine

Pre-heat the oven to 180°C/350°F/GM4.

To make the stuffing, melt the butter and fry the shallot gently for 5 minutes. Add the mushrooms, raise the heat slightly and cook for a further 5-7 minutes. Stir in the breadcrumbs and remove from the heat. Season to taste with salt, pepper and nutmeg, stir in the lemon rind and herbs. Bind with a little beaten egg or cream to form a soft stuffing and spoon into the fish cavity. Secure the opening with wooden cocktail sticks or skewers.

Lay the fish in a buttered ovenproof dish which fits snugly. Brush it generously with melted butter and pour over the lemon juice and wine. Cover lightly with foil and bake for 25-30 minutes depending on the size of fish.

Before serving, remove the cocktail sticks or skewers, then serve the fish, spooning over the cooking juices. Garnish with lemon slices and sprigs of fresh herbs.

Far left: Derwentwater, looking towards Brandelhow Wood, with the lower slopes of Cat Bells
Left: Derwentwater

PIKE AND CHAR SOUFFLÉ
(serves 4–6)

At Troutbeck at the north end of Lake Windermere, the National Trust owns a largely 17th-century solid stone and slate house originally belonging to a wealthy yeoman farming family. Townend contains books, papers, furniture and fascinating domestic implements from the past, largely accumulated by the Browne family who lived here from 1626 to 1943. Amongst the papers is a commonplace book of 1699 with medicinal and culinary recipes including one for roasting pike stuffed with fresh herbs, garlic, spiced butter and anchovies. Freshwater fish such as pike and char would have been abundantly available from nearby Windermere and Rydal Water.

Today anglers can still fish for pike and char on Windermere and for pike on Rydal Water and other waters protected by the National Trust, as long as permits are obtained. You can make this delicious soufflé with your freshly caught fish.

75g (2¾oz) **pike or perch**
75g (2¾oz) **char or trout**
dry white wine to cover
sea salt and freshly ground black pepper
50g (1½oz) **butter**
50g (1½oz) **strong plain flour**
300ml (½ pt) **milk and reserved**
   poaching liquor
pinch of cayenne
pinch of freshly grated nutmeg
4 **free-range egg yolks**
75g (2¾oz) **cheese, grated**
1 **tablespoon fresh fennel**
   or dill, chopped
5 **egg whites**
pinch of cream of tartar

Place the fish in a shallow pan and pour over enough white wine to barely cover. Season lightly with salt and pepper and poach very gently for 2 or 3 minutes until just cooked. Remove the fish and reserve the poaching liquor. Discard the skin and bones and flake the flesh.

Melt the butter in a large pan and stir in the flour. Cook for about 2 minutes, but be careful not to brown, then remove from the heat. Gradually stir in the milk mixed with the poaching liquor and season with salt, pepper, cayenne and nutmeg. Return to the heat and cook for 1 or 2 minutes, stirring continuously until smooth. Remove from the heat again and leave to cool slightly. Beat in the egg yolks, one at a time. (The mixture can be prepared up to this point earlier in the day if you wish, but bring back to a tepid temperature before you start the next stage.)

Pre-heat the oven to 190°C/375°F/GM5. Stir the flaked fish into the sauce with the cheese and herbs. Whisk the egg whites in a large clean mixing bowl with a pinch of salt and cream of tartar until stiff.

Stir 1 large tablespoonful of egg white into the sauce to lighten its texture, then lightly fold in the rest, taking care not to overmix.

Pour the mixture gently into a generously buttered 1.5 litre (2½ pt) soufflé dish. Smooth the surface and mark the top in a criss-cross pattern with a skewer. Stand the dish in a deep roasting tin half-filled with hot water and cook in the centre of the oven for 5 minutes, then reduce to 180°C/350°F/GM4 and cook for a further 40 minutes, or until nicely risen and golden brown on top.

Serve with a crisp green salad for lunch or supper.

Left: The fish market at Kendal, *c.* **1890**
Right: Townend in Troutbeck, home of the Browne family for four hundred years

MORECAMBE BAY SHRIMPS

The development of Morecambe's once significant fishing industry went more or less hand in hand with the town's growth as a centre for holidaymakers and tourists, which made a quantum leap after the railway arrived in 1847. It was the shrimps that provided the mainstay of fishing in the Bay. They were a very fashionable food in Victorian England, much in demand for afternoon tea, and if you have never tasted fresh Morecambe Bay shrimps, you are in for a treat. Tiny, light brown and sweet as honey, they have a limited season from April to the end of November.

Today the Morecambe Bay shrimp industry is small and specialised, providing employment for no more than 10 boatmen and the same number of tractor fishermen who work out of Flookburgh (see p.131). Morecambe Bay, from Fleetwood in the south to Barrow in the north, has been designated a Special Area of Conservation by English Nature because of its mud and sand flats; at low tide well over 125 square miles are exposed, deposited by two large rivers and several smaller streams which empty into the Irish Sea at this point. Extremely dangerous for those without local knowledge, they include areas of quicksand which change unpredictably and the tide comes in fast, trapping the unwary.

Wonderful views of the Bay can be seen from the limestone escarpment of Arnside Knott and Heathwaite and from the cliffs and foreshore of Jack Scout, both on the east side and protected by the National Trust.

All over Lancashire, look out for potted shrimps, which have been a speciality of Morecambe Bay since at least 1799, the date of the foundation of Baxter's, still one of the producers today. Originally, potting was a means of preserving a coastal delicacy for sale inland. Boiled, picked shrimps are cooked briefly in spiced butter – traditionally mace – packed into pots, then sealed with a little more butter. They are utterly delicious and one of my very favourite foods.

SHRIMP TEAS 'UP NORTH'

Shrimp teas are very popular in the North of England. There used to be little seaside cottages with freshly-baked bread and fresh butter, where you could have shrimp teas. Dorothy Hartley in her book *Food in England* published in 1954, describes one such tea served by Betsy Tattershall: 'Betty brought out a pot of tea, with a woollen tea-cosy on it, sugar and cream, a cup and saucer each, two big plates of thin bread and butter – brown and white – a big green plate of watercress and a big pink plate of shrimps. And that was all, except an armoured salt cellar and a robin. Then you "reached to".' What a splendid meal and so simple, but do make sure your shrimps are really fresh and still smelling of the sea. Potted shrimp paste can be served instead of fresh shrimps.

Left: Cockling in Morecambe Bay, *c.* **1920**
Right: Looking from Arnside Knott down into Silverdale and Morecambe Bay

POTTED SHRIMPS WITH LEMON MAYONNAISE
(serves 6)

For a starter, serve 1 small pot of shrimps with hot wholemeal toast and a slice of lemon, straight out of the pot or warmed through. A generous helping with a mixed green salad and lemon mayonnaise makes an excellent lunch.

> 450g (1lb) freshly cooked and
>   picked (peeled) brown shrimps
> 175g (6oz) best quality unsalted butter
> a good pinch of cayenne
> a scant teaspoon of ground mace
> a generous pinch of freshly
>   grated nutmeg
> freshly ground black pepper
> 50g (2oz) clarified butter

For the lemon mayonnaise
> 300ml (½pt) home-made or good-
>   quality mayonnaise (see p.221)
> about 1 tablespoon lemon juice

Melt the unsalted butter in a pan with the spices. Remove from the heat and add the shrimps. Turn them over in the spiced butter, taking care not to break them up. Leave to steep for 10 minutes. Taste for salt and add a little if necessary. Adjust the spices to taste at the same time, then turn into suitable small pots and leave to set.

Melt the clarified butter and spoon over enough to cover the surface of each pot and seal the contents. Cool, chill in the fridge at least overnight before serving. They will keep well for at least 2 weeks in the fridge and may be frozen for up to 3 months; thaw overnight in the fridge before using.

Take out of the fridge about 20 minutes before you want to serve to bring out the flavour. Beat the lemon juice into the mayonnaise. Taste and add more if necessary.

Dip the pots briefly in hot water to melt the butter and turn out on to serving plates. Serve with seasonal salad leaves, lemon mayonnaise and fresh crusty bread.

MORECAMBE BAY SHRIMP TARTLETS
(serves 6)

For the pastry
> 225g (8oz) plain flour
> a pinch of salt
> 150g (5½oz) unsalted butter
> 1 free-range egg, beaten
> a little cold water to mix

For the filling
> 4 x 125g (4½oz) pots of potted shrimps
> 1 small onion, very finely chopped
> 25g (1oz) plain flour
> 300ml (10fl oz) single cream
> ¼ cucumber, finely chopped
>   and drained
> sea salt and freshly ground black pepper
> freshly grated nutmeg
> grated rind and juice of 1
>   unwaxed lemon
> sprigs of fresh fennel or dill to garnish

To make the pastry, sieve the flour and salt into a mixing bowl. Lightly rub in the butter until the mixture resembles fine breadcrumbs. Gradually add the beaten egg and a little water to make a pliable dough, then knead very lightly. Wrap in clingfilm and leave to rest in the fridge for about 30 minutes before using.

Roll out the prepared pastry and use to line 6 x 11cm (4in) individual fluted tart tins with removeable bases. Line with parchment baking paper, greaseproof or foil and fill with baking beans. Chill again for 30 minutes.

Pre-heat the oven to 200°C/400°F/GM6 with a baking sheet inside.

Place the chilled pastry cases on the pre-heated baking sheet and bake blind for about 10 minutes. Remove the paper and beans and prick the bases all over with a fork. Bake for about a further 5 minutes or until the cases are crisp and pale golden.

While the tartlet cases are cooking, prepare the filling. Warm the potted shrimps in a pan until the butter falls from them, then remove the shrimps with a slotted spoon and reserve on one side.

Cook the onion in the shrimp butter until soft and transparent, stir in the flour. Cook for a few minutes, and stir in the cream. Cook over a low heat until the sauce is smooth and thick, add the reserved shrimps and cucumber. Heat through gently and season to taste with salt, pepper, nutmeg, lemon rind and juice.

Just before serving, place a warm pastry case on 6 warm plates and fill with the shrimp mixture. Garnish with a few salad leaves and sprigs of herbs.

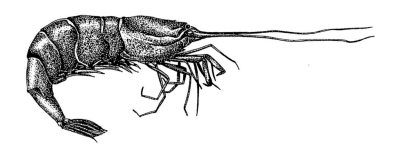

Sandscale Haws in Cumbria, looking towards the southern Lake District

LAKELAND GRILLED TROUT WITH GOOSEBERRY AND MUSTARD SEED SAUCE
(serves 4)

Anglers who come to the Lake District are principally in search of trout. Most of the National Trust lakes, tarns and becks with public access can be fished, provided permits are obtained. On some waters fishing is either privately let or is completely prohibited for conservation reasons.

Serving trout with gooseberry sauce is very traditional to the North West.

4 fresh brown or rainbow trout, cleaned
about 50g (1¾oz) butter, melted
sea salt and freshly ground black pepper

For the gooseberry and mustard seed sauce
2 level teaspoons white
or yellow mustard seeds
about 5 tablespoons dry white wine
225g (8oz) green gooseberries,
topped and tailed
caster sugar or honey to taste
25g (1oz) butter
sea salt and freshly ground black pepper

To make the sauce, soak the mustard seeds in a little of the wine, until they are swollen.

Place the gooseberries in a pan with the remaining wine and bring to a simmer. Cook gently for about 8 minutes until the fruit begins to soften and pop, then remove from the heat. Allow to relax for 10-15 minutes, stir and taste. If too tart, stir in a little sugar or honey, although the sauce is supposed to be on the sharp side. If too thin, cook for a few more minutes, before stirring in the mustard seeds, wine and butter. Season to taste with salt and pepper. Keep warm while you cook the trout.

Leave on the head and tails of the fish, but remove the gills. Wipe the skin well with a damp cloth, but don't wash. Line a baking sheet or grill pan with buttered foil and add the trout. Cut the fish two or three times diagonally across the body on both sides and brush generously with melted butter. Season well with salt and pepper. Place the fish under a hot grill and cook for about 5 minutes on each side, depending on the size, until the skin is just starting to brown. Serve immediately with the warm gooseberry sauce.

MOSS ECCLES NUTTY BROWN TROUT
(serves 4)

Moss Eccles Tarn is a peaceful little lake above the village of Near Sawrey where Beatrix Potter lived. She bought part of the Tarn along with Castle Cottage, her married home, and proceeded to plant water lilies and stock it with brown trout. Her husband, Willie Heelis, was a keen dry-fly fisherman and Beatrix Potter would sometimes accompany him in the boat. In a letter of July 1922 to their niece, Silvie Heelis, Beatrix writes 'Uncle Willie has gone out fishing – or poaching; rather an odd performance occasionally resulting in one pound trouts!' Their boat was recovered from the bed of Moss Eccles Tarn in 1976 and is now one of the many fascinating exhibits at the Bowness Steam Boat Museum on Lake Windermere.

Moss Eccles was given to the National Trust by Beatrix Potter and is still a peaceful, magical place today. You can follow Willie's footsteps by fly-fishing for brown trout; permits are available from the Tower Bank Arms, the pub in the village, and Windermere and Ambleside District Fishing Association. The best trout, whatever the size or variety, is the one you catch yourself and eat within an hour or two – the simpler the cooking the better.

The brown trout has a cleaner, lighter taste than a rainbow trout and paler pink flesh. They are available from some supermarkets, otherwise use rainbow. For a special breakfast, serve this recipe with home-cured bacon, hot wholemeal toast and farm butter.

4 fresh brown or rainbow trout, cleaned
225g (8oz) shelled hazelnuts
sea salt and freshly ground black pepper
a little flour for dusting
2 large free-range eggs
1 dessertspoon milk
100g (3½oz) clarified butter
watercress and French dressing to serve

Grill or roast the hazelnuts until their skins can be rubbed off using a rough tea towel, then chop them. Leave on the heads and tails of the fish, but remove the gills. Wipe them with a damp cloth rather than washing. Rub the fish skins gently with plenty of black pepper and salt and dust lightly with flour.

Beat the eggs with the milk, then dip the trout in the mixture. Finally, roll in the chopped hazelnuts.

Melt the clarified butter in a large, heavy frying pan and fry the fish over a moderate heat for 4-5 minutes on each side, lightly pressing the fish down into the pan so that the skin crisps to a delicious golden brown. The trouts are cooked if the flesh gives when pressed gently in the thickest part with the fingertips.

Remove the trout to 4 serving plates and pour over the pan juices. Serve with watercress, sprinkled with French dressing and plenty of crusty bread.

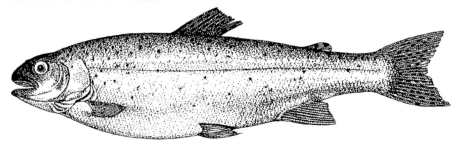

ULLSWATER TROUT MARINATED IN LEMON AND OIL WITH A TOMATO AND CORIANDER SAUCE
(serves 4)

Anglers can fish for trout for free on parts of Ullswater and Brotherswater near Penrith, both protected by the National Trust. There are stunning walks for everyone in this valley around Aira Force Waterfalls. It was after a walk with his sister Dorothy along this shore of Ullswater that William Wordsworth wrote 'I wandered lonely as a cloud'.

Try marinating your freshly caught trout in lemon juice and oil before cooking.

> 4 whole brown or rainbow
>   trout, cleaned
> 2 garlic cloves, crushed
> grated rind and juice of 2
>   unwaxed lemons
> 8 tablespoons olive oil

> For the tomato and coriander sauce
>   6 ripe plum tomatoes, cut into eighths
>   ½ red onion, finely chopped
>   2 fresh red chillis, finely sliced
>   (including seeds)
>   juice of 1 lemon
>   4 tablespoons olive oil
>   3-4 tablespoons fresh coriander leaves,
>   roughly chopped
>   sea salt and freshly ground black pepper

Slash the skin of the trout in three places on each side, then place in a shallow dish. Add the garlic, lemon rind and juice, and olive oil. Coat the fish with the marinade, cover and chill for 2 hours.

For the sauce, mix all the ingredients together and season to taste. Cover and leave on one side.

Remove the fish from the marinade and season well. Grill or barbecue for about 5 minutes on each side, then serve warm with the tomato sauce and plenty of good bread.

WARM SALAD OF POTATO, ROCKET AND ESTHWAITE SMOKED TROUT
(serves 4 as a starter)

When Beatrix Potter's family holidayed in the Lake District in 1896, they kept a boat on Esthwaite Water, close to the village of Near Sawrey, which was to be her future home. Beatrix wrote of how much she enjoyed rowing alone there and indeed Esthwaite was to remain her favourite lake. She sketched and painted it many times – the view from the wood in *The Tale of Jemima Puddleduck* shows Esthwaite, and Mr Jeremy Fisher's adventures are thought to have taken place here.

> 4 organic smoked trout fillets, skinned
>   and boned
> 450g (1lb) waxy new potatoes
>   (Charlotte, Anya or Ratte)
> 175g (6oz) good-quality creamed
>   horseradish
> ½ small red onion, very finely chopped
> 3 tablespoons crème fraîche
> juice of 1 lemon
> 3 tablespoons extra virgin olive oil
> 1 tablespoon fresh flat-leaf parsley,
>   finely chopped
> sea salt and freshly ground black pepper
> 100g (3½oz) rocket leaves, washed
>   and drained

Cook the potatoes in boiling salted water until tender. Meanwhile, make the dressing by mixing together the horseradish, onion, crème fraîche, lemon juice, oil and parsley in a large bowl. Whisk well with a fork, season to taste and set aside. When the potatoes are cooked, drain well and dry over heat, then slice roughly into the dressing.

Warm the trout fillets very gently under the grill, then flake roughly into the bowl with the potatoes. Toss the mixture carefully without breaking up the ingredients. Arrange the rocket leaves on 4 plates and top with the fish mixture. Serve sprinkled with freshly ground black pepper.

Left: Ullswater Trout marinated in Lemon and Oil with a Tomato and Coriander Sauce
Above: Illustration from *The Tale of Mr Jeremy Fisher*, 1906. The water-lilies and reeds are based on sketches of Esthwaite Water made by Beatrix Potter. ©Frederick Warne

FORMBY ASPARAGUS AND SEA TROUT SOUP
(serves 4)

Sand dunes are important sites for a variety of rare plants, insects, reptiles and amphibians. In the North West, the National Trust protects two superb dune systems: Sandscale Haws, 2 miles from Barrow-in-Furness in Cumbria, which is an internationally renowned nature reserve with a strong population of the coral root orchid and the breeding site of the natterjack toad; and further south on the unspoilt Sefton coast near Formby in Merseyside, where you might catch a glimpse of the rare red squirrel in the pine woods behind the dunes.

Freshfield, the National Trust site at Formby, was founded in 1848 by Thomas Fresh who started cultivating the land behind the dunes using night soil (human manure) from the surrounding highly populated area. The high pH shell sand combined with the night soil proved ideal for growing asparagus, which soon took over as the main crop. Bundles were exported all over the world, starting their journey by rail from the old Freshfield station. Formby asparagus was very highly regarded by connoisseurs who enjoyed its 'crunchy' texture and it was always served on Cunard liners.

The last tenants to grow asparagus on National Trust land were the Aindow family who used horses until the late 1980s, but last spring the National Trust planted half an acre to bring back asparagus to this part of the coast. It is an exciting project involving the setting up of an Asparagus Trail to tell the crop's story. Vegetables with a natural habitat on the shoreline seem to go particularly well with fish.

> 600g (1lb 5oz) fresh asparagus
> 50g (1¾oz) butter
> 1 medium onion, chopped
> 200g (7oz) potatoes, peeled and chopped
> 1 litre (1¾ pts) chicken or
>   vegetable stock
> sea salt and freshly ground white pepper
> 350g (12oz) wild or responsibly farmed
>   sea trout or salmon fillet, cut into
>   1cm (½ in) cubes
> 150 ml (5fl oz) double cream or
>   crème fraîche.

Trim off any woody ends from the asparagus and, if necessary, use a potato peeler to remove any tough outer skin layers. Cut off the top 4cm (1½in) including the tips of 16 spears (4 per person) for a garnish. Melt the butter in a large pan. Add the onion and potato, cover closely with a butter paper or greaseproof and sweat gently for about 10 minutes, or until soft. Add the stock, bring to the boil and cook for 15 minutes or until the potatoes have broken down.

While the soup is cooking, blanch the reserved asparagus tips in boiling salted water for 4 minutes, then remove from the water with a draining spoon and refresh immediately in cold water. Drain and put to one side. Cut the asparagus stalks into 2.5 cm (1in) pieces and add to the pan. Cook for about 7 minutes until tender, then liquidise in a blender. Pass the purée through a sieve just in case there are any stringy asparagus bits, and return the soup to a clean pan. Bring to the boil, reduce the heat. Season to taste.

Add the sea trout or salmon chunks and simmer for just 2 minutes. Briefly stir in the cream to marble the soup, pour into 4 warm bowls. Garnish with the asparagus tips and serve with chunks of warm wholemeal bread.

Above: Formby on Merseyside, showing the sand formations created by the tide and the dune system
Right: Formby Asparagus and Sea Trout Soup

BAKED SEA BASS WITH LAVERBREAD SAUCE
(serves 4-6)

Bass is the most beautiful sea fish; it is even called salmon bass as it has a silver belly, which darkens to pale blue-grey on its sides, deepening to charcoal blue-black on the back. It is a great sporting fish and thrives in rough weather. Anglers catch bass off the rocky headlands and beaches of Wales as the fish search for crabs and other foods in the shallows. Farmed sea bass doesn't have the same flavour as wild, but it is good nevertheless, being of consistent quality.

A large red gurnard or sea bream could be used instead.

1 whole sea bass, about 1.5kg (3lb 5oz), line-caught or responsibly farmed, cleaned and scaled
sea salt and freshly ground black pepper
extra virgin olive oil
about 100ml (3¹⁄₂fl oz) dry white wine

For the laverbread sauce
200g (7oz) tin of chopped tomatoes
100g (3¹⁄₂oz) prepared laverbread or puréed spinach
2 tablespoons freshly squeezed lime juice
¹⁄₂ teaspoon celery salt
¹⁄₂ teaspoon Tabasco
sea salt and freshly ground black pepper
1 tablespoon fresh parsley, chopped

Pre-heat the oven to 200°C/400°F/GM 6.

Season the fish inside and out, place in a roasting tin, drizzle with a little olive oil and put in the oven. After 5 minutes, pour over the wine and bake for about 20 minutes, or until the fish is cooked, basting a couple of times with the juices. Meanwhile, put all the ingredients for the sauce in a small pan and bring slowly to the boil. Simmer for a few minutes and season to taste.

Serve the fish whole on a large warm serving dish with the cooking juices poured over. Hand round the laverbread sauce separately and eat with plenty of warm crusty bread.

LAVERBREAD AND ORANGE SAUCE

When made with chicken or lamb stock, this sauce is the traditional Welsh accompaniment for mutton and lamb grazed on seashore pastures, and for salt duck (duck steeped in sea salt for 2 or 3 days before cooking). By substituting cream, the sauce is delicious with salmon and sea trout, or lobster and shellfish. If Seville oranges are not in season, use a sweet orange sharpened with lemon juice.

110g (4oz) freshly prepared, or canned laverbread
15g (¹⁄₂oz) butter
15g (¹⁄₂oz) plain flour
300ml (10fl oz) double cream
juice of 1 Seville orange
a pinch of ground mace

Melt the butter in a pan and stir in the flour. Cook for a few minutes without browning, then gradually stir in the cream. Cook for 5 minutes until smooth and creamy, stir in the laverbread, orange juice and mace.

For real devotees of laverbread, omit the flour and cream and make a purée of laverbread with a knob of butter and Seville orange juice, or sweet orange juice sharpened with lemon juice.

LAVERBREAD

Enjoyment of this red seaweed (*porphyra umbilicalis*), commonly attached to rocks below the high-tide mark on the shores of western Britain, is traditional to South Wales. Laver is eaten to a lesser extent in North Devon and in Ireland and Scotland, where it is known as 'sloke'.

The name laverbread is somewhat of a misnomer, but it is just a literal translation of the Welsh – bara lawr – with the 'bara' in this context meaning sustenance rather than bread. It was well known in 18th-century Bath, sold in china pots, and the great Victorian chef of the Reform Club in London, Alexis Soyer, made laverbread a smart society food for a while.

Today, Glamorgan and Pembroke are the most important areas of production with two large processors and a handful of small family-run businesses. Laverbread is gathered at low-tide at any time of the year, although at its best in the winter. Gathering for large-scale processing can be very frustrating, because the seaweed may grow on a beach one year and not the next. Storms and changes in the level of sand around the rocks can also make the harvest difficult. In fact, supplies are becoming scanty in South Wales, so Scottish laverbread is being brought down for processing.

Once gathered, the seaweed has to be washed at least three times to remove sand and grit, then left to steep in fresh water to reduce saltiness and with a little bicarbonate of soda to remove any bitterness. Then it is stewed in its own juices for up to 7 hours to a soft greenish-black purée, which is ladled into cellophane packets or cartons for sale. Canned or dried, it is available from specialist grocers, Oriental supermarkets and health food shops. Laverbread is extremely nutritious due to its high vitamin and mineral content.

Laver, as 'nori', is used widely in Far Eastern sushi and sauces. In Wales, laverbread is likely to be heated up and served on fried bread as part of a breakfast or tea-time fry-up and used to flavour seafood dishes and sauces (see above and p.158).

COCKLE CAKES WITH LAVERBREAD SAUCE
(serves 4 as a starter or light snack)

Cockle cakes are really batter fritters, a favourite Penclawdd way of preparing the local harvest. Any clams, whelks or winkles can be cooked in the same way.

> 225g (8oz) self-raising flour
> 1 large free-range egg, separated
> 1 tablespoon vegetable oil
> 300ml (½ pt) warm water
> 225g (8oz) cockles or clams, freshly cooked and shelled
> sea salt and freshly ground black pepper
> 2 heaped tablespoons fresh parsley, chopped
> sunflower or ground nut oil for deep-frying
> 1 unwaxed lemon, cut into 4 wedges

For the laverbread sauce
> 225g (8oz) prepared laverbread
> juice of ½ lemon

Sieve the flour and work in the egg yolk and oil. Beat in the water until you have a thick batter. Whisk and leave aside for 30 minutes.

Whisk the egg white until stiff and fold into the batter. Add the cockles and parsley, and season to taste. Deep-fry the batter in spoonfuls until golden and crisp. To make the sauce, heat up the laverbread with the lemon juice.

Serve the cockle fritters piping hot with lemon wedges for squeezing. Accompany with the sauce.

PORTHMADOG COCKLES AND EGGS
(serves 1 or 2)

This recipe comes from the Porthmadog-Criccieth area, where the National Trust owns land close to the Llŷn Peninsula, also noted for its cockles. The women would walk from Penrhydeudraeth in Snowdonia to Porthmadog to gather and sell cockles from door to door, dancing and singing the following rhyme:
> *'Cockles and eggs, thin oat cakes,*
> *The girls of Penrhyn doing the shakes!'*

The rich fish and egg mixture was traditionally eaten between slices of barley bread or oatcakes as a special treat.

> 175g (6oz) freshly cooked and shelled cockles
> bacon fat for frying
> 2 large free-range eggs, beaten
> freshly ground black pepper

Fry the cockles in a little bacon fat for a few minutes, then add the beaten egg to the pan. Stir until the egg is lightly cooked, then season with pepper. Serve immediately with crusty bread for lunch or supper.

Cockles are also excellent cooked with bacon. Sometimes the shellfish are sprinkled with oatmeal before being fried.

DEEP-FRIED COCKLES, MUSSELS AND LAVER WITH SPICY MAYONNAISE
(serves 4 as a starter or lunch)

If you cannot get hold of fresh laver, use the outer leaves of spring cabbage finely shredded or other types of seaweed.

> 225g (8oz) cockles or clams, freshly cooked and shelled
> 225g (8oz) mussels, freshly cooked and shelled
> 110g (4oz) freshly picked laver, well-washed and dried
> 225g (8oz) self-raising flour
> 1 teaspoon paprika
> sunflower oil for deep-frying
> sea salt and freshly ground black pepper
> 1 unwaxed lemon, cut into 4 wedges

For the spicy mayonnaise
> 4 tablespoons home-made mayonnaise(see p.221)
> 2-3 teaspoons good-quality chilli sauce

Drain off excess juice from the shellfish, but don't squeeze them. Cut the laver into 5cm (2in) pieces and squeeze dry in kitchen paper.

Mix together with flour and paprika and dust the shellfish, using a sieve to shake off the excess. Heat the oil and deep-fry the shellfish for about 1 minute until crisp and slightly golden. Drain and reserve, then deep-fry the seaweed, moving it around to keep the pieces separate. Drain and serve with the shellfish. Season with salt and pepper and garnish with lemon wedges.

Mix together the mayonnaise and chilli sauce to taste and serve with the seafoods.

PENCLAWDD COCKLES

Shellfish-gathering has always been important to the Welsh diet, but as the population of South Wales increased during the Industrial Revolution, it developed into a commercial enterprise at Burry Inlet, the estuary of the River Loughor. The main centres for cockle-fishing were Llanelli and Burry Port on the north side and the village of Penclawdd in Gower on the south.

Until the 19th century, Penclawdd was a thriving industrial port. Cockle-gathering became a lifeline for women whose husbands were too ill to work in the mines. They took their catch to Swansea – cockles already boiled and shelled were carried in a wooden pail balanced on the seller's head with live cockles in a large basket covered with a white cloth on her arm. A cockle fair is still held in Swansea every September. Gradually the men left heavy industry, largely displacing the women and today the cockle fishery is the only remaining industry in the village.

The cockles from this area are considered to be amongst the best-flavoured fished around the British coast, and in April 2001 the Burry Inlet Cockle Fishery became the fifth fishery in the world to receive the Marine Stewardship Council Award as a sustainable fishery. Only hand-raking is allowed, although access is now by vehicle rather than horse-drawn cart. Effective management by the South Wales Sea Fisheries Committee has ensured that the stock is consistent and in excellent condition. A limited number of full-time licences (around 55) is issued each year; gathering takes place all week except on Sundays and the level of fishable stock is set at around 2,500-3,000 tonnes.

The cockle-fishers have to cross National Trust Land at Burry Inlet and further up the estuary at Llanrhidian to get to the beds on either side of the estuary. They work with the ebbing tide, using a small knife with a curved blade to scrape the sand to expose the cockles, which are drawn together with a rake and then riddled to separate out those that are too small. After washing in pools on the beach, the shellfish are loaded in sacks.

Locals like to fry fresh breadcrumbs and chopped spring onions in butter in a lidded pan until the crumbs are crisp and golden, then quickly stir in some freshly boiled cockles seasoned with pepper and salt to heat through. They serve them with a generous sprinkling of chopped parsley.

WELSH LEEK, COCKLE AND GOAT'S CHEESE TARTS
(serves 4 as a starter or lunch)

Dairy herds have been a feature of Welsh scenery for centuries, particularly in the fertile Towy Valley, the Vales of Glamorgan and Clwyd and the rolling Radnorshire countryside. Milk provided the staple income for many farms until quotas changed the perspective. Innovative families turned this to their advantage and began producing value-added products such as butter, yoghurt and cheese, so now, alongside the large creameries, there are smaller craft producers of farmhouse cheeses, butter and cream. If you don't enjoy goat's cheese, use a brie style instead, cut into tiny pieces.

For the pastry
    110g (4oz) plain flour
    a pinch of salt
    25g (1oz) lard, at room temperature
    25g (1oz) butter, at room temperature
    25g (1oz) firm goat's cheese,
       without rind
    a little cold water to mix

For the filling
    350g (12oz) leeks, trimmed and cut
       into 1cm (½in) slices
    15g (½oz) butter
    175g (6oz) firm goat's cheese,
       without rind
    3 large free-range eggs, beaten
    200ml (7fl oz) double cream
       or crème fraîche
    sea salt and freshly ground black pepper
    110g (4oz) freshly cooked cockles or
       clams

To make the pastry, sieve the flour and salt into a mixing bowl. Lightly rub in the fat until crumbly, then coarsely grate in the goat's cheese. Sprinkle about 1 tablespoon cold water over and start to mix the pastry with a knife. Finish off with your hands, adding a few more drops of water until you have a smooth dough that will leave the bowl clean. Wrap in clingfilm and chill for about 30 minutes.

Roll out the pastry as thinly as possible and cut out 4 rounds. Line 4 deep 10cm (4in) loose-bottomed flan tins taking care not to stretch the pastry. Prick the bases with a fork and chill again in the fridge for 15 minutes.

Pre-heat the oven to 190°C/375°F/GM5. Line the tarts with baking parchment and fill with baking beans, place on a baking sheet and bake for 10 minutes to set the pastry. Remove the paper and beans and bake for a further 5 minutes.

To make the filling, melt the butter in a frying-pan over gentle heat, add the leeks and a little salt. Cook the leeks gently for 10-15 minutes, then transfer to a sieve set over a bowl to drain off the excess juice. Place a saucer with a weight on top to press out every drop of moisture.

Crumble the goat's cheese and gently combine it with the leeks. Mix the beaten eggs with the cream or crème fraîche and season with pepper and a little salt.

When the pastry cases are cooked, remove them from the oven with the baking sheet. Arrange the leeks and cheese in the tarts, and sprinkle in the cockles. Gradually pour in the egg and cream mixture, and put the baking sheet with the tarts back in the oven. Bake for about 20 minutes until golden brown, but wobbly in the centre.

Remove from the oven and serve warm, not hot, with a tomato and basil salad.

CRAB OR LOBSTER AND LAVERBREAD SOUFFLÉS WITH COCKLE SAUCE
(serves 8 as a starter)

The Gower Peninsula plays host to both crab and lobster potting. This recipe makes a small amount of crab or lobster go a long way.

    175g (6oz) prepared crab meat (mixture
       of brown and white) or lobster, plus
       the shell if possible
    ¼ onion, peeled and sliced
    5cm (2 in) piece of carrot cut into four
    175g (6oz) prepared laverbread,
       or puréed spinach
    50g (2oz) butter
    50g (2oz) plain flour
    425ml (¾pt) full-fat milk
    3 large free-range eggs, separated
    ½ teaspoon freshly grated nutmeg
    sea salt and freshly ground black pepper

For the cockle sauce
    150ml (¼pt) white sauce reserved
       from soufflé mix
    150ml (5fl oz) whipping cream
    110g (4oz) shelled cockles or clams
    50g (2oz) laverbread, or puréed spinach

If the shell is available, pick out the meat and make a stock with the shell, flavoured with the carrot and onion. Boil down to 2 well-flavoured tablespoons, which can replace the equivalent amount of milk in the basic sauce for the soufflé and cockle sauce.

To prepare the sauce, melt the butter in a small pan, stir in the flour off the heat, then continue cooking gently for a few minutes without browning. Stir in the milk gradually (using the crab shell stock if available) and cook over a gentle heat for 5 minutes. Reserve 150ml (¼pt) of the sauce for later.

Pre-heat the oven to 200°C/400°F/GM6.

Stir the crab meat and laverbread into the sauce. Season to taste with salt, pepper and nutmeg, then stir in the egg yolks one by one. Beat the egg whites until quite stiff and stir 1 tablespoonful into the sauce lightly. Fold in the remaining egg white very carefully, then taste and adjust the seasoning if necessary.

Butter 8 small ramekins and spoon in the mixture, leaving a little room for expansion. Bake for 10-12 minutes until puffed up and golden brown.

Meanwhile make the cockle sauce by heating up the reserved white sauce with the cream. Stir in the cockles or clams and the laverbread. Season with salt and pepper. Serve with the soufflés as soon as they are ready.

Previous page: Llanrhidian Marsh, West Glamorgan. The hardy Gower ponies used to pull the carts for the cocklers
Left: Welsh Leek, Cockle and Goat's Cheese Tarts

PORTH MEUDWY CRAB SOUP
(serves 6–8)

The beautiful Llŷn Peninsula is noted for its spectacular coastal scenery and, through successful campaigns, the National Trust has acquired such wonderful places as Porthdinllaen, a charming fishing village on the north coast near Nefyn, the famous 'whistling' sands of Porthor, and the tiny fishing cove of Porth Meudwy (Welsh for hermit) right at the end of the Peninsula opposite Bardsey Island. The rocky coast here is ideal for crabs and lobsters and there are 3 or 4 commercial fishermen based at the cove. A successful initiative encouraged by the Welsh Development Agency involves cooking and dressing crabs and lobsters by the fishermen's wives for sale locally to visitors. An annual seafood festival is held at Nefyn for 2 days at the beginning of July.

Try to buy your crab meat with its shell to add flavour to the stock for this soup.

225g (8oz) brown crab meat
100g (3½oz) white crab meat
2 tablespoons sunflower oil
25g (1oz) butter
**225g (8oz) onions, peeled and
  roughly chopped**
**100g (3½oz) red pepper,
  roughly chopped**
**1 bouquet garni (made with 1 strip
  orange peel, 1 sprig fresh thyme,
  1 sprig fresh parsley and 1 bay leaf
  tied in a piece of muslin)**
200ml (7fl oz) dry white wine
450g (1lb) tin chopped tomatoes
**600ml (1pt) fish stock (see p.222)
  including the crab shell if available**
½ teaspoon paprika
sea salt and freshly ground black pepper
150ml (5fl oz) double cream
1 tablespoon fresh parsley, chopped

Fry the onions and pepper gently in the oil and butter for about 5 minutes until softened, but not coloured. Add the brown and half the white crab meat and the bouquet garni and cook for 1-2 minutes. Stir in the wine, then the tomatoes and stock. Season with paprika, salt and pepper and simmer for 10 minutes, stirring frequently. Allow to cool. Remove the bouquet garni.

Liquidise the soup, then put through a sieve to give a smooth thick texture.

Return the soup to a clean pan and reheat gently, adding the cream. Flake in the remaining white crab meat, sprinkle with parsley, dust with a little more paprika and serve with warm crusty bread. (Make sure you don't overcook the soup because the crab loses its fresh flavour and the crab meat becomes stringy.)

Above: The fishing village of Porthdinllaen on the Llŷn Peninsula, Gwynedd
Right: The whistling sands of Porthor

SMOKED EEL PÂTÉ
(serves 4 as a starter or snack)

National Trust staff and volunteers in South Pembrokeshire have built an eel path to enable thousands of young freshwater eels, born at sea, to migrate to their natural habitat. In April and May, the eels make a grand exodus inland from Broadhaven to the freshwater Bosherton Lily Pools on the Stackpole Estate, but the final leg of their journey can be hampered by sandy terrain which becomes dry in periods of low rainfall and then slows their progress and makes them fast food for seagulls. The 556 metre (1,820 foot) channel, lined with concrete and filled with 30cm (12 in) of water, speeds them on their way. As well as eels, the Lily Pools support a variety of birds, resident otters, a number of coarse fish including pike, roach and tench, and magnificent water lilies. During Pembrokeshire Fish Week, at the beginning of July, visitors are encouraged to 'come and damsel/dragonfly spot'.

Some of the most beautiful and varied scenery in West Wales can be seen at the Stackpole Estate, acquired by the National Trust in 1976. Situated within the Pembrokeshire Coast National Park, the estate has rugged limestone coastline with resident choughs, two beautiful sandy beaches at Broadhaven South and Barafundle Bay, sand-dunes, farmland and woods. From the tiny Stackpole Quay, where the National Trust has holiday cottages, several small boats fish commercially for mackerel, bass and pollack.

225g (8oz) smoked eel fillets, roughly chopped
grated rind and juice of 1 unwaxed lemon or lime
a pinch cayenne
100g (3½oz) low-fat curd or cream cheese
sea salt and freshly ground black pepper

Place the smoked eel in a processor and blitz for a few seconds. Add all the other ingredients except the salt and black pepper. Blitz until you have a smooth paste. Season to taste. Put into individual ramekins or 1 larger pâté dish. Chill for at least 1 hour, preferably overnight, before serving with hot wholemeal toast and sticks of raw vegetables or a few salad leaves.

Left: The freshwater lily ponds on the Stackpole Estate, Pembrokeshire
Above: Wreckage on the beach at Barafundle Bay, with Stackpole Head in the distance

LAVER SCRAMBLED EGGS WITH SMOKED SALMON
(serves 4)

Any smoked fish or shellfish can be used instead of salmon, or, as a change, try flaked fresh fish and shellfish. Thinly sliced Carmarthen air-dried ham would also be excellent.

6 free-range eggs
50ml (2fl oz) full-fat milk
  or single cream
sea salt and freshly ground black pepper
25g (1oz) butter
100g (3½ oz) prepared laverbread
½ teaspoon Tabasco
2 teaspoons fresh chives, chopped
4 slices wholemeal toast
4 slices organic or good-quality smoked
  salmon

Lightly beat the eggs with the milk and season to taste. Melt the butter in a non-stick pan without colouring, then add the egg. Over a medium heat, cook the egg, stirring continuously with a wooden spoon. When it begins to thicken, add the seaweed and continue to stir until it is cooked, but is still very creamy. Remove from the heat and stir in the Tabasco and chives.

Spoon onto hot buttered toast and top with a slice of smoked salmon.

LOBSTER POT THERMIDOR
(serves 4)

This is a favourite dish of The Lobster Pot in picturesque Church Bay, 11 miles from Holyhead. Lobsters and crabs are caught all around the rocky coast of Anglesey. Two lobstermen work from Cemaes Bay, three out of Holyhead and a few are based in Beaumaris.

4 freshly cooked lobsters
  (about 450g [1lb] each)
25g (1oz) butter
25g (1oz) shallots, finely chopped
150ml (¼pt) dry white wine
1 teaspoon English mustard
1 teaspoon Dijon mustard
1 tablespoon fresh flat-leaf parsley
150ml (5fl oz) double cream
600ml (1pt) Béchamel sauce (see p.219)
sea salt and freshly ground black pepper
50g (1¾ oz) Parmesan cheese, grated
extra fresh parsley, chopped to serve
4 lemon wedges to serve

Pre-heat the oven to 180°C/350°F/GM 4.

Remove all the meat from the lobsters and cut into large pieces. Put the shells to one side for later.

Melt the butter and cook the shallots gently for at least 10 minutes until soft, but not coloured. Add the wine and reduce to one quarter of the volume. Stir in the mustard, parsley, cream and sauce. Season to taste. Carefully add the lobster meat and heat slowly for 1-2 minutes, but don't overcook.

Divide the lobster equally between the reserved shells and sprinkle with Parmesan. Cook in the oven for about 10 minutes to just heat through.

Serve sprinkled liberally with parsley and garnished with lemon wedges.

Above and right: Llanbadrig in Cemaes, on the most northern part of Anglesey

ST BRIDE'S BAY BAKED MACKEREL WITH FRESH HERBS AND MUSTARD
(serves 4)

The National Trust owns about 15½ miles of the coastline at St Bride's Bay in Pembrokeshire, including the spectacular Marloes Peninsula with its glorious remote stretch of beach at Marloes Sands, backed by superb rock and cliff scenery with offshore views of the nature reserves of Skomer and Stokholm Islands. At the western extremity of the peninsula is the attractive rocky cove of Martin's Haven, which is the starting place for boat trips to Skomer, across the treacherous currents of Jack Sand. The tiny cove with its shingle beach has long been used by local people for fishing and lobster potting. Crabs and lobsters are caught all around these rocky shores, while mackerel is fished in the Bay from late June to early September.

The Pembrokeshire Fish Week is held annually at the end of June. The programme includes fishing lessons and competitions, sea-fishing trips, cookery demonstrations, sushi tasting and celebratory fishy meals at local restaurants and pubs. For further information, contact 01437 776168.

The traditional Welsh ways of cooking mackerel include baking with herbs and mustard: Pembrokeshire's Food Officer, Kate Morgan, gave me this recipe. She suggests serving the mackerel with new potatoes from South Pembrokeshire, often the earliest crop in Britain. Sea bass, grey mullet, red gurnard and sea bream all can be used.

4 very fresh line-caught mackerel, cleaned
75g (3oz) butter, softened
grated rind and juice of 1 small unwaxed lemon
4 spring onions, finely chopped
1 tablespoon fresh thyme, chopped
2 tablespoons fresh flat-leaf parsley, chopped
2 teaspoons sweet grain mustard
1 teaspoon good-quality horseradish sauce
sea salt and freshly ground black pepper

Pre-heat the oven to 190°C/375°F/GM5.

Wipe the mackerel with a damp cloth and cut off the fins. Blend the butter with the lemon rind and juice, spring onion, herbs, mustard and horseradish. Season with salt and pepper, then stuff the body cavity of each fish with the mixture.

Cut 4 pieces of foil large enough to enclose the mackerel. Place a fish on each, season lightly and wrap in the foil to make a parcel to prevent the juices escaping.

Bake the parcels in the pre-heated oven for 15-20 minutes, until the fish is just cooked. (Alternatively, cook on a barbecue over a moderate heat.)

Serve the mackerel in the foil parcels with new potatoes, a good tomato salad and fresh crusty bread to mop up the juices.

Marloes Peninusla in Dyfed, looking towards St Anne's Head

GRATIN OF WELSH SEAFOOD WITH LAVERBREAD AND CAERPHILLY
(serves 4 as a starter or lunch)

Vary this dish using a combination of seafoods – e.g. cockles and mussels with salmon or smoked mackerel. The iron flavour of the seaweed and the crunchy herb topping give a good contrast of flavours and textures. You can use any combination of herbs, although basil combines well with fish.

> 225g (8oz) grey or red mullet fillets, skinned
> 100g (3½) dive-caught scallops
> 100g (3½oz) fresh North Atlantic prawns, shelled
> juice of ½ lemon
> a dash of Tabasco
> 225g (8oz) prepared laverbread, or puréed spinach
> 4 slices stale wholemeal bread
> 4 sprigs fresh flat-leaf parsley, chopped
> 1½ teaspoons fresh basil, chopped
> 2 garlic cloves, peeled
> 50g (1¾oz) butter, chilled and diced
> 75g (2¾oz) Caerphilly or Cheddar cheese, grated
> freshly ground black pepper

Pre-heat the oven to 200°C/400°F/GM6. Cut the mullet into 1cm (½in) slices and halve the white meat of the scallops horizontally, leaving the orange roes whole.

Put the prepared fish and scallops in a bowl with the prawns, lemon juice and Tabasco. Mix well and leave for a few minutes.

Spoon the laverbread into 1 large or 4 small gratin dishes.

Blitz the bread in a processor or blender to make breadcrumbs. Add the herbs, garlic and butter and process to form a crumbly mixture. Stir in the grated cheese.

Cover the laverbread with the fish and lemon juice, pressing it slightly into the seaweed. Sprinkle over the breadcrumb and cheese mixture to cover completely, but don't press it into the fish.

Grind some pepper over the top, then bake in the pre-heated oven for about 10 minutes (20 minutes if using a large dish) until the fish is just cooked and the top is crisp and golden. Finish under the grill if necessary, then serve immediately.

GLORIOUS GOWER PIE
(serves 4 as a starter or 2 for lunch)

The National Trust owns about 2,025 hectares (5,000 acres) in Gower, ranging from salt-marsh at Llanrhidian on the north coast, to the limestone cliffs between Port Eynon and Rhossili in the south. At Port Eynon and nearby Oxwich, the Trust has recently built two slips for small fishing boats that catch mainly mackerel, bass and sewin (sea trout), but cockles, mussels, winkles, prawns, crabs and lobster are also abundant.

In this adaptation of a very traditional Gower recipe, you could use any shellfish or combination of shellfish and white fish instead of the mussels.

> 1.2 litres (2 pts) fresh live mussels, scrubbed and bearded
> 225g (8oz) prepared laverbread
> 40g (1½oz) butter
> ½ bunch of spring onions, chopped
> 1 glass dry white wine
> grated rind and juice of ½ unwaxed lemon
> 50g (1¾oz) brown breadcrumbs
> 1 tablespoon fresh parsley, chopped
> 1 garlic clove, peeled
> 110g (4oz) Llanboidy or strong Cheddar, grated
> freshly ground black pepper

Melt 15g (½oz) of the butter in a large pan with a tight-fitting lid and fry the chopped spring onions without colouring. Add the wine and lemon juice and bring to the boil. Put the cleaned mussels into the pan, cover and shake over a high heat for about 3 minutes until they have opened. Discard any that remain closed. Drain the mussels in a large sieve, reserving the liquor and remove the shells. Keep the mussels warm.

Add 40g (1½oz) of the breadcrumbs, the parsley and the lemon rind to the cooking liquor and mix well. Butter a 17.5cm (7in) ovenproof dish or 4 ramekins and rub with the garlic clove. Put the breadcrumb mixture into the base of the dish, or dishes, then spread with half the mussels, half the laverbread, half the cheese, with a grinding of pepper. Repeat the layers and top with the remaining breadcrumbs. Dot with the remaining butter, then grill until the top is crisp, the cheese has melted and the layers have warmed through, or bake in a moderate over (180°C/350°F/GM4) for about 20 minutes.

Three Cliffs Bay on the Gower Peninsula

STEAMED CONWY MUSSELS
WITH WELSH CIDER
(serves 2 as a main course)

Mussels are found all around the coast of Wales, particularly at the low ebb of a spring tide. The largest producers are in the Conwy Estuary and the Menai Strait where they have been harvested since Roman times, although many other fishermen gather them by hand from West Wales, Carmarthen Bay and Gower.

Before the First World War, Conwy Fisheries Laboratories pioneered a process to purify shellfish; by immersion for 42 hours in large tanks filled with chlorinated seawater. The mussels were then washed, shovelled into sacks and transported by train to markets in Manchester, the Midlands and London. Until the 1970s up to 50 men and women earned a living from fishing for mussels but, during the construction of the tunnel under the River Conwy, the beds were severely damaged and only 5 mussel men were left, scratching a living.

After the tunnel's completion the Conwy Mussel Development Group was set up to try to restore musselling to its original status. Unfortunately, about the same time, the original purification tanks were closed down by MAFF (now DEFRA) because they didn't meet European health and hygiene regulations. The local fishermen were forced to set up their own modern purification system without the use of chemicals; the seawater is sterilised by ultra-violet light. Once purified, the mussels are washed, graded, weighed and packed before being sent overnight to the traditional markets.

Conwy mussels are fished during the winter months from September to April by licensed fishermen in the traditional way, from small, 16-foot boats using the long rakes first employed by monks centuries earlier.

1kg (2lb 4oz) fresh live mussels, scrubbed and bearded
50g (1³⁄₄oz) butter
1 shallot, finely chopped
2 garlic cloves, skinned and finely chopped
1 stick celery, finely chopped
300ml (½pt) cider
100ml (3½fl oz) double cream
2 tablespoons fresh flat-leaf parsley, chopped
freshly ground black pepper

Melt half the butter in a pan and gently sauté the shallot, garlic and celery for about 10 minutes.

Heat up a large tightly lidded pan, then add the mussels and cider. Cover with the lid and raise the heat. Cook, shaking the pan from time to time, for about 3 minutes or until the mussels have opened. Discard any that are tightly closed. Ladle the mussels into 2 warmed bowls and pour the liquor through a sieve lined with 2 layers of muslin onto the cooked vegetables.

Boil the soup until reduced a little to intensify the flavours, then remove from the heat and add the cream. Whisk in the remaining butter, then add the parsley. Taste and season with black pepper – add sea salt if necessary. Pour over the mussels and serve immediately with fresh warm bread.

ANGLESEY JAMES' CAKES
These thin shortbread biscuits, marked with a scallop shell, were made at Aberffraw on the west coast of Anglesey and are often called 'Berffro cakes' (Welsh for shortbread) instead of their correct name, which reflects the pilgrims' scallop shell motif for the shrine of St James in Northern Spain.

Left: An itinerant fish dealer using mule transport
Right: The east front of Plas Newydd in Gwynedd, with the Menai Strait and Snowdonia beyond

ANGLESEY OYSTERS IN SPINACH
(serves 4 as a starter)

Native oysters were once plentiful around Wales, particularly in Swansea Bay where the Romans established a fishery at Mumbles and in the waters of Milford Haven. Unfortunately, 200 years of over-exploitation, pollution and disease introduced with non-native species led to their depletion, although recently they have been making a slow revival in both places. However, most of the native beds have already been replenished with farmed Pacifics. Two large fisheries are found in Anglesey; one off the north-west coast at Trearddur Bay near the National Trust's beautiful Mynachdy Estate; the other in the Menai Strait close to Plas Newydd, the Marquess of Anglesey's home, now owned by the National Trust.

The Anglesey Oyster and Welsh Produce Festival takes place at a weekend in October at the end of the native oyster season, organised by Menter Môn and sponsored by the Welsh Development Agency with seafood dinners, live entertainment and Welsh dancing. For details contact 01407 860301/01248 752474

A local chef, Scott Bowdler, contributed this recipe to Menter Môn's promotion of Anglesey seafood.

12 fresh Native or Pacific oysters, opened (retaining all the juices and the deep shells)
6 black peppercorns
a few parsley stalks
12 large spinach leaves
25g (1oz) butter
1 teaspoon fresh ginger, crushed
180ml (6fl oz) sweet white wine
500ml (18fl oz) double cream
3 sprigs fresh dill, chopped
sea salt and freshly ground black pepper
1 unwaxed lemon, cut into 4 wedges
12 extra sprigs fresh dill, to garnish

Poach the oysters in their liquor with the peppercorns and parsley stalks for 3 minutes. Remove and refresh in cold water, reserving the poaching liquor. Wrap each oyster in a spinach leaf and put on one side.

Gently sauté the ginger in half the butter, then add the strained poaching liquor, wine, cream and chopped dill. Reduce until moderately thick, then season to taste. Just before serving, gently sauté the oysters in the remaining butter until warmed through.

Pour the sauce onto 4 warm serving plates and arrange 3 washed oyster shells symmetrically on each plate. Place an oyster parcel in each shell and garnish in between with sprigs of fresh dill. Serve with lemon wedges and fresh wholemeal bread.

TEIFI SALMON WITH SPARKLING WINE SAUCE
(serves 4)

The coast from Fishguard, the ferry port for Ireland, to Aberystwyth is gentle with high cliffs and large bays interspersed with tiny coves, several protected by the National Trust. The Teifi Valley dominates the area and the river itself has probably the most exciting salmon and sewin fishing to be found in Wales. Geraldis Cambrensis, Gerald the Welshman, wrote in 1188 that 'The noble river Teivi flows here and abounds with the finest salmon, more than any other river in Wales…'. He also commented on the spectacular sight of fish leaping the great falls at Cenarth.

The most interesting feature of salmon or sewin fishing in the upper Teifi has been the traditional use of coracles and nets, a craft thought to have been used for thousands of years in Britain. The fishermen operate in pairs, each in his own coracle, steering with a paddle in one hand and holding one end of a drag net in the other. Working at night, or when the river is in spate, they move downstream with the current, to catch the fish as they swim upstream. Once a fish is caught, the net is lifted out of the water, the two coracles draw together and the salmon is removed. The fishermen continue for a mile or more, then, at the end of the trawl, they carry the coracles on their backs to start again.

Coracle fishing is fast disappearing although some people keep them for leisure purposes. The craft requires skilful handling and has been discouraged by those responsible for fishing rights. There is now much competition from the growing breed of leisure anglers, so fishing licences for coracle men are expensive and strictly limited in number. Their season in general has also been restricted (1 March to 1 September) and there is talk of further restriction. Nevertheless, the tradition survives and long may it continue.

Welsh vineyards produce some excellent wines, with sparkling enjoying a particularly good reputation. The combination of salmon and sparkling white wine is superb.

Accompany with new potatoes and broad beans as served traditionally with salmon and sewin in the Cenarth area.

4 x 175g (6oz) wild Pacific or responsibly farmed Atlantic salmon or sewin steaks or fillets
1 tablespoon olive oil
25g (1oz) butter
2 shallots, finely chopped
300ml (10fl oz) sparkling white wine
a small pinch of saffron strands
150ml (5fl oz) double cream or crème fraîche
sea salt and freshly ground black pepper

Steep the saffron strands in the cream and leave on one side. Season the fish, then heat the olive oil and half the butter in a frying-pan. Fry the salmon for 4-5 minutes on each side, then remove and keep warm.

Melt the remaining butter in the frying-pan and soften the shallots gently for about 10 minutes. Add the sparkling wine and boil for 5 minutes until reduced, then add the cream and saffron. Boil for a further 3-5 minutes until thickened.

Season the sauce and serve with the salmon.

Far left: Fishguard Bay, Pembrokeshire
Left: Coracle fishermen at Cenarth in Cardiganshire

HOT-SMOKED SALMON KEDGEREE WITH QUAILS' EGGS
(serves 6)

Penrhyn Castle is a huge neo-Norman fantasy castle sitting dramatically between Snowdonia and the Menai Strait. Built by Thomas Hopper between 1820 and 1845 for the wealthy Pennant family, who made their fortune from Jamaican sugar and Welsh slate, the castle is crammed with fascinating things. The Victorian Kitchen, scullery and larders have been restored to show the preparations for the banquet during the Prince of Wales' visit in 1894.

Kedgeree, an Anglicised version of an Indian dish of rice and lentils called 'Khichri', was popular on the Victorian and Edwardian breakfast menu, when British-Indian cuisine was a chic novelty. It must have graced the sideboard at many house-party breakfasts in Penrhyn Castle's breakfast room.

Recently, kedgeree has enjoyed a revival and although smoked haddock is traditional and excellent, try using fresh or hot-smoked salmon or smoked eel for a change. You could add other seafood, such as scallops, mussels or prawns. It is the perfect comfort food and a complete meal for breakfast, lunch or supper, or as a starter at dinner.

For the stock
- 1 undyed smoked haddock fillet
- 1 onion, peeled and halved
- 600ml (1pt) full-cream milk
- 850ml (1½pt) water

For the kedgeree
- 700g (1lb 9oz) hot-smoked or kiln-roasted salmon, skinned
- 12 quails' eggs, hard-boiled
- 5 cardamon pods
- ½ level tablespoon cumin seeds
- ½ level tablespoon mustard seeds
- ½ level tablespoon coriander seeds
- 100g (3½oz) butter
- 1 medium red onion, peeled and finely sliced
- 6 cloves
- ½ cinnamon stick
- 1 piece blade mace
- 2 good pinches saffron strands
- 350g (12oz) white basmati rice
- 2 tablespoons fresh flat-leaf parsley, roughly chopped
- 2 tablespoons fresh coriander, roughly chopped
- grated rind and juice of 1 unwaxed lime
- freshly ground black pepper
- 4-5 tablespoons single cream (optional)
- lime wedges to serve
- mango chutney to serve

To make the stock, put the haddock, onion, milk and water into a pan. Bring to simmering point, then take off the heat and leave to cook completely. Strain into a jug. (Use the fish to make fish cakes if you wish.)

To make the kedgeree, split open the cardamon pods and remove the black seeds inside. Put them with the cumin, mustard and coriander seeds in a small frying-pan and place over a medium heat. Dry-roast the spices for 2-3 minutes, by which time you should be able to smell them. (They will also start to jump around a bit.) Tip the spices into a mortar and grind to a fine powder with a pestle.

Melt 25g (1oz) butter in a large sauté pan or saucepan with a lid and cook the onion for about 10 minutes, until softened. Add the ground spices, cloves, cinnamon stick, blade mace, saffron and rice. Stir together well, then pour in enough of the reserved stock to come about 2.5cm (1in) above the level of the rice in the pan. Don't stir once the liquid has been added. Cover the pan with a tea-towel, which will absorb the steam, and then the lid, and cook over a gentle heat for 5 minutes. Take the pan off the heat and leave it for 15 minutes (still covered). By this time the liquid should have been absorbed by the rice and the grains tender. Remove and discard the cloves, cinnamon and mace.

Flake the salmon into large pieces and halve the eggs. Using a fork, carefully fold into the rice with half the chopped herbs and the lime rind and juice. Season well with black pepper and add the remaining butter cut up into small pieces. Fork everything together over a gentle heat until the salmon and eggs are heated through. Taste and adjust seasoning, then stir in some cream if you like. Pile into a large warm serving dish and scatter over the remaining herbs.

Serve with lime wedges, mango chutney and hot buttered English muffins, or triangles of toast. Add a dressed green leaf salad if serving for lunch or supper.

Far left: Hot-smoked Salmon Kedgeree with Quails' Eggs
Left: The Victorian China Room in Penrhyn Castle, Gwynedd

SMOKED SALMON AND LAVERBREAD CREMPOG
(serves 4-6 as a starter)

Crempog is Welsh for pancakes, which in this recipe have been layered with smoked salmon and laverbread. Any smoked fish may be used. The batter recipe will make far more pancakes than you need, but you can't really make a smaller amount and they freeze very successfully wrapped in foil.

For the pancakes
110g (4oz) plain flour
a small pinch of salt
1 free-range egg
300ml (½ pt) full-cream milk
25g (1oz) unsalted butter, melted
vegetable oil for frying

For the filling
110g (4oz) soft goat's cheese or cream cheese
30ml (1fl oz) double cream
freshly ground black pepper
150g (5½ oz) good-quality sliced smoked salmon
50g (1¾) prepared laverbread
50g (1¾ oz) rocket leaves
shell-on prawns for garnish (optional)

To make the pancakes sieve the flour and salt together into a bowl. Whisk the egg and the milk into the flour, followed by the melted butter. Heat a frying-pan, then add a little oil. Pour in some of the batter mixture, making sure the pan has only a thin layer of mix by tilting and rotating the pan to make the batter spread out. Cook for 30-40 seconds until golden brown, then turn over and cook for a further 20-30 seconds. Remove from the pan and cool on greaseproof paper while you cook the remainder. (You will need 5 thin 15-20cm [6-8in] pancakes for this dish.)

While the pancakes are cooling, mix the goat's cheese with the cream to make a smooth spreadable mixture. Season with black pepper.

Arrange one cold pancake on a large plate and spread with a quarter of the cheese mixture, topped with a quarter of the smoked salmon. Spread with a little laverbread, then top with a few rocket leaves. Put a second pancake on top and repeat until 4 layers have been made, finishing with a pancake. Refrigerate for 1-2 hours, then cut into wedges like a cake. Garnish with a few salad leaves and decorate with extra goat's cheese and shell-on prawns if you wish.

HOT POACHED SEWIN WITH FENNEL SAUCE
(serves 6)

Wales is famous for its sea trout, known locally as sewin, although nobody seems to know why as the Welsh word is *gwyniedyn*. It is a member of the brown trout family, going to sea to feed and returning to the river to spawn. Sewin feeds more locally than salmon and is therefore more distinctive from region to region, depending on the feeding grounds. Of course, Wales is not the only part of Britain where sea trout is caught, but in certain Welsh rivers like the Teifi, Dyfi and Conwy it has always been particularly plentiful.

The season for sewin begins around Easter and continues throughout the summer: under 900g (2lb) are known as 'shinglin'; 900g (2lb) to 1.4kg (3lb) are 'twlpyn'; and the larger fish from 1.4g (3lb) up to 9kg (20lb) are called 'gwencyn'. The best flavoured are considered to be from 1-2kg (2¼-4½lb) and these appear in the estuaries from May onwards. The larger sewin tend to have less flavour and the flesh may have turned a pale fawny pink instead of a good clear pink.

The traditional fishing for sewin on Welsh rivers was in coracles. In E. Donovan's *Descriptive Excursions through South Wales and Monmouthshire, 1805,* there is an interesting account of Swansea Market: 'Half a dozen families seated upon the panniers of their ponies….rode hastily down the market place with a supply of sewen…conveyed from Pontardulais, about ten miles to the westward…abounding with fish during the summer, being caught in the coracle fisheries by peasantry.' Only about 700-800 sewin are landed by coracle each year now; most are caught with hand-nets in the estuaries, weirs and basket traps in the rivers and, of course, by rod and line.

Sewin used to be so plentiful in the past that it was not considered a luxury by the English gentry living in Wales. Hence, there are genuine Welsh traditions for its cooking. In South Pembrokeshire, wild fennel was added to melted butter or a white sauce and poured over poached sewin.

Salmon or sea bass can be used.

1 whole fresh sewin, weighing about 1.4kg (3lb) or a tail from a larger fish
court bouillon to cover (see p.222)
a handful of fresh fennel

For the fennel sauce
110g (4oz) unsalted butter
150ml (5fl oz) double cream
sea salt and freshly ground black pepper
a squeeze of lemon juice
about 2 tablespoons fresh fennel fronds, chopped

Wipe the fish well and place the fennel inside the body cavity. Pour the court bouillon into a fish kettle or pan large enough to take the fish. Bring to simmering point, then add the fish. Just return to simmering point, then switch off the heat and allow to stand for 20 minutes. After this time, the fish will be cooked. Remove it from the water and leave on a warm serving plate for 5 minutes. The skin will come off easily now, (only remove the body skin). Keep warm while you make the sauce, which will only take about 5 minutes.

Melt the butter in a frying-pan 20-25cm (8-10in) across. When it has melted, stir in the cream. Continue to stir until the sauce bubbles into a thick consistency. This will take about 5 minutes at the most, depending on the amount of heat used, but make sure you don't overheat and curdle the sauce.

Season with salt, pepper and lemon juice, then stir in the fennel. Serve immediately with the fish. New potatoes and a green vegetable or salad are all you need.

John Powell Ponsonby Lewes of Llanerchaeron, Ceredigion, showing his magnificent catch

BAKED SEWIN WITH CUCUMBER AND TARRAGON SAUCE
(serves 6)

Afon Glaslyn in Snowdonia is a renowned sewin river. Netting is carried out in the estuary into Tremadog Bay where the view is fantastic, looking north to Snowdon itself. The National Trust allows anglers with permits to fish for salmon and trout 10 miles up the river in the Aberglaslyn Pass near the village of Beddgelert. There is a famous view here, looking north from the stone bridge, Pont Aberglaslyn.

A whole sea trout makes a wonderful dinner party dish and is easy to cook if baked in the oven – also superb cooked this way on the barbecue. Sewin's flavour is more delicate than salmon, so a fresh-tasting cucumber sauce, its traditional accompaniment in Wales, is ideal. Dill, fennel or basil are as successful as tarragon.

Salmon or sea bass can be used.

> **1 whole fresh sewin or salmon weighing about 1.5kg (3-3¹/₂lb), cleaned**
> **50g (1³/₄oz) melted butter**
> **sea salt and freshly ground black pepper**
> **4 tablespoons white wine**

> **For the cucumber and tarragon sauce**
> **1 firm medium-sized cucumber**
> **75g (3oz) butter**
> **4 tablespoons double cream or crème fraîche**
> **¹/₂ teaspoon lemon juice (if using cream)**
> **sea salt and freshly ground black pepper**
> **1 teaspoon fresh tarragon, chopped**

Pre-heat the oven to 180°C/350°F/GM4.

Leave the head and tail of the fish intact, but cut off the gills. Wipe with a damp cloth, then place in the centre of a large piece of buttered foil. Brush the fish generously with the melted butter on both sides and season well inside and out. Pour over the wine, then wrap up the fish in the foil to make a parcel. Place on a baking sheet and bake for 30-40 minutes or until the fish is tender. Test with a skewer in the thickest part.

Meanwhile, make the sauce. Wipe the cucumber and chop it coarsely, then melt the butter over a low heat. Add the cucumber and cook for a few minutes until heated through, then cool. Purée in a blender or processor with the cream or crème fraîche. (Add the lemon juice if using cream.) Season well to taste and return the purée to the pan. Cover and leave on one side until needed.

When the fish is cooked, unwrap it and leave for 5 minutes, then skin the body. Transfer to a warm serving dish and keep warm while you finish the sauce.

Reheat the sauce gently, stirring in the tarragon. Serve separately from the fish with new potatoes and a green vegetable or crusty wholemeal bread and salad.

WELSH TROUT WRAPPED IN BACON
(serves 4)

Wild brown trout from the turbulent Welsh streams and rivers have a fine clean flavour and were once so plentiful they were cooked with home-cured bacon for breakfast. Quarrymen and miners would go down to local streams on Sunday mornings and tickle enough trout for the family.

The National Trust owns unique Roman gold mines in Carmarthenshire, set amid wooded hillsides overlooking the beautiful Cothi Valley. Mining resumed here in the 19th century and continued until 1938. Visitors to Dolaucothi Gold Mines are taken underground to see the workings and have a go at gold-panning. They can also fish for trout, sea trout and salmon; day permits can be obtained from the Dolaucothi Hotel.

Freshly caught trout and home-smoked bacon would make this dish superlative, but the method of cooking does improve farmed trout as long as the bacon is good quality.

> **4 medium fresh brown or rainbow trout, cleaned**
> **about 50g (1³/₄oz) butter**
> **4 sprigs fresh parsley**
> **4 thin slices unwaxed lemon**
> **freshly ground black pepper**
> **8 thin rashers dry-cured smoked streaky bacon, de-rinded**
> **a little extra butter**
> **2 tablespoons fresh chives, chopped**
> **2 tablespoons fresh parsley, chopped**

Pre-heat the oven to 200°C/400°F/GM6.

Pack the cavity of each fish with a knob of butter, a sprig of parsley and a slice of lemon. Add a twist of black pepper. Stretch the bacon a little with the back of a chef's knife, then wind 2 rashers in a spiral around each fish and brush with melted butter. Arrange the fish in a shallow ovenproof dish which fits them snugly with the loose ends of bacon underneath so they can't unwind. Season with plenty of black pepper, then bake for 15-20 minutes until tender. Place on 4 warm serving plates.

Melt a little extra butter with the juices from the fish, add the herbs and pour over each fish. Eat with warm crusty bread or new potatoes.

Far left: Afon Glaslyn, the great sewin river, in Gwynedd
Left: The Head Set of the Gold Mine at Dolaucothi, Carmarthenshire

FRIED TROUT IN OATMEAL
(serves 4 as a starter)

This is the second traditional Welsh way of cooking fresh trout. The seasoned oatmeal is used as a covering to protect the fish.

> 4 fresh brown, rainbow or
>   sea trout fillets, skinned and boned
> fine oatmeal seasoned with salt
>   and black pepper
> 4 rashers dry-cured smoked back bacon
> 1 shallot, finely chopped
> 4 tablespoons dry white wine
> 4 tablespoons double cream
> 1 tablespoon fresh parsley, chopped

Lightly toss the fish fillets in seasoned oatmeal. Cut the rind off the bacon and chop it finely. Heat the bacon with the rind very gently in a frying-pan until the fat starts to run, then increase the heat and cook until the bacon is crisp and golden brown. Discard the rind, lift the bacon pieces out with a draining spoon and put on one side.

Fry the fish in the bacon fat for a few minutes, turning them once. Lift out of the pan and arrange on a warm serving dish. Keep warm while you fry the shallot gently in the remaining fat until softened. Add the wine and boil until reduced by half. Stir in the cream and bring to the boil, then stir in half the bacon and half the parsley. Pour over the trout fillets and scatter with the remaining bacon and parsley.

ROAST TURBOT WITH ORANGE HOLLANDAISE
(serves 4)

An Anglesey turbot farm, jointly run with Greece, is attracting huge international interest. It was the Greeks who initiated marine fish farming – if you eat bass in Greece, it will have been farmed – so they have the necessary experience.

The fish are housed in a large purpose-built building in a disused granite quarry. They are reared under very strictly controlled conditions so are not exposed to pollutants, or under stress from overcrowding or from seals banging into their cages, so they grow very quickly and are in excellent health when harvested. The turbot are sold in a range of sizes, going out directly to wholesalers, restaurants and supermarkets all over the world.

Because this fish farm is land-based, waste is not poured into the sea. The small amount of organic waste can be utilised as fertiliser and to construct saline wetlands, which are important wildlife habitats. For the falcons and choughs which nest in the quarry, the presence of the farm has provided extra protection from the huge local problem of egg collectors; they can now live undisturbed.

> 4 x 225g (8oz) turbot steaks
> 25g (1oz) unsalted butter
> sea salt and freshly ground black pepper
> 50ml (2fl oz) fish stock (see p.222)
> 1 teaspoon fresh parsley, tarragon
>   and chives, chopped
> juice of ½ lemon

> **For the orange hollandaise**
> 3 tablespoons white wine,
>   or tarragon vinegar
> 2 tablespoons water
> 10 whole white peppercorns
> 3 large organic/free-range eggs yolks
> 175g (6oz) best quality unsalted butter,
>   cut into 12 pieces
> sea salt
> Seville orange or orange juice sharpened
>   with lemon juice to taste

Make the sauce first, before you cook the fish. Put the vinegar, water and peppercorns into a small pan and boil down to about 1 tablespoon of liquid. Leave to cool

Beat the egg yolks in a bowl, then add the reduced vinegar mixture. Pour this into the top of a double saucepan, or set the bowl over a pan of barely simmering water. Add the pieces of butter one at a time stirring all the time. Cook very slowly adding the butter gradually once the last piece has melted. If by any chance the mixture curdles, the remedy is the same as for mayonnaise; stir in 1 tablespoon of boiling water. If this doesn't work, start with another egg yolk, whisk it, then add a tiny trickle of curdled sauce, whisking hard, then add the rest drop by drop whisking as you go. When the sauce is glossy and thick enough to coat the back of a spoon, remove from the heat, then season with salt and orange juice to taste. Keep the sauce warm while you cook the fish.

Pre-heat the oven to 230°C/450°F/GM 8.

Quickly brown the turbot steaks on both sides in a frying-pan with a small piece of butter, then transfer them to a baking tray, or roasting tin. Season with salt and pepper, then roast in the oven for about 15 minutes, or until cooked.

Remove from the oven and arrange on 4 warm plates. Keep warm while you bring the stock, herbs, lemon juice and remaining butter to the boil in a small pan. Pour over the turbot and divide the warm hollandaise between the plates (or serve separately).

Serve with a simply cooked green vegetable such as samphire, asparagus, purple-sprouting broccoli, or spinach depending on the season.

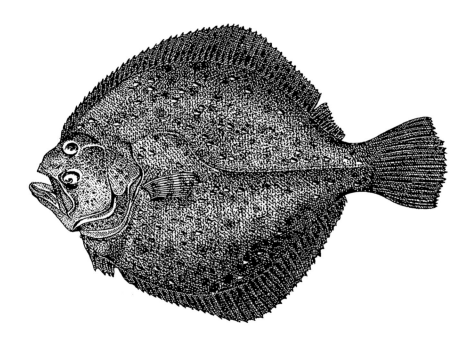

Roast Turbot with Orange Hollandaisee

NORTHERN IRELAND

The National Trust owns some of Northern Ireland's most spectacular coastline, stretching from the extraordinary Giant's Causeway on the North Antrim coast round to the unspoilt beauty of Fair Head and Murlough Bay and south to the less dramatic, but nevertheless beautiful, coastline of County Down with the loughs of Belfast, Strangford and Carlingford. Many of the National Trust's properties are important for their wildlife interest, offering a wide range of opportunities to enjoy unspoilt habitats and fascinating flora and fauna. Strangford Lough is one of Europe's most important wildlife sites and the Trust operates a Wildlife Scheme embracing the entire foreshore of the lough, as well as some 50 islands. Depending on the season, visitors may see vast flocks of wintering wildfowl and nesting birds as well as seals, otters and other marine animals. As the National Trust warden reminded me, the really skilled fishermen of the Lough are the wildfowl, especially the cormorants and terns.

Northern Ireland is surrounded on three sides by clean, cold seas providing the best possible conditions for seafood. Inland, it is dotted with loughs and threaded by rivers to form a habitat for first-class wild salmon and trout. Nowhere else in the UK is game angling so cheap and uncrowded. Until recently fish has been in good supply, playing an essential part in the local diet. Even today, Northern Ireland consumers eat 55 per cent more seafood than the rest of the UK. The current annual total value of the Northern Ireland seafood market is about £22.7million, employing around 1,000 people, so the fishing industry is still vital to the economy.

There are very few active fishing ports on the North Antrim coast apart from Ballycastle because of over-fishing, although, ironically, huge Russian and Spanish factory ships can be seen fishing offshore. The main fishing ports are in County Down – Kilkenny, Northern Ireland's premier port, Portavogie and Ardglass. A taskforce for this area was set up by the Government in 2003 to review the impact of recent EU measures for fisheries management on the local communities and to propose an action plan to address the economic and social challenges identified.

Aquaculture will play an increasingly important part in Northern Ireland's fishing industry. At the moment there are a number of ongoing initiatives backed by European money. Large shellfish farms have been set up in County Down in the clean waters of Carlingford and Dundrum Bays and in Belfast and Strangford Loughs. There is significant development in bottom-grown mussels, which are not harvested during spawning from April to August. They are bigger and tastier than the rope-grown kind, which are available all year. Funds have also been used to encourage the joint marketing of oysters between Northern Ireland and Donegal and Sligo in Eire.

Many representative bodies and agencies are striving to promote Northern Ireland's seafood. Most of the fishing ports hold annual fish festivals with cooking demonstrations, tastings and promotions in local restaurants, while a huge seafood festival is held at Hillsborough in County Down. To increase consumption and encourage the home-cooking of fish, 'Northern Ireland Seafoods', which represents the processing and aquaculture sectors of the fishing industry, provides cooking demonstrations in schools, hotels and supermarkets. A replica trawler, *Seafood Voyager*, is taken around the villages.

Previous pages: Alta Corry Bay on Rathlin Island, County Antrim
Left: A souvenir seller on the Giant's Causeway, County Antrim, *c*. 1860

CUSHENDUN SEA BASS WITH WINE AND TARRAGON SAUCE
(serves 4)

Although there is very little commercial fishing on the North Antrim coast today, it provides excellent sea angling for the amateur. The Causeway Coast Sea Angling Festival is held annually in September at Portrush, a busy seaside resort west of the Giant's Causeway. Further round the coast is the lovely village of Cushendun in the heart of the Antrim Glens, with its distinctive style of buildings designed by Clough Williams-Ellis, the celebrated architect of Portmeirion in North Wales. Most of the village is managed by the National Trust, including the harbour, from which one bag-net salmon fisherman works.

Sea bream would also be delicious in this recipe.

4 x 175g (6oz) pieces line-caught or responsibly farmed sea bass fillet, skinned and boned
a little butter
sea salt and freshly ground black pepper

For the sauce
300ml (½pt) fish stock (see p.222)
125ml (4fl oz) good- quality dry white wine
15g (½oz) mushrooms, chopped
15g (½oz) shallots, finely chopped
180ml (6fl oz) double cream
1 tablespoon fresh tarragon leaves, torn

To make the sauce, put the fish stock, white wine, mushrooms and shallots in a small pan and reduce by half over a high heat. Stir in the cream and reduce until it coats the back of a spoon. Pass through a sieve, then keep warm while you cook the fish.

Place the fish on buttered and seasoned pieces of greaseproof paper. Lightly salt the fish and place in a steamer over a pan of simmering water. Cover with a lid and steam for 4-5 minutes until just firm and tender to the touch.

While the fish is cooking, finish the sauce by adding the chopped tarragon and seasoning to taste. Arrange pieces of bass on 4 warm serving plates and spoon over some sauce.

Left: The medieval stronghold of Carrickfergus Castle, guarding the entrance to Belfast Lough, County Antrim
Above: Cottages designed by Clough Williams-Ellis in the village of Cushendun, County Antrim

CHOCOLATE CARRAGHEEN PUDDING WITH IRISH COFFEE SAUCE
(serves 4)

Carragheen is an important source of alginates – vegetable gelatines – which are used for thickening soups and stews, emulsifying ice creams and setting sweet and savoury jellies, mousses, jams and marmalades. Alginates can also be made into thin, durable films for use as edible sausage skins.

Traditionally in Ireland carragheen is used to thicken blancmanges and milk drinks. Most Irish people like to eat the blancmange with no extra flavouring, just large quantities of rich farm cream, but you can flavour it with vanilla, almond, elderflowers, fruit juice, especially lemon or ginger. This chocolate version is excellent.

20g (³⁄₄oz) **cleaned, well-dried**
   carragheen moss
600ml (1pt) **full-cream milk**
1 tablespoon **caster sugar**
110g (4oz) **good-quality dark chocolate**
½ teaspoon **groundnut oil**

For the Irish coffee sauce
90ml (3fl oz) **cold water**
225g (8oz) **caster sugar**
250ml (9fl oz) **strong ground coffee**
1 tablespoon **Irish whiskey**
softly whipped cream to serve

Soak the carragheen in tepid water for 10 minutes. Strain off the water and put into a pan with the milk and sugar. Slowly bring to the boil, stirring to dissolve the sugar, then simmer very gently with the lid on for 20 minutes until most of the seaweed has dissolved.

Meanwhile, chop the chocolate into small pieces or grate roughly.

Remove the milk from the heat and stir in the chocolate until it has all melted. Strain through a fine strainer into a clean pan, rubbing all the jelly through. Beat it well to mix in.

Very lightly grease 4 teacups or individual pudding moulds, then pour in the chocolate mixture. Chill until set.

To make the sauce, pour the water and remaining sugar into a heavy-based pan. Heat gently, stirring until the sugar dissolves. Remove the spoon and continue to heat the syrup until it turns a pale golden colour. Pour in the coffee and stir over a gentle heat until smooth. Remove from the heat and cool, then stir in the whiskey. Leave to cool.

Turn each pudding onto a serving plate and pour some sauce around each one. Serve with the cream.

DUNDRUM CARPETSHELL SOUP
(serves 4)

Many of the cockles exported from Northern Ireland to France at an alarming rate are really members of the clam family. Their Latin name is *Venerupis decussata*, but they are known locally as 'carpetshells'. They have a smooth surface with a slight ridge running vertically over the shell. Other types of clams, mussels, winkles, whelks or a mixture of small shellfish can also be used for this soup, which comes from the village of Dundrum in County Down.

Just south of Dundrum is Ireland's first nature reserve, cared for by the National Trust since 1967. Murlough is an extraordinarily beautiful landscape with unusually high dunes calculated to be 6,000 years old. From Norman times, these contained a rabbit warren for meat and fur. Rabbit grazing has had a major influence on the development of the heathland and grassland, providing a haven for wildlife. It's a great place for seal and bird-watching.

1.5kg (3lb 5oz) **carpetshell clams**
   or cockles, scrubbed and cleaned
150ml (5fl oz) **medium dry white wine**
75g (2³⁄₄oz) **butter**
2 large **leeks, white part only, washed**
   and sliced
1 small **fennel bulb, chopped**
1 tablespoon **plain flour**
400ml (14fl oz) **fish stock (see p.222)**
a pinch of **saffron strands**
sea salt and freshly ground black pepper
150ml (5fl oz) **whipping cream**
1 level tablespoon **fresh tarragon, torn**

Tip the clams into a large tightly lidded pan and pour over the wine. Put the lid on and bring to the boil, then cook for 3-4 minutes, shaking the pan, until the clams have opened. Drain into a colander over a bowl. Discard any closed shellfish and shake the colander to get out any remaining liquor. Remove the meat from the shells and reserve the liquor.

Wipe out the pan and melt the butter. Sweat the leeks and the fennel in the butter for about 10 minutes until soft and golden. Stir in the flour and allow it to cook gently for a couple of minutes, then stir in the reserved clam liquor strained through a sieve lined with a double layer of muslin to remove any sand. Add the fish stock and simmer gently for about 20 minutes. Liquidise in a blender and pass through a fine sieve into a clean pan.

Add the saffron and season to taste. Stir in the cream and tarragon, then the reserved clam meat.

Reheat gently and serve with warm wholemeal soda bread.

CARRAGHEEN MOSS
The purplish-red fronds of this lovely seaweed are common on the rocks and stones of the western coasts of Scotland, and in the Channel Islands, but its real home is Ireland, where the village of Carragheen on the west coast has provided its most common name – Irish moss.

For centuries women have gathered carragheen in large wicker baskets from the rocky shores all around the coast of Ireland. It is found at the lowest tidal level and is easily recognised because its fronds have a distinctly flat stalk and branch repeatedly into a rough fan shape. The seaweed is best gathered young in April and May and either used immediately, or carefully dried. It is thought by many parents to be essential in the diet of growing children, as it is bursting with minerals and goodness. Eat as a vegetable like spinach or use as a thickening agent.

TO DRY CARRAGHEEN MOSS
In Ireland, the seaweed used to be spread out to dry on the cliffs, bleaching to a creamy-white colour. If you want to dry it yourself, wash it very well in fresh water, then lay it outside to dry somewhere out of the wind. Wash it from time to time with fresh water or simply leave it out in the rain until it changes colour, when it is ready to bring inside. Trim off any rough stalks, then dry thoroughly indoors. Store in paper bags hanging in a dry place.

Commercially prepared dried carragheen is available from health food shops. Soak the carragheen in water for 10-15 minutes before using.

The beach of Murlough Bay, looking towards the Mourne Mountains, County Down

COCKLE, MUSSEL AND WHILLICK CHOWDER
(serves 6)

Small shellfish like cockles, mussels and whillicks (local name for winkles), together with clams, limpets and whelks, have always played an important role in the diet of the people living on the shores of Strangford Lough. There is still a considerable amount of hand-gathering today.

Any combination of shellfish can be used in this chowder.

2 tablespoons sunflower oil
1kg (2¼lb) live cockles or clams, prepared
1kg (2¼lb) live mussels, scrubbed and bearded
100g (3½oz) winkles, cooked and removed from their shells
150ml (¼pt) dry white wine
75g (2¾oz) butter
125g (4½oz) dry-cured smoked bacon, cut into 1cm (½in) strips
3 large waxy new potatoes (e.g. Charlotte, Pink Fir Apple, Ratte or Anya), diced into 1cm (½in) cubes
2 sticks celery, finely sliced
1 carrot, finely sliced
1 sprig fresh thyme
1 bay leaf
75g (2¾oz) plain flour
1 litre (1¾pts) full-cream milk
a pinch of saffron strands
150ml (5fl oz) double cream
sea salt and freshly ground black pepper

Heat the oil in a large tightly lidded pan until smoking. Add the cockles and mussels, put on the lid and shake well. Pour on the wine and steam the shellfish for 3 minutes until the shells open. Discard any that remain closed, tip into a colander suspended over a bowl, reserving the cooking liquor.

Take the shellfish meat out of most of the shells, reserving about 18 of each in their shells.

Melt the butter in a clean pan over a medium heat and cook the bacon for 4-5 minutes. Add the vegetables and herbs, turn down the heat and cook for a further 5 minutes. Stir in the flour and cook for a further 5 minutes, then gradually stir in the milk. Strain the reserved cooking liquor into the pan through a strainer lined with two layers of muslin to remove any sand.

Add the saffron, bring slowly to the boil. Simmer gently for 20 minutes, stirring occasionally. Remove the thyme and bay leaf, stir in the cream. Season to taste and add the shellfish meat (including the winkles) and the remaining fish in their shells. Reheat gently and serve in 6 warm bowls dividing the cockles and mussels in their shells between the bowls. Ladle over the rest of the soup and eat with warm wholemeal soda bread and a glass of Guinness.

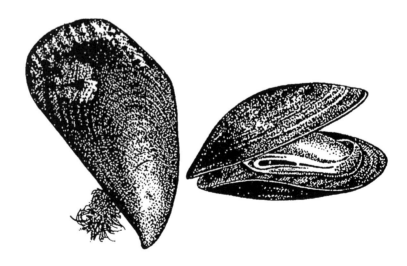

The harbour of the village of Strangford Lough, County Down

BARBECUED DUBLIN BAY PRAWNS AND CHILLI LIME BUTTER
(serves 4 as a starter)

Barbecue or grill on skewers or fry over a high heat without the skewers and quickly toss in the butter before serving.

> 16 large raw Dublin Bay prawns
> 100g (3½oz) unsalted butter, softened
> 1 red chilli, seeded and finely chopped
> 1 garlic clove, peeled and crushed
>   with a little sea salt
> grated rind of 2 unwaxed limes
> juice of 1 lime
> 2 tablespoons fresh coriander leaves,
>   finely chopped
> freshly ground black pepper

Beat together the butter, chilli, garlic, lime rind and coriander. Add the lime juice and season to taste. Thread the Dublin Bay prawns on to skewers and brush with a little of the flavoured butter. Barbecue or grill for about 3 minutes, then brush again with butter. Turn over and cook for a further 3 minutes.

Serve with more flavoured butter, a crisp leaf and herb salad and crusty soda bread.

IRISH FISH STEW
(serves 4)

A variety of fish caught off the coast of Northern Ireland is used to make this traditional stew. It's very quick and easy and all you need to make a meal are chunks of warm soda bread and a glass of Guinness.

> 8 small raw whole Dublin Bay prawns,
>   peeled and intestines removed (see
>   p.197)
> 1300g (10½ oz) clams or cockles,
>   scrubbed and cleaned
> 350g (12oz) sea bream or gurnard
>   fillets, unskinned
> 2 tablespoons extra virgin olive oil
> 350g (12oz) medium waxy new potatoes
>   (e.g. Ratte, Pink Fir Apple, Anya
>   or Charlotte), peeled and cut into
>   large chunks
> 2 large garlic cloves, peeled
>   and freshly sliced
> 2 dried chillies, crumbled
> 1 x 400g (14oz) tin chopped tomatoes
> sea salt and freshly ground black pepper
> 50g (1¾oz) fresh root ginger, grated
> juice of 1 lemon
> 150ml (¼pt) medium dry white wine
> 2 tablespoons fresh, flat-leaf parsley,
>   roughly chopped
> extra virgin olive oil, to serve

Heat the olive oil in a large, heavy-bottomed pan with a lid. Add the potatoes, garlic and chilli and cook for about 5 minutes until coloured. Add the tomatoes and season well. Cook for a further 15 minutes, until the potatoes are soft. Stir in the ginger.

Add all the fish, then pour over the lemon juice and wine. Season to taste, then cover with a lid and simmer gently for 5 minutes. The clams should be open and the Dublin Bay prawns firm. Discard any clams that are tightly closed and remove the intestines from the prawns.

Ladle into 4 warm soup or pasta plates, dividing the fish evenly.

Sprinkle with parsley and drizzle with olive oil.

Irish Fish Stew

WARM SMOKED EEL, NEW POTATO AND BACON SALAD
(serves 4 as a starter or lunch)

Smoked salmon's status, according to a supermarket survey, is floundering because it is mass-produced in offshore farms and no longer a rarity. Smoked eel, however, has wriggled its way into a niche market where it is now considered a refined delicacy.

4 smoked eel fillets, skinned
700g (1lb 9oz) new waxy potatoes (Ratte, Charlotte, Belle de Fontenay or Jersey Royals), scrubbed
4 rashers dry-cured smoked streaky bacon
200g (7oz) tub crème fraîche
1 teaspoon good-quality horseradish cream
juice of 1 medium lemon
freshly ground black pepper
85g (3oz) watercress, trimmed (optional)
1 unwaxed lemon, quartered to serve

Cook the potatoes in boiling salted water for 15-20 minutes, or steam, until tender.

While the potatoes are cooking, mix the crème fraîche in a large bowl with the horseradish cream and lemon juice. Season well with black pepper, but don't add any salt because of the saltiness of the eel and bacon.

Drain the potatoes and dry off over heat. Halve them and leave to cool for a few minutes. Meanwhile, grill the bacon until crisp and cut into strips. Warm the eel fillets for a few seconds under the grill and chop into 2.5cm (1in) pieces. Keep bacon and eel warm. Tip the potatoes into the cream dressing and stir until it coats them and becomes quite runny. Add the eel fillet, bacon and watercress if using. Toss gently together, then pile into 4 warm serving bowls or plates and serve straight away with lemon wedges (and warm crusty bread if serving for lunch).

DULSE CHAMP

Cook the dulse in milk as below. Mash some floury potatoes, season to taste, then add the dulse with enough of the cooking liquor to make the dish creamy and smooth. You can add as much dulse as you like to suit your personal taste. Put the champ into a deep warmed dish, make a well in the centre and pour some hot melted butter into it.

DULSE

'Did you treat your Mary Anne to dulse and yellowman
At the Ould Lammas Fair, at Ballycastle?'

Near the Giant's Causeway is the seaside resort of Ballycastle, where for over 350 years Lammas Fair has been held at the end of August. Sheep and ponies are sold and there are the usual fair day delights. The two traditional foods are 'yellowman', a brittle yellow toffee that has been made by the same family for hundreds of years, and dulse, an edible seaweed. Also called dillisk and dillesk, dulse is a reddish-brown seaweed common all around the coast of Britain, but only eaten in the remoter parts of Ireland and Scotland.

Seawater contains minerals and trace elements in exactly the same proportions as our bodies. Growing in such a rich environment, seaweeds like dulse naturally absorb the minerals and are an excellent source of valuable iron, calcium and iodine. If gathering your own dulse, look for it growing on stones, or often on other seaweeds, fairly low down the tidal level on an unpolluted beach. The best months to gather it, as with most seaweeds, are April, May and June when the plant has produced new shoots. Cut the dulse leaving plenty of the stem-like part which is attached to the stone, so that it continues to grow, or gather leaves, which have been washed free of their moorings. Wash the dulse very thoroughly in fresh water to remove sand, shells and other beach debris.

TO DRY DULSE

Dulse used to be eaten raw in salads, but it is usually sold dried. All over Ireland it is dried on low stone walls and beaches, while in Portaferry, at the entrance to Strangford Lough, it can be seen drying on the pavements. To dry it yourself, leave the seaweed hanging outside on a sunny wall for a day or two until it is virtually dry, then bring it in and hang it for another day in a warm place, such as the airing cupboard. When it is crisp, store in air-tight jars in a dry place.

TO COOK DULSE

Soak the weed in cold water for 3 hours, then simmer in milk or water for 3-5 hours, or until tender. It is extremely tough, so the long cooking is really necessary. Add a good knob of butter and freshly milled pepper. Serve as a vegetable with any meat or fish, or add a few fronds to vegetable and fish soups and stews to give them body and a wonderful flavour.

The strange basalt rock formations of the Giant's Causeway, County Antrim

AROMATIC IRISH HERRING
(serves 4)

At one time the herring was the most common fish caught off the coast of Northern Ireland. In the 1890s the fishing smacks followed the shoals of herring and mackerel down the coast and into Strangford Lough where there was plenty of food. Many of the traditional fish recipes use herring, which was salted and pickled in vast quantities. Red herrings, salted and heavily smoked, were hung up by skewers from the kitchen rafters until needed, then they were grilled over a turf fire, or steamed on top of a pot of potatoes.

There were plenty of herring and mackerel in the Lough in 2003, providing sport for anglers from boats or rocks, but there is no longer any commercial fishing. However, herrings are reappearing in fishmongers as the ban on herring fishing was lifted in 1984. They are probably the cheapest and most highly nutritious food available to us; as high in protein as lean beef and rich in vitamins A, B and D. Sadly, we seem to have forgotten how to cook them; try this recipe to enjoy a really fresh herring, or any other oil-rich fish, such as mackerel, sardine or pilchard.

4 very fresh herrings, cleaned and heads removed
4 tablespoons olive oil
2 tablespoons coriander seeds
2 dessertspoons cumin seeds
1 teaspoon black peppercorns

Pre-heat the grill or barbecue.

Wipe the fish and dry well with kitchen paper. Score each diagonally across 3 times on both sides. Brush lightly with oil. Lightly crush the coriander, cumin and peppercorns together in a pestle and mortar, then roll the fish in the spice mixture.

Grill for about 5 minutes on each side until cooked through with a crisp skin. Serve with a leaf and herb salad, soda bread and mango chutney or a sweet relish.

DUBLIN LAWYER
(serves 4 as a starter or 2 as a main course)

This is a famous Irish recipe for lobster and although it originates in Dublin, it is often served in Northern Ireland, where the rocky Atlantic coast is a haven for both lobsters and crabs. They are landed at Ballycastle, nestling between high cliffs on the famous Antrim coast road.

2 freshly cooked lobsters
50g (2oz) butter
sea salt and freshly ground black pepper
3-4 tablespoons Irish whiskey
150ml (5fl oz) double cream
½ teaspoon fresh lemon thyme leaves
1 teaspoon fresh parsley, chopped
a few sprigs fresh flat-leaf parsley or watercress to garnish

As soon as the lobsters are cool enough to handle, split them in half and extract all the meat from the body, tail and large and small claws. Scrape out all the soft greenish tomalley (liver) from the part of the shell nearest the head and put it with the firmer meat into a warm bowl. Cut the meat into chunks. Warm up the lobster shells in a low oven.

Melt the butter in a pan and when it is foaming, toss the lobster in it until it is cooked through and the juices turn pink. Season well. Heat the whiskey in a small pan and pour over the lobster meat. Set it alight and when the flames have died down, add the cream and herbs. Gently heat through without boiling, then spoon back into the hot shells.

Serve immediately on hot plates, garnished with parsley or watercress and eat with chunks of warm soda bread.

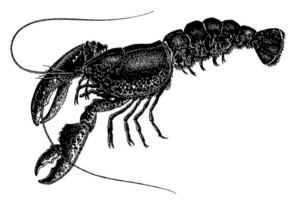

Far left: Ballymoran Bay on Strangford Lough
Left: A fisherman's cottage at White Park Bay, County Antrim

SMOKED MACKEREL AND POTATO GRATIN
(serves 4-6)

Fair Head is one of the great headlands of Ireland, its sheer face rising some 200 metres (600 feet) above sea level, with views over the gentler slopes, wooded areas and white sands of Murlough Bay. There is no commercial fishing from here, but amateur anglers catch a variety of fish including mackerel in the summer.

1kg (2lb 4oz) even-sized main crop potatoes (e.g. King Edward, Maris Piper or Desirée)
2 small garlic cloves, crushed
sea salt and freshly ground black pepper
250g (9oz) locally smoked line-caught mackerel fillets, skinned and boned
300ml (10fl oz) full-cream milk
300ml (10fl oz) double cream
1 tablespoon local grain mustard (optional)
freshly grated nutmeg
50g (1³⁄₄oz) butter

Pre-heat the oven to 150°C/300°F/GM2.

Peel the potatoes and slice them very thinly (about 3mm [¹⁄₈in] thick). Dry them off with a cloth, then arrange half in a well-buttered shallow baking dish. Sprinkle over half the garlic and season well.

Flake the mackerel into bite-sized pieces and sprinkle over the potatoes in the dish, then cover with the remaining potatoes and garlic. Season again.

Mix the milk, cream and mustard (if using) together and pour over the potatoes. Grate over a generous amount of nutmeg, then dot with the butter. Bake on the highest shelf in the oven for about 1¹⁄₂ hours or until the potatoes are tender and the gratin is bubbly and golden brown on top.

Serve with a leaf and herb salad.

MUSSELS IN MURPHIES
(serves 4)

The Irish consume more potatoes than any other nation in Europe: Ireland's bleakest period of history was in 1845-46 when the national crop failed, causing the great famine. The potato makes an appearance not just in savoury dishes, but in Irish cakes and desserts.

Scotland and Ireland both have traditional and ingenious recipes for cooked mussels held in portable, edible containers. Hot bread rolls were used in Scotland; the crumb was taken out and the mussels packed in its place. In Ireland, the container was a potato baked in its jacket and then hollowed out. The whole meal could be wrapped in a cloth and taken to work in a man's pocket.

4 large baking potatoes (a floury variety such as King Edward or Maris Piper), scrubbed and dried
olive oil
sea salt
2kg (4¹⁄₂ lb) fresh live mussels, scrubbed and bearded
6 tablespoons water
1 sprig fresh parsley
1 sprig fresh thyme
1 small onion, peeled and chopped
50g (1³⁄₄oz) butter
2 shallots, peeled and finely chopped
a large pinch saffron strands
4 tablespoons dry white wine
150ml (5fl oz) double cream
1 tablespoon fresh flat-leaf parsley, roughly chopped

Pre-heat the oven to 200°C/400°F/GM6.

Rub the potatoes all over with olive oil and sprinkle with salt. Bake in the oven for about 1 hour. Meanwhile, put the mussels into a large pan with a tight-fitting lid with the water, herbs and onion. Cover and cook over a high heat for about 3 minutes until the mussels have opened, shaking the pan frequently (you will need to cook in several batches). Remove from the heat, and, when the mussels are cool enough to handle, remove them from their shells, discarding any that are tightly closed. Strain and reserve the cooking liquor.

When the potatoes are almost cooked, melt the butter in a small pan and sauté the shallots very gently for about 8 minutes until they are very soft and sweet. Stir in the saffron and wine and reserved cooking liquor. Simmer until the liquid is reduced by half, then add the cream. Simmer for 1 minute, then add the mussels. Simmer very gently uncovered for about 3 minutes, stirring occasionally, until the sauce has thickened and the mussels are hot.

Remove the potatoes from the oven, cut each in half and fill with the mussel sauce. Serve sprinkled with parsley.

Far left: Looking across Murlough Bay to Fair Head
Left: Smoked Mackerel and Potato Gratin

BAKED STRANGFORD OYSTERS WITH IRISH SLOKE
(serves 4 as a starter)

Strangford Lough, on the eastern coast of Northern Ireland, is the largest sea lough in the British Isles. Almost totally landlocked, apart from its connection to the Irish Sea through the treacherous Strangford Narrows, the lough has over 70 small islands and countless tidal rocky outcrops called 'Pladdies'.

Northern Ireland's Department of Agriculture and Rural Development has recently completed a strategy for Aquaculture in Strangford Lough with the co-operation of the National Trust, who owns its entire foreshore and islands and is committed to the lough's protection through the Strangford Lough Wildlife Scheme. Both oyster- and mussel-farming exists now, but there is a project to increase the Native oyster population by releasing oyster seed into the seabed. The Lough's waters are Class A and rich in plankton, so shellfish-farming should have a great future.

16–24 Native or Pacific oysters, opened, reserving the juices and deep shells
1 tablespoon olive oil
4 garlic cloves, chopped, then crushed
100g (3¼oz) 1 or 2 day-old brown bread
5 large sprigs fresh coriander
2 spring onions, green part only, roughly chopped
1 tablespoon sesame oil
100g (3¾oz) prepared sloke (laverbread)
½ teaspoon Tabasco
16-24 slices lemon, to secure the oysters while grilling
2 unwaxed lemons, cut into wedges

Pre-heat the oven to 230°C/450°F/GM8.

Heat the oil in a small frying-pan and fry the garlic for a few minutes until very golden and quite crisp. Remove from the pan to cool, reserving the oil.

Blitz the bread in a processor or blender to make breadcrumbs, then add the garlic. Reserving a few coriander leaves for garnish, chop the remainder and add to the processor with the spring onion greens. Blitz again until all the ingredients are finely chopped, then add the reserved garlicky oil and the sesame oil, blitz finally to form a herb crumble.

Mix the sloke, or laverbread, with some of the reserved oyster juice and the Tabasco to make a thick, flowing relish.

Place the reserved oyster shells on slices of lemon set on a baking tray, then put a tablespoon of the sloke into each shell and top with an oyster. Sprinkle the herby crumble onto each. Bake for 3–4 minutes to just heat the oysters through and to crispen the crust.

Garnish gently with roughly chopped coriander leaves and lemon wedges and enjoy with a glass of Guinness.

Left: Selling oysters at the market in Clifden, County Galway, 1900
Right: The characteristic drumlin landscape of Strangford Lough

BEEFSTEAK, GUINNESS AND OYSTER PIE
(serves 4)

By the 18th century the earlier rigid demarcation between fish and meat dishes was becoming blurred and shellfish, especially oysters, began to be added to the latter. This classic Victorian pie was probably heavy on the oysters and light on the beef, as the shellfish were so cheap until the closing years of the 19th century when they were becoming over-fished. The addition of oysters adds a special savour to the pie, while Guinness gives body to the gravy. This dish takes 24 hours to prepare.

> 12 fresh Native or Pacific oysters
> 700g (1lb 9oz) rump steak, cut into
>   2.5cm (1in) cubes
> about 2 tablespoons beef dripping
> 2 medium onions, sliced
> 25g (1oz) flour
> 200ml (7fl oz) Guinness
> 200ml (7fl oz) beef stock
> ½ teaspoon Worcestershire sauce
>   (optional)
> 1 teaspoon dark brown sugar
> 1 bouquet garni
> sea salt and freshly ground black pepper
> 350g (12oz) puff pastry
> 1 free-range egg, beaten

Pre-heat the oven to 180°C/350°F/GM4.

Heat a little of the dripping in a flameproof casserole dish and quickly fry the meat in batches until nicely browned, adding more dripping as necessary. Remove the browned meat to the lid of the casserole so that no juices escape and leave on one side. Fry the onions for a few minutes until lightly browned, then stir in the flour. Remove from the heat and gradually stir in the Guinness and the stock. Add the Worcestershire sauce, sugar and bouquet garni. Season well, and cook in the oven for about 1½ hours or until the meat is tender. Remove from the oven, cool and chill overnight.

Next day, open the oysters and add them, with their juice, to the meat. Remove the bouquet garni and check the seasoning, then transfer to a 1.2 litre (2 pt) pie dish.

Roll out the pastry to 5cm (2in) larger than the top of the pie dish, then cut off a 2.5cm (1in) strip from around the edge. Brush the edge of the pie dish with water, press the pastry strip onto it, and brush the strip with water. Cover the pie with the remaining pastry, pressing the edges together to seal. Trim and decorate the edge. Glaze with the beaten egg and make a small hole in the centre of the pie to let out the steam. Chill while you heat up the oven to 230°C/450° F/GM8.

Bake for 25-30 minutes then cover the pie loosely with foil to prevent further browning. Reduce the oven temperature to l60°C/325°F/GM3 and cook for a further 20-25 minutes until the pastry is cooked. Serve immediately with a glass of Guinness.

OATMEAL-CRUSTED GLASHAN FROM PORTAFERRY
(serves 4)

The fishery in Strangford Lough was flourishing in the early 19th century, supplying part of the Belfast market, but had become uneconomic by the end of the century due to competition from steam trawlers working more extensive grounds elsewhere. At Portaferry, at the entrance to the lough, traces of the industry remain in the architecture along the Strand and in the local names for various fish. Sand smelt is sold as 'Portaferry chicken', while coley or saithe (black pollack) is known as 'glashan'. Coley doesn't have a wonderful flavour, but true pollack (green pollack) is tastier and available in sustainable quantities. Anglers fish for it from rocks at the mouth of the lough along with whiting, codling and ling. Any of these could be used for this very traditional Northern Irish recipe. You can buy pinhead oatmeal from the better supermarkets and health food shops, but any oatmeal or porridge oats would work just as well.

> 4 x 175g (6oz) thick pieces of line-caught
>   pollack fillet, skinned and boned
> sea salt and freshly ground black pepper
> a little flour for dusting
> 1 free-range egg, beaten with a little
>   milk
> 110g (4oz) pinhead oatmeal
> 1 teaspoon dry English mustard
> a little butter for frying

Season the fish with salt and pepper and dust with a little flour. Mix the oatmeal with the mustard and tip on to a baking tray. Pour the beaten egg into another tray. Dip the fish pieces into the beaten egg and then into the oatmeal to coat both sides.

Melt a little butter in a non-stick frying-pan and gently fry the fish for about 3 minutes on each side, depending on thickness, until lightly brown. The oatmeal coating should be nice and crispy to form a crunchy crust around the soft fish centre.

Serve straight from the pan with boiled potatoes and a green vegetable (curly kale would be traditional). A Béchamel sauce (see p.219) flavoured with grain mustard is excellent with this fish.

Crown Liquor Saloon, Belfast, where oysters are on offer along with Guinness

MANOR HOUSE SALMON WITH A RED PEPPER SAUCE
(serves 4)

Bought by the National Trust in 1967, Carrick-a-Rede on the North Antrim coast means the 'rock in the road' because the island and the narrow channel between it and the mainland act as barriers to migrating salmon seeking the fresh waters of the rivers Bush and Bann. The fish were deflected north into the nets laid by local fishermen who erected the original 20-metre (60-foot) rope bridge more than 300 years ago to reach the fishery. The new bridge is much more heavily used by the many thousands of visitors who come to this glorious spot each year. Suspended over a 30-metre (90-foot) chasm, the bridge sways and wobbles underfoot and crossing it requires nerves of steel.

In the early 19th century, the bag net, which until recently was used to catch salmon here, was introduced from Scotland. The net was set and the fish trapped themselves by swimming into the bag. Sadly, today there are so few salmon that the Fisheries Board is buying up all the licences for bag nets to stop the fishing. At the moment, the National Trust still holds one, but soon this will be bought from it. Consequently, there is very little commercial salmon fishing here. Recreational anglers with rod and line are allowed further up the rivers, although many are polluted by intensive agriculture.

At the Georgian guest-house owned by the National Trust on nearby Rathlin Island, wild salmon is on the menu whenever possible. Penny Sewell, who runs Manor House, likes to use fresh local ingredients, including fish caught by an islander and also by a fisherman from Ballycastle on the mainland, and vegetables and herbs from the old walled garden. She gave me this recipe, a favourite at the guest-house, which was devised by a recent chef, Roger Robinson.

4 x 175g (6oz) pieces of wild Pacific or responsibly farmed Atlantic salmon fillet
about 50g (1³/₄oz) butter, melted
sea salt and freshly ground black pepper
4 teaspoons Demerara sugar

For the red pepper sauce
   2 red organic peppers, halved lengthways, and seeded
   150ml (5fl oz) single cream
   a dash of sherry
   sea salt and freshly ground black pepper

For the parsley oil (optional)
   150ml (¹/₄pt) olive oil
   about 40g (1¹/₂ oz) fresh flat-leaf parsley, finely chopped
   a little extra fresh flat-leaf parsley chopped to decorate

To make the parsley oil, process the chopped parsley with the oil in a blender. Once made, it will keep for up to 2 weeks in a fridge and can be used in many fish dishes.

To make the red pepper sauce, line a baking tray with baking parchment and put the red pepper halves on it, skin-side uppermost. Grill until uniformly blackened and softened. Leave to cool, then the skins should peel away easily. Remove and discard the stalks, then chop into large chunks. Blitz in a food processor or blender, or place in a bowl and whisk to a purée with an electric hand whisk. Transfer the purée to a small pan and stir in the cream and sherry. Leave on one side while you cook the salmon.

Pre-heat the oven to 210°C/425°F/GM7. Brush a baking tray with melted butter and place the fish on it. Brush each piece with melted butter and sprinkle with sugar. Season well. Roast in the oven for 8-10 minutes.

Warm the sauce through gently and season to taste. Place pieces of salmon on 4 warm serving plates and add spoonfuls of sauce. Drizzle a little parsley oil around the border and sprinkle with freshly chopped parsley.

Serve with new potatoes and fresh young broad beans, or peas.

Left: Salmon fishing at Carrick-a-Rede, off the Antrim coast
Right: The fishermen make their catch by hanging their nets from hoists during the season between May and September

PEPPERED SALMON WITH BUSHMILLS WHISKEY CREAM SAUCE
(serves 4)

The Giant's Causeway on the treacherous north coast has attracted the curiosity of travellers for centuries and is now Northern Ireland's top tourist attraction and only World Heritage site. Legend has it that the Causeway was built by the Irish giant, Finn MacCool, so that he could cross the sea to Scotland to challenge a rival giant, Benandoner. In fact, the famous basalt columns were created during a period of volcanic activity some 60 million years ago, when lava cooled quickly as it flowed into the sea. But visitors who see only the columns of the Causeway miss some of the finest coastal scenery in Ireland. The National Trust protects part of the North Antrim Coastal Path and the spectacular cliffs and headlands are easily accessible. The Causeway Coastal Path starts at Blackrock, where an old slipway once serving the salmon fishery can be seen nearby, and extends 14 miles east to the famous Carrick-a-Rede rope bridge (see p.210).

In 2002 the narrow gauge railway running the 2 miles from the Giant's Causeway to the world's oldest distillery at Bushmills was opened. This recipe celebrates two of the best North Antrim ingredients; salmon and single malt whiskey.

4 x 175g (6 oz) wild Pacific or responsibly farmed Atlantic salmon steaks
2 level teaspoons Dijon mustard
$^{1}/_{2}$-1 level tablespoon mixed 4-colour peppercorns, crushed in a pestle and mortar
freshly ground sea salt
25g (1oz) butter
2 tablespoons Irish whiskey
300ml (10fl oz) double cream
2 tablespoons fresh chives, roughly chopped

Wipe the salmon steaks with a damp cloth and pat dry. Remove as many small bones as possible with tweezers, then smear one side with half the mustard. Press half the crushed peppercorns into the mustard to give a nice thin coating. Season with salt.

Heat a frying-pan until hot, then add the butter. As soon as it starts to foam, put in the salmon steaks, peppered-sides down. Reduce the heat to low and fry for about 5 minutes until brown.

While the fish is cooking, smear the raw side with the remaining mustard and crushed peppercorns. Season with salt. Turn the steaks over and cook the other side for another 5 minutes, until the fish is cooked through. Turn up the heat and splash in the whiskey. Continue to cook for a few seconds until it has almost disappeared, then take the pan off the heat. Remove the fish to 4 warm plates and keep warm.

Pour the cream into the pan, stirring in any bits from the fish frying that are sticking to the pan. If using a cast-iron frying-pan, you will find that the residual heat will probably thicken the sauce sufficiently so that only the briefest of cooking will be necessary, so watch carefully or your sauce may end up a gooey mess. Put back on the heat and carefully bring to a fast bubble. Cook for just a few seconds until the sauce starts to thicken, then taste and season with a little more salt if necessary. Stir in most of the chives. Pour over the salmon and sprinkle with the extra chives. Serve with new potatoes and a leaf salad.

The Giant's Causeway. The enormous scale can be seen in the photograph, near left, where the little girl is dwarfed by enormous pipe-shaped boulders known as the Organ

LIME-MARINATED GLENARM FRESH AND SMOKED SALMON
(serves 4 as a starter)

Trading under the brand name of 'Glenarm', Northern Salmon (see p.234) is based in the pretty coastal North Antrim village of Glenarm with its ancient castle. In the farmed salmon world, Glenarm fish is renowned for its quality derived from clean water, unusually strong tides and natural rearing using larger enclosures and lower stocking densities.

> 225g (8oz) Glenarm organic salmon fillet
> juice of 4 limes
> 8 thin slices smoked Glenarm
>   organic salmon
> 2 tablespoons tartare sauce (see p.222)
> assorted salad leaves to serve

With a very sharp knife, slice the fresh salmon across very thinly, then cut into fine dice. Put into a shallow dish and mix well with the lime juice. Leave to marinate for several hours, preferably overnight – stirring once or twice. During this time the fish is 'cooked' by the acid in the lime juice.

Later, or next day, drain the salmon well and mix with the tartare sauce. Divide between the slices of smoked salmon and roll up loosely.

Arrange a few salad leaves on 4 plates and 2 salmon rolls on each and serve with thin brown bread and butter.

GRILLED SCALLOPS WITH IRISH SLOKE
(serves 4 as a starter)

In the past, dredging for scallops and queenies in Strangford Lough seriously damaged the horse-mussel beds said to be left over from the Ice Age, so 'no take' zones were set up in the lough for conservation. Now, there are just a few small boats dredging on a modest scale for the shellfish in established 'take' areas only.

Scallops are landed in all the County Down fishing ports; either king or queen scallops can be used for this recipe although you will need twice the number of queenies.

> 8 dive-caught scallops
>   (ask your fishmonger for 4 deep shells)
> 25g (1oz) butter
> 200g (7oz) button mushrooms, sliced
> 1 teaspoon anchovy essence or Thai
>   fish sauce
> 100g (3½oz) prepared sloke
>   (laverbread, see p.157)
> 100ml (3½fl oz) home-made or good-
>   quality mayonnaise (see p.221)
> 1 tablespoon good-quality chilli
>   garlic sauce
> juice of 1 lime
> a little washed seaweed (if available),
>   to serve
> 4 lime wedges, to serve

Rinse the scallops and pat them dry, then slice the white flesh of each into 2 or 3 pieces, keeping the orange roes whole.

Lightly fry the mushrooms in the butter and divide amongst 4 scallop shells if you have them, or 4 individual gratin dishes. Top with the scallop pieces and put under a hot grill for 1-2 minutes. Remove from the grill and spread a small amount of anchovy essence on the scallops. Top with the sloke.

Mix the mayonnaise with the chilli sauce and the lime juice, blending well, then spread over the sloke. Put back under the grill and cook for a few minutes until the top is golden.

On 4 serving plates arrange some seaweed if available, or use a few salad leaves, then add the scallop shells or gratin dishes. Serve with the lime wedges.

An old Irish kitchen, *c. 1888*

ULSTER CHAMP WITH BUTTERED SEA TROUT
(serves 4)

Ulster champ is a traditional potato dish made by mashing potatoes with home-made butter and shredded leeks, or scallions (spring onions). Sometimes young nettle tops, parsley or young green peas replaced the leeks. A heavy wooden pestle or 'beetle' was used to mash large wooden tubs full of potatoes in the days when they were Ireland's staple food. For a supper dish, scrambled eggs, if available, would be served with the champ. Today, the dish has become fashionable all over Britain and in America.

Northern Ireland has excellent sea trout that provides good sport for anglers. Permits can be obtained from the National Trust to fish stretches of river under their protection and in Strangford Lough. The Danes are currently working on a pioneer project involving a sea trout hatchery. If this is successful, Strangford Lough will be restocked in the near future.

Sea trout are not as affected by agricultural pollution as salmon, because they can spawn in small becks. Although they go out to sea, they don't travel as far as the salmon, so are not as vulnerable to over-fishing by huge factory trawlers.

4 x 175g (6oz) pieces of wild,
  or responsibly farmed sea trout fillet,
  skinned and boned
50g (1¾oz) butter
sea salt and freshly ground black pepper
extra butter for serving

For the Ulster champ
  450g (1lb) floury potatoes
    (e.g. King Edward or Maris Piper),
    peeled and cut into large chunks
  8 scallions or spring onions, washed
    and trimmed
  75ml (2½fl oz) double cream
  50g (1¾oz) butter
  sea salt and freshly ground black pepper

To make the champ, cook the potatoes in salted water for about 20 minutes, or until tender. Drain and dry off over the heat.

Meanwhile, cut off 5cm (2in) of the green part of the spring onions, chop finely and set aside. Finely chop the remaining onions and put in a small pan with the cream.

When the potatoes are almost cooked, cook the sea trout. Season with salt and then place, skinned-side down, in a frying-pan of gently bubbling melted butter. Cook on a low heat for about 5 minutes, allowing the fish to colour just a little. Season with pepper, then turn the fish over. Remove from the heat and allow the trout to finish cooking in the pan while you finish the champ.

Mash the potatoes really well until light and smooth. Bring the double cream and spring onions to the boil, then pour onto the mash. Beat in the remaining butter and season to taste.

To serve, place a generous dollop of champ on 4 serving plates. Sprinkle over the reserved chopped spring onion green, then top with sea trout. Add a small knob of butter to each piece of fish to melt down onto the champ, or, to gild the lily, serve with hollandaise sauce (see p.220).

Young broad beans or fresh garden peas would be an ideal vegetable accompaniment.

IRISH CORACLE FISHING

Coracles, or 'curraghs' as they are known in Ireland, are believed to go back to Neolithic times. Sea-going curraghs, which are still used on the west coast, range from 5-8 metres (16-24 feet) long and are rowed by two, three or four oarsmen, while river curraghs are much smaller and occupied by just one person. The latter is often referred to as a Boyne Curragh, as it was on the River Boyne in the Republic of Ireland where they were last built and used for commercial fishing

There were two fishing techniques. The most popular used a long net, with one end tied to a tree, or post, on the river bank. As the curragh was paddled in a large circle to the far side of the river and back again, the net was let out from the stern. It was then pulled ashore. The other method used a short net between two curraghs as they drifted downstream. The minimal disturbance to the water with both methods undoubtedly contributed to the success of the catch.

The traditional river curragh was built using locally grown coppiced hazel rods forming a framework, which was then covered with a tanned cowhide, although in more recent times, canvas treated with bitumen became popular. The last person building curraghs in any number was Michael O'Brien who died in 1931 – he lived near Navan on the Boyne. Around this time, fish stocks in most Irish rivers were becoming badly depleted and in 1937, curragh fishing was banned for conservation. The boats virtually died out after this and it was only in the mid-1990s that there was a revival of interest (see p.240).

SEA URCHINS WITH MAYONNAISE
(serves 4 as a starter)

The sea urchin takes its name from an old English meaning of urchin – hedgehog. Poor people living on the coast of Ireland and remote parts of Scotland often used the flesh of sea urchins instead of butter. The main demand now for Irish sea urchins comes from France, where it is common to see basketfuls on display alongside varieties from the Mediterranean. Usually one urchin is cut open to show the star-shaped orange ovaries, which are the edible part. In fact, in many European languages the sea urchin's name means 'sea-egg'.

Sea urchins are common in all the rocky areas of the Northern Ireland coast and in Strangford Lough. They are delicious eaten raw with lemon juice, crusty bread and plenty of white wine, or the bright orange creamy inside can be scooped out and added to sauces to serve with fish. They can also be cooked in the same way as a boiled egg and mixed with cream, mayonnaise or lemon juice. However you serve them, they must be very fresh or they are not worth eating. If you live in London they can be obtained quite easily most of the year from a fish merchant at Billingsgate who specialises in unusual fish and shellfish.

> **12 very fresh sea urchins**
> **2 tablespoons home-made or good-quality mayonnaise (see p.221)**

Cook the sea urchins for about 4 minutes in boiling water and remove the prickles from the top of the shell. Remove the plug with the point of a knife or kitchen scissors. Cut out a large hole and scoop out the meat. Sieve it into a small basin and mix with the mayonnaise. Put back into the shells and serve chilled with fingers of warm buttered brown toast.

DERRYMACROW TROUT WITH COLCANNON
(serves 4)

By the tranquil waters of Upper Lough Erne in County Fermanagh lies one of the most important nature conservation sites owned by the National Trust – the Crom Estate. A romantic landscape of islands, wooded peninsulas and ruins on the lough shores, Crom is a popular destination for visitors seeking natural beauty and tranquillity.

The estate boasts 7 comfortable holiday cottages with complimentary permits for coarse fishing on Lough Erne (contact 0870 458 4422 for bookings); day tickets are available for all visitors and boats can be hired. Anglers can fish for pike in Green Lough and until recently a trout syndicate fished from Derrymacrow Lough. The small speckled brown trout, which are found in many Irish loughs and rivers, have a delicate sweet taste. Traditionally, they were simply dipped in oatmeal and fried, but try them enriched with cream and served with colcannon, a famous Irish dish. Made from 'praties' and kale with yellow cream and a melting 'lake of clover-flavoured butter', colcannon, originally associated with Hallowe'en, now appears on the smartest restaurant menus.

> **4 very fresh trout, cleaned and filleted, but unskinned**
> **sea salt and freshly ground black pepper**
> **75g (2¾ oz) butter**
> **175ml (6 fl oz) double cream**
> **2 tablespoons fresh dill, chopped**
>
> **For the colcannon**
> **450g (1lb) floury potatoes (e.g. King Edward or Maris Piper), peeled and cut into large chunks**
> **225g (½lb) Savoy or spring cabbage, shredded finely**
> **1 small leek, finely chopped**
> **150ml (¼pt) full-cream milk**
> **sea salt and freshly ground black pepper**
> **a pinch of grated nutmeg**
> **40g (1½oz) butter**

To make the colcannon, boil the potatoes until tender, drain and dry well over heat, then mash. Season to taste with salt, pepper and nutmeg.

Simmer the cabbage and leeks in the lightly salted milk until soft, then add to the potatoes. Beat well with the butter. Check the seasoning. Keep the colcannon warm while you cook the fish.

Season the trout well and fry flesh-side down in melted butter for a few minutes until golden brown. Turn over onto the skin-side and add the cream and dill. Simmer gently for 3-4 minutes, or until the trout is tender. Adjust seasoning. Spoon a generous dollop of colcannon on to 4 warm serving plates and top with the trout and cream.

Serve immediately with a leaf salad.

Left: Crom Castle in County Fermanagh
Right: Derrymacrow Trout with Colcannon

SAUCES, BUTTERS AND STOCKS

BÉCHAMEL SAUCE
(makes about 300ml [1½pt])

- 300ml (½pt) milk
- 1 bay leaf
- 1 blade mace
- 1 shallot, chopped
- 25g (1oz) butter
- 25g (1oz) plain flour
- sea salt and pepper

Put the milk, bay leaf, mace and shallot into a small saucepan and very gently bring to the boil. Remove from heat and allow to infuse for 20 minutes. Strain the milk into a jug. Melt the butter very slowly in a small saucepan. As soon as it is melted, take off the heat and stir in the flour. Stir to a smooth paste, return the pan to a medium heat and add the milk, a little at a time, making sure that all the milk is incorporated before adding any more. When all the milk is incorporated, turn the heat to very low and let the sauce cook for about 20 minutes. Season to taste with sea salt and freshly milled pepper.

Photograph of fishermen taken in 1880 by Frank Meadow Sutcliffe

VARIATIONS

Anchovy Sauce
Add 3-4 pounded anchovy fillets or a few drops of anchovy essence to the finished sauce. Serve with whiting, turbot, brill and sole.

Caper Sauce
Add 1 tablespoon capers and a little chopped parsley to the finished sauce. Serve with skate, halibut, turbot and whiting.

Crab Sauce
Add 125g (4½oz) of crab meat to the milk for the white sauce. Liquidise in a blender and add to the roux in the normal way. Serve with brill, turbot, sole and plaice.

English Lobster Sauce
Stir 2 tablespoons of chopped lobster meat, including the coral, into the white sauce. Season with a little anchovy essence and cayenne pepper. Serve with sole, turbot and brill.

Herb Sauce
Add 2 tablespoons of fresh herbs, finely chopped (dill, tarragon, fennel leaves, chervil or coriander) to the finished sauce. Serve with bass or salmon.

Mustard Sauce
Whisk 1-3 teaspoons of prepared English or French mustard into the sauce at the last minute with a generous squeeze of lemon juice before serving with fish rich in oil such as herrings and mackerel.

Parsley Sauce
Add 25g (1oz) of chopped fresh parsley to the basic white sauce. Season with lemon juice and add a little melted butter. Serve with any white or smoked fish, salmon or sea trout.

Prawn or Shrimp Sauce
Add 125g-175g (4½-6oz) of peeled and chopped prawns or shrimps, a squeeze of lemon juice and 2 tablespoons of prawn or shrimp stock if available. Serve with turbot, brill, sole and plaice.

Cheese Sauce
Add 50-75g (1¾-2¾oz) of grated Cheddar cheese and 25g (1oz) of grated Parmesan cheese with 1 teaspoon of English mustard to the prepared sauce and serve with any white fish or shellfish.

VELOUTÉ SAUCE
(makes about 300ml [½pt])

This is made in the same way as the Béchamel (previous page), but fish stock and sometimes wine is substituted for all or half the milk. Many of the seasonings used to flavour white sauce, such as mustard or shellfish, can also be used with a velouté sauce. Serve with any fish.

> 25g (1oz) butter
> 25g (1oz) flour
> 300 ml (½pt) fish stock (see p.222)
> 25g (1oz) mushroom stalks, chopped
> sea salt and black pepper

Melt the butter, stir in the flour and cook for a minute. Gradually add the heated stock and continue cooking to make a smooth sauce. Add the chopped mushrooms and cook until creamy. Season to taste.

HOLLANDAISE SAUCE
(makes about 300ml [½pt])

> 3 tablespoons white wine vinegar
> 2 tablespoons water
> 10 white peppercorns
> 3 large egg yolks
> 175g (6oz) unsalted butter, cut into
>   12 pieces
> sea salt and lemon juice to taste

Put the vinegar, water and peppercorns into a small pan and boil down to about 1 tablespoon (15ml) of liquid. Leave to cool.

Beat the egg yolks in a basin and add the reduced vinegar mixture. Pour the egg yolks and vinegar mixture into the top of a double saucepan or set the basin over a pan of barely simmering water on a low heat.

Cook slowly without letting the water boil, or the sauce will get too hot and curdle. Add the butter, knob by knob, stirring all the time. The sauce is finished when it coats the back of the spoon and looks thick. Season to taste with salt and lemon juice. Keep warm on a very low heat until ready to serve.

Variations

Orange Hollandaise (see p.185)

Cucumber Hollandaise
> basic hollandaise sauce
> 1 cucumber, sliced
> 1 teaspoon fresh fennel, chopped
> sea salt
> a few drops of Tabasco sauce

Put sliced cucumber in a colander, sprinkle with salt and leave to drain for at least an hour. Rinse if the slices are too salty, squeeze them dry in a clean tea towel, then chop them roughly. Add the chopped fennel to the cucumber, then add the Tabasco to the basic sauce and fold in the cucumber just before serving. Adjust the seasoning if necessary. Serve with poached salmon, sea trout, scallops or John Dory.

Hollandaise Sauce with Herbs
Add 1 teaspoon of French mustard and 1 tablespoon of mixed finely chopped chives, fennel, parsley and thyme in the finished sauce.

Quick Hollandaise Sauce
(makes about 425ml [¾pt])

You can make hollandaise very easily in a liquidiser, although it will be lighter in texture, especially if you include the white of one egg. If you want a richer sauce, omit the whole egg.

> 1 whole egg plus 2 egg yolks
> lemon juice
> 1 tablespoon water
> 225g (8oz) unsalted butter,
>   cut into pieces
> sea salt and cayenne pepper to taste

Put the egg, egg yolks, a squeeze of lemon juice and the water in a liquidiser. In a heavy-bottomed pan, gently heat the butter until melted and foaming. Blend the egg mixture, then with the motor running at medium speed, drizzle in a continuous stream the hot butter into the liquidiser through the small hole in the lid of the goblet. The sauce will thicken almost immediately.

Process for another 5 minutes, and pour back into the pan. Don't return to the heat but stir gently for 30-60 seconds – the heat from the pan will finish thickening the sauce. Season with salt, cayenne and more lemon juice if necessary. Keep warm over a pan of hot, but not boiling, water.

BEURRE BLANC
(makes about 350ml [12fl oz])

Although this classic French butter sauce has a reputation for being difficult to make, it is far easier than hollandaise and if it does separate, all you do is add a little more water and boil vigorously to emulsify the butter and water. Beurre blanc is used with freshly poached and grilled fillets of bass, turbot, brill, sole and scallops.

> 50g (1¾ oz) shallots or onions,
>   finely chopped
> 50ml (1¾ fl oz) white wine vinegar
> 100ml (3½fl oz) dry white wine
> 30ml (1 fl oz) double cream
> 225g (8oz) unsalted butter, diced and
>   straight from fridge
> lemon juice, sea salt and cayenne pepper
>   to taste

Place the shallots, vinegar and wine in a thick-bottomed pan. Bring to the boil quickly and reduce over a high heat with just over 2 tablespoons (30ml/1fl oz) remains. Add the cream and boil for 1 minute to reduce a little, then remove from the heat. Whisk in the chilled butter a piece at a time, keeping the sauce just warm enough to absorb the butter. The resulting sauce should be smooth and shiny, but not oily. Season with lemon juice, salt and cayenne and keep warm until needed. Either transfer to a basin over a pan of hot, but not boiling, water, or store in a thermos flask.

Serve 2-3 tablespoons per person.

Variations

Lobster, Crab, Shrimp or Prawn Butter Sauce
Add 175g (6oz) diced cooked lobster or crab meat, flat fish, peeled shrimps or prawns to the above sauce. Serve with fish mousse or poached and baked fish.

Ginger Butter Sauce
Add 3.5cm (1½in) piece of fresh ginger peeled and finely diced to the wine, shallot and vinegar mixture. Continue as before. Excellent with poached bass and pan-fried or grilled scallops.

Orange Butter Sauce
Add the finely grated rind of 1 or 2 unwaxed/organic oranges to the finished sauce. Serve with poached sole, turbot, John Dory or scallops.

MAYONNAISE
(makes 300ml [½pt])

The quality of your mayonnaise depends totally on the quality of the egg yolks and oil. I think extra virgin olive oil is too strong in flavour, and that a good-quality light olive oil mixed with a best-quality flavourless oil is best. Your ingredients and utensils should be at room temperature. Use a bowl and whisk for the lightest mayonnaise, or beat with a wooden spoon for a more solid result. Salt doesn't dissolve in oil, so dissolve it in lemon juice.

> **2 large free-range, preferably organic, egg yolks**
> **a pinch of sea salt**
> **1 teaspoon lemon juice**
> **100ml (3½fl oz) sunflower, groundnut, grapeseed or other flavourless oil**
> **200ml (7 fl oz) light olive oil**
> **sea salt, freshly ground black pepper and lemon juice to taste**

Dissolve the salt in the lemon juice, then put the egg yolks into a medium-sized glass or china bowl. Add the lemon juice and stir briefly with a whisk or spoon. Drip the oil onto the egg yolks, a drop at a time, whisking or beating at the same time, making sure that each is absorbed before adding the rest. As the mixture begins to thicken, speed up to a trickle, but don't stop beating or whisking and don't rush the process or it will suddenly curdle, because the egg yolks can only absorb the oil at a certain pace.

To rescue the mixture if it does curdle, start again with a new egg yolk or 1-2 tablespoons of boiling water in a clean bowl, then very gradually whisk in the curdled mayonnaise, starting a drop at a time.

Once all the oil is incorporated and the mixture is thick enough to wobble, give it another really good beating or whisking. Season to taste with extra salt, a little pepper and more lemon juice if necessary.

The mayonnaise will keep for at least a week in the fridge depending on the freshness of the eggs. If you want a thinner mayonnaise, let it down with a little cream, milk, fromage frais, soured cream or hot water.

Variations

Cucumber and Mint Mayonnaise

> **1 cucumber**
> **about 20 fresh mint leaves**
> **300 ml (½ pt) mayonnaise**
> **150ml (5 fl oz) fromage frais**
> **sea salt, black pepper and lemon juice to taste**

Cut the cucumber in half lengthways, then peel it and scoop out all the seeds with a teaspoon. Grate coarsely into a colander, salt lightly and leave to drain for at least 20 minutes.

Chop the mint, mix the mayonnaise and fromage frais together. Stir in the mint.

Squeeze the cucumber firmly to remove as much liquid as possible, then fold it into the mayonnaise. Season to taste with salt, pepper and lemon juice.

Serve with cold poached fish such as salmon, sea trout, or bass.

Garlic Mayonnaise (see p.30)

Green Mayonnaise (see p.51)
Add 2-3 tablespoons of your chosen chopped fresh herb (dill, tarragon or coriander) to the finished mayonnaise.

Horseradish and Anchovy Mayonnaise

> **1 rounded tablespoon hot horseradish cream**
> **1 x 50g (1¾oz) tin anchovy fillets in olive oil**
> **2 heaped tablespoons capers, drained**
> **3 tablespoons lemon juice**
> **300ml (½pt) mayonnaise**
> **freshly ground black pepper**

Put all the ingredients in a food processor. Blend for about 30 seconds until well combined, but still with texture. Season with pepper to taste.

Serve with grilled meaty white fish such as Dover sole, turbot or halibut.

Saffron Mayonnaise

> **300ml (½pt) mayonnaise**
> **2 garlic cloves, roughly chopped**
> **½ teaspoon cayenne pepper**
> **a large pinch of saffron threads infused in 1 tablespoon hot water**

Follow the instructions for the main recipe for mayonnaise, above, adding garlic that has been pounded with the salt. Stir the cayenne and dissolved saffron into the finished sauce. Particularly good with crab, lobster and other shellfish.

CRAGSIDE TARTARE SAUCE

A lovely old-fashioned sauce to serve with scampi, fried fish or fish cakes. In the restaurant at Cragside, Northumberland (see p.121), they serve it with their home-made salmon cakes.

- 2 large free-range, preferably organic, egg yolks
- 2 level teaspoons Dijon mustard
- 1 tablespoon white wine vinegar
- 200 ml (7 fl oz) vegetable oil
- 50ml (2 fl oz) mild olive oil
- 2 level tablespoons fresh parsley, chopped
- 1 level tablespoon capers, rinsed and chopped if large
- 2 gherkins or 4 cornichons, rinsed and chopped
- sea salt and freshly ground black pepper

Put the egg yolks into a bowl and stir in the mustard with a whisk. Add ½ teaspoon salt dissolved in the vinegar, then slowly and carefully beat in the oils, drop by drop, starting with the vegetable oil. When all the oil has been added, stir in the parsley, capers and gherkins. Check the seasoning.

Variation

Crème fraîche Tartare

- 1 free-range egg yolk
- 1 teaspoon Dijon mustard
- sea salt
- a little Tabasco
- 6-8 heaped dessertspoons crème fraîche
- 2 teaspoons tarragon vinegar
- 1 teaspoon fresh tarragon, chopped
- 1 heaped tablespoon fresh flat-leaf parsley
- 1 teaspoon fresh chives, chopped
- 1 tablespoon rinsed baby capers, chopped
- 1 tablespoon cornichons (small gherkins), chopped

Beat the egg yolk with the mustard, salt and a few dashes of Tabasco until emulsified. Add the crème fraîche a dessertspoonful at a time, and 1 teaspoon of the tarragon vinegar, whisking with a small balloon whisk until thick but pourable. Stir in the other ingredients with the second teaspoon of vinegar. Taste and adjust the seasoning.

FISH STOCK
(makes about 1.2 litres [2 pts])

Ask your fishmonger for bones from sole, brill, turbot, whiting or plaice which make the best-flavoured stock. The secret is not to cook the fish stock for too long, or the unpleasant flavours will be released. It can be prepared in advance and kept in the fridge for up to 1 week or several weeks in the freezer. Use as the base for soups and sauces.

- 1 kg (2¼lb) fish bones
- 1 small onion, finely chopped
- 50g (1¾oz) butter
- 8 tablesppons dry white wine
- 2 litres (3½pts) cold water
- 1 bouquet garni

Remove any specks of blood or skin from the fish bones and wash well. Roughly snip into pieces with scissors and put on one side. Melt the butter in a large pan and sweat the onion for 10-15 minutes. Add the white wine and increase the heat. Reduce the liquid by half, then add the fish bones. Cover with the water, then bring very slowly to the boil, skimming the surface frequently. After 5 minutes cooking time add the bouquet garni, then simmer, uncovered, for no more than 25 minutes.

Strain through a muslin-lined sieve into a bowl. Leave to cool, then use as required.

COURT BOUILLON

This is used instead of water for poaching fish and shellfish. It can be prepared in advance and kept for 2-3 days in the fridge, or stored in the freezer for several weeks.

- 2 medium carrots
- white part of 1 leek
- ½ celery stick
- ½ small fennel bulb
- 4 shallots, peeled and sliced
- 4 button onions, peeled and sliced
- 25g (1oz) butter
- 2 tablespoons white wine vinegar
- 425ml (15fl oz) dry white wine
- 1 litre (1¾pts) cold water
- 25g (1oz) sea salt
- 1 bouquet garni
- 1 garlic clove, unpeeled
- freshly ground black pepper

Wash the vegetables and slice thinly. Melt the butter in a pan and add the vegetables. Stir until buttery, then cover with the lid and sweat for 10 minutes. Add the vinegar, wine and water, then the salt, garlic and bouquet garni. Bring very slowly to the boil, then lower the heat and simmer gently for 20 minutes. At the last minute, add plenty of pepper, then leave to cool before using, to bring out all the flavour.

FLAVOURED BUTTERS

These butters are used as toppings for grilled fish, stuffings for whole fish, or for flavouring sauces and soups.

To make them, beat softened butter with the flavouring ingredients or blend together in a food processor. Turn out on to a sheet of greaseproof paper, clingfilm or foil, then roll up into a sausage shape and chill. Slice into rounds as required. Flavoured butters also freeze well. Defrost for 1-2 hours before using.

Parsley or Maître d'Hôtel Butter

100g (3½oz) butter, softened
2 rounded tablespoons fresh parsley, chopped
juice of 1 lemon
sea salt and freshly ground black pepper to taste

Tarragon Butter

100g (3½oz) butter, softened
1 level tablespoon fresh tarragon, chopped
juice of ½ lemon
sea salt and freshly ground black pepper to taste

Garlic Butter

100g (3½oz) butter, softened
2 large garlic cloves, crushed
1 tablespoon fresh parsley, chopped
1 teaspoon lemon juice
sea salt to taste

Mustard Butter

Excellent with herrings, sardines, pilchards or mackerel.

100g (3½oz) butter, softened
1 tablespoon French mustard
juice of ½ a lemon
sea salt and freshly ground black pepper to taste

Lime, Lemon or Orange Butter

Good with any white fish, salmon, trout and shellfish.

100g (3½oz) butter, softened
4 teaspoons lime, lemon or orange juice
4 good teaspoons appropriate grated rind
freshly ground black pepper to taste

Shrimp or Prawn Butter

Excellent with any grilled white fish or as a stuffing for white fish.

100g (3½oz) butter, softened
100g (3½oz) unshelled shrimps or prawns
1 teaspoon lemon juice
pinch of cayenne pepper

After pounding together, push the butter through a sieve to remove pieces of shell.

Smoked Salmon Butter

This makes a super pâté as well as a delicious topping for white fish.

100g (3½oz) butter, softened
100g (3½oz) smoked salmon trimmings
1 teaspoon lemon juice
pinch of cayenne pepper

Anchovy Butter

This is delicious spread on hot toast or made into sandwiches, as well as being excellent on grilled white fish or as a flavouring for fish pies.

100g (3½oz) butter, softened
6-8 salted anchovy fillets or 2 salted pilchard fillets, drained and soaked in milk to remove excess salt

Spiced Butter

100g (3½oz) butter
3 small spring onions, white parts only, finely chopped
2 plump garlic cloves, peeled and chopped
1 tablespoon cumin seed
1 teaspoon coriander seed
½ teaspoon chilli powder
a small handful of chopped parsley
sea salt

Toast the cumin and coriander seeds in a dry pan over a low heat until they smell fragrant. Add the chilli powder and warm for a few seconds, then grind them all to a fine powder. Stir all ingredients into the butter.

SUPPLIERS

**Information current at time of going to press.
This list represents a list of suppliers known
to me: it is by no means comprehensive.**

THE SOUTH WEST

BRIDFISH SMOKERY

**Unit 1, The Old Laundry Trading Estate,
Sea Road North, Bridport, Dorset DT6 3BD
(01308 456306)
www.bridfishsmokery.com**

Patrick Gubb sells hot- and cold-smoked
farmed Scottish salmon and mackerel as well
as local hot-smoked silver eels, trout, prawns,
haddock and cod's roe. Will smoke customers'
own fish for them. All the preparation, curing
and smoking, using no dyes or additives, is
done behind the shop's counter.

BRITANNIA SHELLFISH LTD.

**The Viviers, Beesands, Nr Kingsbridge,
Devon TQ7 2EH
(01548 581186)**

Nick and Anita Hutchins run this wholesale
and retail business selling fish and shellfish.
They have storage tanks that can keep crabs
and lobsters alive for weeks.

BROCKHILL FISH FARM

**Cecily Cottage, Cecily Lane, Brockhill,
Wareham, Dorset BH20 7NH
(01929 471552)**

Suppliers of fresh and smoked rainbow trout
and trout products from their farm on the
River Piddle, as well as fresh watercress.

BROWN & FORREST

**The Smokery, Bowdens Farm, Hambridge,
Nr Curry Rivel, Somerset TA10 0DR
(01458 250875)
www.smokedeel.co.uk**

A smokery/restaurant on the Somerset Levels;
the watery setting is appropriate to their most
famous product, hot-smoked eels. Michael
Brown collects them from the upper reaches
of the Rivers Avon, Itchen, Stour and Test,
where they are caught on rocks straddled
across the water. He brine-cures the eels for
2-3 hours, then hot-smokes over beechwood.
In the restaurant, the eel comes with rye
bread, creamy horseradish sauce from
Tracklements (p.227)and a beetroot salad.
A great example of a place where good produce
speaks for itself – served simply in comfortable
surroundings. Mail order available.

CAMEL VALLEY VINEYARD

**Little Denby Farm, Nanstallon, Bodmin,
Cornwall PL30 5LG
(01208 77959)
www.camelvalley.com**

Produces excellent white and award-winning
sparkling wines, although the red is a little
thin.

CATCH OF THE DAY

**54 Fore Street, Kingsbridge, Devon TQ7 1NY
(01548 852006)**

Best known for their Salcombe Smokies, hot-
smoked mackerel with a firmer than usual
texture and a powerful punch of salt, they
also smoke farmed Scottish salmon, trout,
cod's roe, haddock and halibut. A good range
of wet fish from Looe and Plymouth, Pacific
oysters and mussels farmed in the nearby
River Avon, dressed Salcombe crab and –
in season – samphire.

**Man choosing turbot at Billingsgate Market in the
City of London, photograph *c.* 1930**

CORNISH SMOKED FISH CO. LTD.
**Charlestown, St Austell, Cornwall PL25 3NY
(01726 72356)**
www.cornishsmokedfish.com
As well as smoked eel and mackerel, their range includes hot- and cold-smoked trout, Scottish salmon and gravadlax, mussels, prawns, haddock and cod's roe plus an unusual gravad mackerel and a sublime cold-smoked mackerel, thinly sliced and delicious eaten cold as an hors d'oeuvre with creamed horseradish. Mail order available.

COTEHELE MILL
**Cotehele, St Dominick, nr Saltash, Cornwall PL12 6TA
(01579 351346)**
Tucked away in dense woodland, this manorial water mill has been restored by the National Trust and is once again grinding corn for the local community. Bags of the stone-ground wholemeal flour can be purchased at Cotehele (p.237) and at local shops.

THE DARTMOUTH SMOKEHOUSE
**Nelson Road, Dartmouth, Devon TQ6 OBR
(01803 833123)**
www.smokehouse.uk.com
Philip Watts runs his family business employing traditional methods to produce a range of cured and smoked fish. I can particularly recommend the kiln-roasted salmon – the fish is marinated in sea salt, cane sugar, dill and black pepper, before being slowly smoked in the kiln over hickory and oak chips, gently cooked and basted with honey. Mail order available.

Philip, a trained chef, suggests mixing Dartmouth Smokehouse Honey and Mustard Dill sauce with a little harissa paste and mayonnaise as an ideal accompaniment for all smoked fish.

DENHAY FARMS LTD
**Broadoak, Bridport, Dorset DT6 5NP
(01308 458963)**
www.denhay.co.uk
Run by George and Amanda Streatfeild, this group of farms uses a traditional West Country cycle; grass is grown for the cows to produce milk for cheese, the whey is fed to the pigs, which produce the muck to fertilise the grass to feed the cows... .The air-dried hams are made by curing the pork legs in a brine flavoured with Dorset apple juice, honey and local herbs, then lightly smoking them over oak chippings before air drying for up to a year. The result is a cross between an Italian Parma and a German Westphalian. Also produce dry-cured bacon, sausages and gammon.

FALMOUTH BAY OYSTERS LTD.
**The Docks, Falmouth, Cornwall TR11 4NR
(01326 316600)**
www.falmouthoysters.co.uk
Suppliers of the finest Cornish Native and Pacific oysters to the House of Commons dining rooms. Mail order available including champagne and oyster gift boxes.

FISHWORKS
**10 Church Street, Christchurch, Dorset BH23 IBW
(01202 487000)**
www.fishworks.co.uk
A fishmongers/restaurant set up by Mitchell Tonks who has a passion for fish. Produce delivered daily from Newlyn and Brixham, with langoustines and scallops from Scotland. Staff will advise on preparation and cooking. Branches in Bristol, Bath and Chiswick in London.

FOWEY FISH
**37 Fore St, Fowey, Cornwall PL23 1AH
(01726 832422)**
www.fowey.com
A shop selling a good range of local Cornish fish, fresh and smoked, from day boats working out of Fowey and Looe. Mail order available. Also a stall every Sunday in a covered market just outside St Austell.

FOWEY SEA FARMS
**The Old Bath House, Fowey Docks, Fowey, Cornwall PL23 1DH
(01726 832333)**
Specialists in local rope-grown mussels and fresh live cockles, clams, razor clams and oysters.

FRANK GREENSLADE
**16 New Quay Road, Poole, Dorset BH15 4AF
(01202 672199)**
Sells mostly locally caught fish in and around the Bay of Bournemouth, including live brown crabs and lobsters kept in tanks, winkles from September to May, whelks all year round and dive-caught scallops.

HEAD MILL TROUT FARM LTD.
**Head Mill, Umberleigh, North Devon EX37 9HA
(01769 580862)**
Situated on the Kings Nympton estate owned by the Wildfowl Trust, at an old mill on the River Mole. Sells trout up to 2.25-2.7kg (5 or 6lb) and has its own smokehouse and farmshop. Smaller trout are hot-smoked while the larger fish are cold-smoked over oak chips in the traditional way.

MARTIN'S SEAFRESH
St Columb Business Centre, St Columb, Cornwall TR9 6BU
www.martins-seafresh.co.uk
Run a company called Fish Direct (0800 027 2066), who deliver fish of good quality by post.

OAKFORD SHELLFISH LTD.
**Mountview Farm, Shillingstone, Blandford, Dorset DT11 0QT
(01258 861173)**
Sells shellfish farmed on privately owned beds in Poole Harbour and harvested with their own boat. Oysters, clams and mussels are purified, graded and packed at Shillingstone.

OYSTER FARM SEAFOOD RESTAURANT (formerly ABBOTSBURY OYSTERS)
**Ferry Bridge, Weymouth, Dorset, DT4 9YU
(01305 788867)**
Pacific and a few Native oysters are grown in the Fleet Lagoon, a natural estuary that runs from the island of Portland to Abbotsbury village. The site used to be managed as a private nature reserve, but has now been designated a Special Area of Conservation and is being used as a case study to provide guidelines on water quality of lagoons. Here, the water is clean and plankton-rich, ideal for oysters. Take the shellfish away or enjoy them ready-opened with crusty bread and a glass of wine. Prices are kept very low as the policy is 'to encourage everyone to try'.

THE OYSTER SHACK
**Milburn Orchard Farm, Stakes Hill, Bigbury, Kingsbridge, Devon TQ7 4BE
(01548 810876)**
www.oystershack.com
Peter Lewis farmed oysters and mussels for 17 years before selling up. He has recently sold up again to new owners Chris Yandell and Simon Warner who now run this informal bistro specialising in locally caught fish and seafood including dive-caught scallops, crabs and lobsters from Salcombe and 12 different dishes of farmed oysters. Also a small shop selling seafood, including smoked fish from Dartmouth Smokehouse and local mussels and oysters.

PENGELLYS FISH SHOP
2 The Arcade, Fore Street, Liskeard,
Cornwall PL14 3JA
(01579 340777)
PENGELLY'S
The Fish Market, The Quay, East Looe,
Cornwall, PL13 1DX
(01503 262246)
My local fish shop which is family owned and
run. All the fish and shellfish are locally caught
by small boats working out of Looe. Staff are
always very helpful and friendly, supplying
recipes, preparing the fish and generally
educating their customers.

THE PILCHARD WORKS
Tolcarne, Newlyn, Penzance,
Cornwall TR18 5QH
(01736 332112)
www.pilchardworks.co.uk
An award-winning working museum telling
the story of the Cornish pilchard that provided
'money, meat and light, all in one night' –
families would sell them, eat them and use the
oil in their lamps. Visitors will see traditional
salt fish processing in full swing. You can talk
to the staff, taste the products and buy the
salted fish vacuum-packed or in jars with
brine, or olive oil. Canned Cornish pilchard
fillets also recently available, and sometimes
salt cod.

Nick Howell also runs a specialist delivery
service, Cornish Fish Direct, with fish from
small, inshore boats using environmentally
friendly techniques. Ring for advice on the
seasonal catch.

PLATTERS SEAFOOD
RESTAURANT
12 Southside Street, The Barbican,
Plymouth, Devon PL1 2LS
(01752 227262)
Situated right on the Barbican Fish Quay
this informal seafood restaurant serves the
freshest fish, carried through the restaurant
in large plastic boxes while you dine. It's a fun
place to eat – noisy and full of fishermen –
saying a lot for the freshness of the fish. Their
take-away fish-and-chip shop is next door.

QUAYSIDE FISH CENTRE
The Harbourside, Porthleven,
Cornwall TR13 9JU
(01326 562008)
www.quaysidefish.co.uk
Former fisherman, John Strike, has been
selling fish here for 25 years and his work has
paid off – he is holder of 'Britain's Best
Fishmonger' award from Seafish Industries.
He only buys Cornish fish from day or inshore
boats landing at Porthleven and Newlyn –
no netted fish, only line caught. A large range
of fish including octopus and cuttlefish, John
Dory, pilchards, wolf fish and crawfish. John
also owns a smokehouse producing a large
range of smoked locally caught fish – the
best prawns I've ever tasted.

RIVER EXE SHELLFISH FARMS
Oak Farm, Kenton, Exeter, Devon EX6 8EZ
(01626 890133)
Sells Pacific oysters farmed in the Exe Estuary
and will deliver anywhere in mainland Britain
within 24 hours. In season, sometimes have
freshly picked samphire.

RIVERSIDE RESTAURANT
West Bay, Bridport, Dorset DT6 4EZ
(01308 422011)
Friendly informal restaurant specialising
in local seafood cooked skilfully and
imaginatively, but also offering traditional
British dishes such as fish and chips and
grilled Dover sole.

SEVERN AND WYE SMOKERY
Chaxhill, Westbury-on-Severn,
Gloucestershire, GL14 1QW
(01452 760190)
www.severnandwye.co.uk
Horace Cook has been supplying Lough Neagh
in Northern Ireland with eel fry from the River
Severn in Gloucestershire for the past 20 years.
His son Richard now runs the Severn and Wye
Smokery employing 40 people. A substantial
part of his business involves smoking eels –
about 18 tonnes a year – many of them
shipped back as mature silver eels from Lough
Neagh. At the smokery they are gutted and
smoked for 7 hours. Finally, the skins are
peeled off. The resulting flesh is buttery and
rich. The company also smokes fresh Glenarm
salmon which is dry-cured and smoked over
oak chips.

MATTHEW STEVENS & SON
Back Road East, St Ives, Cornwall TR26 INW
(01736 799392)
www.mstevensandson.co.uk
A fishmonger with a good reputation locally
for supplying very fresh fish landed at St.Ives
and Newlyn. Mail order available.

TRACKLEMENTS
The Dairy Farm, Pinkney Park, Sherston,
Malmesbury, Wiltshire SN16 ONX
(01666 840851)
www.tracklements.co.uk
Family-run business named after a
Lincolnshire word for meat accompaniments.
William Tullberg started Tracklements 30
years ago with a 17th-century recipe for
mustard by John Evelyn. With his son Guy's
help, the range of mustards has increased,
along with jellies, sauces and condiments,
including their famous onion marmalade.
To accompany fish, try their tartare,
horseradish, horseradish and dill, and dill
and mustard sauces which are available at
good supermarkets and food shops.

WING OF ST MAWES
4 Warren Road, Indian Queens, St Columb,
Cornwall TR9 6TL
(01726 861666)
www.cornish-seafood.co.uk
A fishmonger with a reputation for supporting
sustainable fishing. Supplies fresh Cornish
fish from day boats, including line-caught
mackerel, spider crabs, red gurnard and
pollack, as well as the more usual varieties.
Mail order available.

ADNAMS BREWERY Plc
**Sole Bay Brewery, Southwold,
Suffolk, IP18 6JW,
(01502 727200)
www.adnams.co.uk**
East Anglia, with its dry climate and soil, has a tradition of growing top-quality malting barley and Suffolk is particularly strong on beer. Adnams brewery puffs away in the centre of Southwold producing excellent bitter, which some say has the tang of the sea. They also run a high-quality wine business, have a wine shop in the town and another shop which has kitchenware alongside the range of drinks.

BUTLEY ORFORD OYSTERAGE
**Market Hill, Orford, Woodbridge,
Suffolk IP12 2LH
(01394 450277)
www.butleyorfordoysterage.co.uk**
The Oysterage Restaurant serves very fresh and simply prepared fish, own-smoked fish and oysters, with daily specialities chalked up on a blackboard. Tucked behind the restaurant is their shop selling fresh and own-smoked fish – bloaters, kippers, farmed Scottish or wild Irish salmon, trout, sprats, mackerel, cod's roe and fat eels caught in the local dikes and ditches, all smoked over oak logs.

CLEY SMOKEHOUSE
**High Street, Cley-next-the-Sea, Holt,
Norfolk NR25 7RF
(01263 740282)
www.cleysmokehouse.com**
Undyed oak-smoked kippers and bloaters available, as well as River Tay smoked wild salmon, smoked Icelandic cod's roe, pots of delicious home-made taramasalata and lightly spiced crab pâté. Also on sale are potted shrimps made from brown shrimps caught in The Wash, sweet pickled herring, a fresh herring roe pâté and bags of frozen whitebait, caught in nets by a local fisherman off Blakeney Point.

COLCHESTER OYSTER FISHERY LTD.
**Pyefleet Quay, East Mersea, Colchester,
Essex CO5 8UN
(01206 384141)
www.colchesteroysterfishery.com**
Christopher Kerrison runs the only company farming Native oysters in Colchester. The oyster beds were decimated by the disease *Bonamia* in 1982, but are slowly recovering. The native Colchesters are wild stock dredged by fishermen from disease-free waters and held in the Pyefleet Channel. After purification, they are graded from 1-3, packed in tubs with seaweed and distributed. Pacific oysters from Ireland also available. The staff are happy to open them for you.

J.T. COLE
**Newcombe Road, Lowestoft,
Suffolk NR32 1XA
(01502 574446)**
An old-fashioned smokehouse started by the present owner's great-grandfather. Terry Jones cold-smokes red herrings, bloaters and kippers over oak dust and haddock, cod and whiting over white shavings.

COLMAN'S MUSTARD SHOP
**Bridewell Alley, Norwich, Norfolk NR2 1NQ
(01603 627889)
www.mustardshop.com**
Visit this splendid Victorian-style emporium dedicated to mustard to see how the Norwich firm of Colman's has developed since 1914. Their greatest mustard is the dry powder known as Genuine Double Superfine, which you mix with water, but Colman's also manufacture prepared English mustards of various strengths and flavours, plus versions of German, American and French mustards.

THE COMPANY SHED
**129 Coast Road, West Mersea, Colchester,
Essex CO5 8PA
(01206 382700)**
A fish shop and shellfish bar selling a good range of wonderfully fresh locally caught fish. Owners, Richard and Heather Haward, buy direct from boats that land in Wivenhoe, Brightlingsea, Harwich and Mersea. Cockles from Leigh are bought in and there are herrings, eels from the Fens and locally smoked kippers, bloaters and buckling. Oysters farmed by Richard are also available as well as locally caught crabs and lobsters. In the freezer Heather keeps fish stock from trimmings, crab soup, fish stew packs and fishcakes.

CRONE'S CIDER
**Fairview, Fersfield Road, Kenninghall,
Norfolk NR16 2DP
(01379 687687)
www.crones.co.uk**
Robert Crone makes both apple juice and cider in the traditional way, using apples grown to Soil Association standards. Norfolk cider is different from its West Country cousin in that it is made predominantly from a mixture of dessert fruit and cooking apples rather than cider apples, and tends to have a lower alcoholic content. Robert produces 3 types of cider – Original Strong, a milder User-Friendly, and Special Reserve with 8 per cent alcohol content. Sales preferred by appointment.

RICHARD & JULIE DAVIES
**7 Garden Street, Cromer, Norfolk NR27 9HN
(01263 512727)**
A fish shop in the town centre specialising in Cromer crabs, which are cooked daily and sold both whole and dressed. (The staff are happy to give you a bag of ice to keep them chilled on the way home.) Lobsters also available, as well as King's Lynn shrimps, local herrings, samphire, smoked fish from Cley and a selection of fresh fish, usually bought from Lowestoft.

DONALDSONS
**Hextable Road, King's Lynn,
Norfolk PE30 2AE
(01553 772241)**
A fish shop in King's Lynn selling locally caught brown shrimps, Cromer crabs, lobsters and samphire as well as other excellent locally caught fish.

ALFRED ENDERBY LTD.
**Fish Dock Road, Grimsby Fish Docks,
Grimsby, Lincolnshire DN31 3NE
(01472 342984)
www.alfredenderby.co.uk**
One of the few independent family fish-smoking firms left in England, with a smokehouse that is about 100 years old (see p.70). Deals direct with the Faroe Islands for large line-caught haddock, and specific farms in the Shetland Islands for top-quality salmon.

THE FISH SHED
**Brancaster Staithe, Nr King's Lynn,
Norfolk PE31 8YB
(01485 210532)**
Run by Margaret and Stephen Bocking and selling fresh local fish and shellfish. They smoke herrings and ham, pot crabs and shrimps and make good fishcakes.

FLORA'S TEA ROOMS
Dunwich Beach, Saxmundham,
Suffolk IP17 3DR
(01728 648433)
A wooden shack on the beach renowned for its locally caught fish and chips, salads and home-made cakes.

GURNEY'S SEAFOODS LTD.
The Market Place, Burnham Market,
King's Lynn, Norfolk PE31 8HF
(01328 738967)
During the season from May to September, you will find Cromer crabs, lobsters, local brown shrimps, mussels, fresh fish including grey mullet, Dover soles, local herrings and bunches of freshly picked samphire in this friendly fish shop. They have another small shop in Brancaster marked by a 2-foot luminous prawn!

JOHN'S FISH SHOP
5 East Street, Southwold, Suffolk IP18 6EH
(01502 724253)
www.johns-fish-shop.co.uk
The white-tiled shop, run by John Huggins, has a well-earned reputation for its range of wet fish and a serious selection of herrings, both fresh and cured. In autumn, when the local long-shore herrings are in season, John has fish caught 4-5 miles offshore in drift nets. He also sells fresh herring roe, the soft male roe as well as the hard and darker roe from the female.

THE LIGHTHOUSE
77 High Street, Aldeburgh, Suffolk IP15 5AN
(01728 453377)
A classic neighbourhood restaurant open every day of the week and not afraid to serve well-cooked, straightforward food, like their excellent local fish and chips. Owners Sara Fox and Peter Hill believe in using good local ingredients and cooking them simply.

MAYNARD HOUSE ORCHARDS
Bradfield St Clare, Bury St Edmunds,
Suffolk IP30 0DX
(01284 386264)
Started juicing their own apples several seasons ago, most of them between August and Christmas. Their unfiltered juices include a blend of Cox and Bramley, a refreshing Bramley, well-rounded Cox, flowery Discovery, Russet and James Grieve.

MORSTON HALL HOTEL
Morston, Holt, Norfolk, NR25 7AA
(01263 741041)
www.morstonhall.com
Take a boat trip from Morston Quay to see the seals, then pop into this Michelin-starred, 17th– century farmhouse-turned-hotel on the edge of Morston Marshes for a leisurely dinner. The owners Galton and Tracy Blakiston have made it into one of Britain's leading country hotels. Galton spent his childhood summers on nearby Blakeney Spit collecting mussels and shrimping. Now he turns such ingredients – Blakeney lobsters, Cromer crabs and Morston mussels – into delicious modern British dishes with the menu changing daily.

RAGLIN SMOKEHOUSE
The Old Smokehouse, Raglin Street,
Lowestoft, Suffolk NR32 2JP
(01502 581929)
An old-fashioned smokehouse hidden down an alleyway in the town. Here you can buy meaty kippers and red herrings direct from the smokeroom.

REGATTA
171-173 High Street, Aldeburgh,
Suffolk IP15 5AN
(01728 452011)
A colourful, friendly restaurant specialising in local seafood dishes. In season, sprats straight off the beach are fried in garlic butter and parsley – simply fresh and delicious.

RICHARDSONS SMOKEHOUSE
Bakers Lane, Orford, Suffolk IP12 2LH
(01394 450103)
A traditional smokehouse producing bloaters, mackerel, sardines, trout, haddock, prawns and Alaskan salmon. Steve Richardson also smokes a variety of meat, game, cheese and garlic and makes fishcakes from his own smoked salmon.

RIVER FARM SMOKERY
Junction Wilbraham Road & A1303,
Bottisham, Cambridgeshire CB5 9BU
(01223 812577)
Smokery with a shop selling fresh fish from Lowestoft as well as smoked. Sometimes smoked pike is available as well as smoked eel, salmon, halibut and kippers.

JAMES WHITE DRINKS LTD.
White's Fruit Farm, Helmingham Road,
Ashbocking, Suffolk IP6 9JS
(01473 890111)
www.jameswhite.co.uk
Produces intensely flavoured apple juices made from fresh English fruit, each apple type giving a distinctive flavour: Bramley is dry and crisp; Cox is far fuller with a deep fruity bouquet; and Russet is superbly rich and sweet. English pear and English grape juices also produced, as well as cider vinegar and a range of ciders. Mail order available as well as the farm shop.

BAY FISHERIES
Robin Hood's Bay, North Yorkshire YO22 4SG
(01947 880665)
An excellent fishmongers owned by local
fisherman, John Brown, who also sells from a
van in neighbouring villages. The shop is only
open for 1 hour on Wednesday mornings in
the winter, but 7 days a week at Easter and
during the summer for holidaymakers.

BIG MUSSEL
15 The Side, Newcastle, Tyne & Wear NE1 3JE
(01912 321057)
www.bigmussel.co.uk
Attractive casual restaurant on the busy rake
to the Quayside, specialising in fresh local fish
and seafood, particularly mussels, which are
served in fourteen different ways. Open
lunchtime and evenings.

BRYAN'S
6 Weetwood Lane, Headingley,
Leeds LS16 5LT
(0113 278 5679)
A celebrated place to eat fish-and-chips in
Headingley, just outside Leeds. Both take-
away and restaurant are always very busy.

CROSS OF YORK
3-4 Newgate Market, York Y01 2LA
(01904 627590)
Fishmonger highly rated in trade.

FORTMAYNE FARM DAIRY
Fortmayne Cottage, Newton-le-Willows,
Bedale, North Yorkshire DL8 1SL
(01677 450660)
Makes the excellent Richard III Wensleydale
with unpasteurised milk from the next-door
Friesian herd. The cheese is eaten young at
only two weeks.

FORTUNE'S KIPPERS
22 Henrietta Street, Whitby,
Yorkshire YO22 4DW
(01947 601659)
Have been making kippers in the same way for
five generations, although today the herrings
come frozen from Iceland. Fortune's kippers
are only available from their shop in Whitby;
they don't supply any other retail outlets.

Recently given a Les Routiers award as one
of the finest traditional food retailers in the
North of England.

THE JOLLY FISHERMAN
Craster, Alnwick, Northumberland NE66 3TR
(01665 576218)
Enjoy excellent local seafood in this charming
pub with views over the sea – crab meat,
whisky and cream soup, crab sandwiches
and kipper pâté.

MAGPIE CAFÉ
14 Pier Road, Whitby,
North Yorkshire YO21 3PU
(01947 602058)
www.magpiecafe.co.uk
Famous for its fish-and-chips, cooked in the
traditional Yorkshire way in beef dripping.
Also other traditional fish dishes available.

HARRY RAMSDEN'S
White Cross, Guiseley, Nr Leeds LS20 8LZ
(01943 874641)
www.harryramsdens.co.uk
'T' biggest chip 'oile i' Yorkshire' and the
biggest fish-and-chip shop in the world is
Harry Ramsden's at Guiseley, between Leeds
and Ilkley, a vast place employing 200 people
in shifts and visited with reverence by millions
of people each year.

The history of the place is fascinating. In
1928 Mr Harry Ramsden borrowed £150 to
open a small green and white painted hut as
a fish shop. He stood at the serving hatch in
front of two pan fryers – a large man in a wing
collar, Arthur Askey glasses, starched apron
and a ribboned straw boater. The coming of
the motor car and the potential of the location,
a natural gateway to the Lake District and the
Yorkshire Dales, inspired Mr Ramsden to
embark on an ambitious scheme to build the
largest fish-and-chip shop in the country,
which he achieved in 1931. In 1954 Harry
decided to sell out to Eddie Stokes, a
restaurateur from Blackpool, who changed
Harry Ramsden's from a popular attraction
into the unique attraction it is today. Open all
week, 11.30am-10pm.

RIDLEY'S FISH & GAME
2 Battle Hill, Hexham,
Northumberland NE46 1BB
(01434 603138)
Very good selection of local fish and game.

RIVERVIEW FISHERIES
2 Union Quay, North Shields, Tyne & Wear
NE30 1HU
(0191 259 2366)
An excellent fishmongers near Souter
Lighthouse, which sells really fresh local fish.
Will also give advice on cooking and recipes.

L. ROBSON & SONS LTD.
Haven Hill, Craster, Alnwick,
Northumberland NE66 3TR
(01665 576223)
www.kipper.co.uk
A fourth-generation family business
specialising in the traditional method of
oak-smoking kippers and salmon using both
Scottish farmed and local wild fish. Can be
delivered next day to all parts of the UK
mainland and weekly deliveries throughout
the North East.

In the summer, treat yourself to a kipper
tea in the restaurant – kippers, brown bread
and butter and a pot of strongly brewed tea.

THE SWALEDALE CHEESE COMPANY
Mercury Road, Richmond,
North Yorkshire DL10 4TQ
(01748 824932)
www.swaledalecheese.co.uk
Like 'the other Dales' cheeses, Swaledale
was originally made by the monks using ewes'
milk. Both ewes' and cows' milk versions made
now, eaten young at three weeks, although
it is probably at its best when matured on to
five weeks.

SWALLOW FISH LTD.
2 South Street, Seahouses,
Northumberland NE68 7RP
(01665 721052)
www.swallowfish.co.uk
Only traditional smokehouse in Seahouses,
smoking plump and meaty kippers, Scottish
and local wild salmon from Beadnell Bay,
cod and haddock from Peterhead, plus local
mussels and prawns. Smokes over beechwood
logs. Also sells freshly boiled crabs and
lobsters and local wild salmon and sea trout.

WENSLEYDALE CREAMERY
Gayle Lane, Hawes, North Yorkshire DL8 3RN
(01969 667664)
www.wensleydale.co.uk
The creamery has a visitor centre, which tells
the history of the cheese and a viewing gallery
where you can watch it being made. Also a
café and shop.

THE NORTH WEST

JAMES BAXTER & SON

Thornton Road, Morecambe,
Lancashire LA4 5PB
(01524 410910)

Bob Baxter's family has been potting shrimps for over 200 years. Once the family had their own boats; now Bob buys in his shrimps, although they are still processed in the same time-honoured way and picked by hand. Baxter's Morecambe Bay potted shrimps have a special sweet fresh nuttiness. Bob will send them anywhere in the world.

GEORGE DEVEREAU & SON LTD.

33 Castle St, Douglas, Isle of Man IM1 2EX
(01624 673257)
www.isleofmankippers.com

Producer of Manx kippers, established in 1984. Peter Canipa, who smokes for them, uses a smoke temperature higher than that used elsewhere, and remarks that timing is crucial to quality.

THE FISH PLAICE STALL

Abingdon Street Market, Blackpool,
Lancashire FY1 1DE
(01253 293687)

Good variety of local fish.

HAWKSHEAD RELISH COMPANY

The Square, Hawkshead, Cumbria LA22 0NZ
(01539436614)
www.hawksheadrelish.com

Mark Whitehead originally made sauces and relishes using local ingredients for his café in Hawkshead, but due to popular demand he now produces them for retail sale. All made from either his garden or the local market. The lemon chutney is an ideal accompaniment for fish.

HAWKSHEAD TROUT FARM

The Boat House, Hawkshead,
Cumbria LA22 0QF
(015394 36541)
www.hawksheadtrout.com

Organic trout farm and smokehouse run by Nigel Woodhouse, a Trustee of the Soil Association. Buy from a shop on the premises or fish for your own. Boats available for hire.

MORECAMBE BAY POTTED SHRIMPS

Stockbridge Lane, Off Daltongate,
Ulverston, Cumbria LA12 7GB
(01229 585037)
www.morecambebayshrimps.com

A family business started by Les Salisbury who has been fishing for shrimps since he was a lad, going out on horse and cart. In the past, Young's Seafoods and Flookburgh Fishermen were the two factories taking in shrimps for potting; Les sent his to Flookburgh to be processed under the brand name of Morecambe Bay Potted Shrimps. When the members of the co-op decided to retire, Furness Fish bought the factory and the name. Mail order available and a market stall at Borough Market, Southwark St. London SE1 every Thursday, Friday and Saturday selling a wide range of fresh fish and gourmet produce.

THE OLD SMOKEHOUSE AND TRUFFLES CHOCOLATES

Brougham Hall, Brougham, Penrith,
Cumbria CA10 2DE
(01768 867772)
www.the-old-smokehouse.co.uk

Jo Hampson and Georgina Perkins run two units from the courtyard of Brougham Hall, an old castle that was converted into a house in the 19th century. From one they make chocolates and from the other run a smokery, producing a range of smoked fish including both wild char from Windermere and farmed from Gilcrux Springs at Wigton near Carlisle. A small proportion of their smoked salmon is wild, caught by haaf-netters in the Solway Firth.

JAMES PEET

66 Station Road, Banks Village, Southport,
Lancashire PR9 8BB
(01704 229266)

Shrimps are netted in a sustainable way off the Formby coast and landed at Southport. Award-winning sweet, spicy potted shrimps are produced by this company.
Mail order available.

TOWER BANK ARMS

Near Sawrey, Nr Hawkshead, Ambleside,
Cumbria LA22 0LF
(01539 436334)
www.towerbankarms.co.uk

Traditional Lakeland village pub made world famous in *The Tale of Jemima Puddleduck*. Enjoy an excellent local Cumberland sausage here before buying your permit to fish in Moss Eccles Tarn (see p.144).

WALES

THE ANGLESEY SEA SALT COMPANY

Brynsiencyn, Anglesey LL61 6TQ
(01248 430871)
www.seasalt.co.uk

Britain's only organically certified sea salt, Halen Môn is produced from the fresh Atlantic waters around Anglesey. Carefully prepared by hand with no additives whatsoever, it has a unique flavour and crisp texture ideal for culinary and table use. Also available mixed with organic spices.

E. ASHTON (FISHMONGERS)

200 Central Market, St Mary's Street, Cardiff,
South Glamorgan CF10 2AU
(029 2022 9201)
www.ashtonfishmongers.co.uk

Ashton's sells a varied selection of wet fish, an assortment of clams, freshly boiled crabs and freshly prepared laverbread.

BLACK MOUNTAINS SMOKERY LTD.

Leslie House, Elvicta Park, Crickhowell,
Powys NP8 1DF
(01873 811566)
www.smoked-foods.co.uk

A family-run business using traditional curing methods with modern smoking equipment to produce a delicious selection of quality smoked foods including salmon, trout, gravadlax and haddock.

CAWS CENARTH

Fferm Glyneithinog, Pontseli, Boncath,
Carmarthenshire SA37 OLH
(01239 710432)
www.welshorganiccheese.com

Acknowledged to have instigated and led the revival of farmhouse Caerphilly-making in Wales. Also produce a wide selection of other farmhouse cheeses.

THE CHARTHOUSE RESTAURANT

The Old Sail Loft, Midford Docks, Milford
Haven, Pembrokeshire SA73 3AF
(01646 690098)
www.thecharthouse.co.uk

Waterfront restaurant playing a big part in the Pembrokeshire Fish Week. Specialises in fresh seafood and local produce. Jan Mathias and her staff will give you a warm welcome, so enjoy excellent food beside the bustling docks and trawlers!

Also sells fresh fish daily and locally farmed meats and cheeses.

CIG MOCH PENLLYN
Cig Moch, Yffor, Pwllheli,
Gwynedd LL53 7HG
(01766 810044)
Produces delicious dry-cured bacon.

COAKLEY GREEN
Stall 4/c, the Market, Oxford Street,
Swansea SA1 3PF
(01792 653416)
Huge range of local fish from day boats as well
as uncooked and processed local cockles and
laverbread, with an emphasis on freshness.
Very knowledgeable staff. No mail order.

THE CONWY MUSSEL COMPANY
Mussel Purification Centre, The Quay,
Conwy, Gwynedd LL32 8BB
(01492 592347)
Set up to promote the high-quality mussels
found in the Conwy Estuary and keep alive
the traditional methods of the fishery. At
present there are 16 fishermen licensed for
Conwy mussels, renowned for their flavour
and quality.

THE FISH PLACE
Walter Davies & Sons, The Docks,
Milford Haven, Pembrokeshire SA73 3AE
(01646 692331)
A fish shop down by the docks next door to the
fish market. The fish is straight off the small
trawlers fishing along the Welsh coastline and
in the Irish Sea – brill, turbot, sand soles, dabs,
red and grey mullet and sea bass.

GORWYDD CAERPHILLY
Gorwydd Farm, Llanddewi brefi, Tregaron,
Ceredigion SY25 6NY
(01570 493516)
www.gorwydd.com
Produce a mature traditional Caerphilly
cheese with a fresh lemony taste and creamy
texture. Recent holder of the Gold Award for
Caerphilly and Best Welsh Cheese in the World
Cheese Awards.

LLŶN AQUACULTURE LTD.
Afonwen Farm, Chwilog, Pwllheli,
Gwynedd LL53 6TX
(01766 810904)
A farm run by Kath and Mike Rigby,
producing freshly prepared portion-sized
sea bass delivered direct to your door.
Perfect for a weekend treat, dinner party
or celebratory meal.

THE LOBSTER POT
Church Bay, Nr Holyhead, Anglesey LL65 4EY
(01407 730241/588)
www.thelobsterpot.net
A quaint white-washed, oak-beamed
restaurant specialising in local seafood,
especially lobsters from their own hatchery.
Open for lunch-time snacks and evening
dinners, April-October.

MENAI OYSTERS
Tal y Bont Bach, Dwyran, Anglesey LL61 6UU
(01248 430878)
A commercial oyster farm occupying a prime
position in the picturesque Menai Strait
between the mainland and Anglesey. Strong
tidal currents coupled with a plentiful food
supply produce succulent meaty Pacific
oysters and mussels that are delicious all
the year round. Mail order available.

MERLIN CHEESES
Tyn-y-llwyn, Pontrhydygroes, Ystrad
Meurig, Ceredigion SY25 6DP
(01974 282636)
www.merlin-cheeses.co.uk
Merlin cheese, a hard, cheddar-type cheese,
is made on the farm using unpasteurised
goats' milk. Gill Pateman makes 16 different
varieties including garlic and chive, and pear
and cinnamon.

MYTI MUSSELS LTD
Porth Penrhyn, Bangor, Gwynedd LL57 4HN
(01248 354878)
Farm mussels in the fast flowing waters of the
Menai Strait. Graded, cleaned, de-bearded and
distributed live.

THE OLD FORGE TROUT FARM
Mold Road, Bodfari, Nr Denbigh,
Denbighshire LL16 4WD
(01745 710305)
Producers of high-quality Welsh rainbow trout
with their own farm shop.

PEMBROKESHIRE FISH FARMS
Vicar's Mill, Llandissilio Clynderwen,
Pembrokeshire SA66 7LS
(01437 563553)
Owners, Brian and Margot Bateman, have been
farming trout since 1970, breeding their own
juveniles to give complete traceability.
Stocking rates are low and there is a first-class
natural water supply. Products range from the
freshest portion size trout, cleaned ready for
use, to large trout of 1.5-2.5kg (3-5lb). Hot-
smoked trout also available and smoked trout
pâté can be ordered from farm shop.

PSYGOD LLYN SEAFOODS
Y Maes, Pwllheli, Gwynedd, LL53 5HA
(01758 614292)
Very small but busy fish shop in the centre
of Pwllheli, run by Katherine Williams. Sells
a good variety of local fish and locally caught
crabs, lobsters and other shellfish.

RALPH'S CIDER
Old Badland Farm, New Radnor, Presteigne,
Powys LD8 2TG
(01544 350304)
Only licensed cider producer in Wales making
traditional farmhouse cider from apples
grown in orchards where no pesticides or
herbicides are used. The whole cider-making
and bottling process is carried out on the farm.

ALBERT REES
Arfryn, Uplands, Carmarthen,
Carmarthenshire SA32 8DX
(01267 237687)
www.carmarthenham.co.uk
A small family business specialising in hams
and bacon, dry salt-cured in the traditional
Welsh farmhouse way. Their Carmarthen
hams are air-dried to mature, then sliced
very thinly and pre-packed for convenience.

Main shop is in Carmarthen Market, but
trade in many others, also selling home-made
sausages, faggots and home-cooked meats.

RHOSCOLYN SHELLFISH OYSTER FARMS
The Ravens, Bod Lardour, Trearddur Bay,
Anglesey LL65 2TU
(01407 860264)
One of two designated shellfish growing sites
on the western coast of Britain producing
high–quality oysters. Mail order available.

SELECTIVE SEAFOODS
Ffridd Wen, Tudweiliog, Pwllheli,
Gwynedd LL53 8BJ
(01758 770397)
www.selectiveseafoods.com
Family-run business in a redundant farm
building, hand-processing locally caught crabs
and lobsters supplied by 2 fishermen; Steve
Harrison at Aberdaron near Porth Meudwy,
and Sean Williams working from Porth
Colmon on the north coast. Customers can
order by mail or the internet for next day
delivery or, better still, make a pilgrimage
down the narrow lane lined with wild flowers.

SELWYN'S SEAFOODS
Lynch Factory, Marsh Road, Llanmorlais,
Swansea SA4 3TN
(01792 850033)
Present owner's grandmother, Sarah Jones, was one of the Penclawdd women who relied on cockle-gathering for an income after her husband died of 'dust' from the coal mines. Burry Inlet cockles and locally gathered laverbread processed on a daily basis. Mussels available in season. Factory open to the public for wholesale and retail sales.

THE SHED
Porthgain, Haverfordwest,
Pembrokeshire SA62 5BH
(01348 831518)
Small family-run tea room and evening bistro on Porthgain quayside on the Pembrokeshire Coast Path. Slate and granite used to be shipped out from this small fishing village and the owner of the shed, Rob Jones, a shell-fisherman working from Porthgain and the larger ports of Fishguard and Milford Haven, will take visitors out in his boat *The Colleen* to discover the industrial history of fishing and quarrying in this area. The Shed's specialities include dressed crab and lobster caught and cleaned by the owners, and local fish.

SWANSEA MARKET
Oxford Street, Swansea SA1 3AG
One of the best markets in Britain, specialising in foods from the Gower Peninsula; local producers set up on wooden tables to sell their wares. The market is renowned for its fish – stalls are piled high with Penclawdd cockles, cooked mussels and prepared laverbread in big buckets. Ladies cook up Welsh cakes and pancakes on griddles on nearby bakery stalls.

TEIFI VALLEY FISH FARM
Ty Manr, Llanybydder,
Carmarthenshire SA40 9RE
(01570 480789)
A working trout farm supplying brown and rainbow trout for re-stocking lakes and rivers throughout Wales. Trout, locally caught sea fish and local salmon also on sale fresh to the customer.

TWNTI SEAFOODS RESTAURANT
Rhyd-y-Clafdy, Llanbedrog, Nr Pwllheli,
Gwynnedd LL53 7YH
(01758 740929)
Situated in a tiny village between the fish shop at Pwllheli and the village of Llanbedrog just down the coast, specialising in seafood with only two non-fishy dishes.

VIN SULLIVAN FOODS LTD.
2 Gilchrist Thomas Industrial Estate,
Blaenavon, Torfaen, Abergavenny NP4 9RL
(01495 792792)
www.vin-sullivan.co.uk
Vin Sullivan has been supplying specialist food for over 40 years with an enormous range of Welsh produce, including an impressive choice of fresh local sea fish and a regular supply of sewin in season. Also sells fresh laverbread from Swansea.

NORTHERN IRELAND
CROWN LIQUOR SALOON
46 Great Victoria Street, Belfast,
Co. Antrim BT2 7BA
(028 9027 9901)
This National Trust pub is the most famous in Belfast and one of the finest examples of a high-Victorian public house to survive, with rich ornamentation and snugs still intact. Visitors can sample Bushmills whiskey or enjoy fresh oysters with a glass of Guinness, thought by many, and not just Irishmen, to be better with oysters than Chablis or Muscadet. Another speciality is fresh, locally caught inshore cod.

CUAN SEA FISHERIES
Skettrick Island, Killinchy,
Co. Down BT23 6QH
(028 9754 1461)
www.cuanoysters.com
Largest producer of oysters in the UK, but also specialise in the supply of other live, fresh shellfish – mussels, winkles and scallops. Guaranteed 'shore to door' next-day delivery service within the UK and also distributes throughout Europe, the Middle East and the Far East. Has a sister company, Cuan Oysters Ltd., which offers same-day delivery in Central London.

DUNDRUM BAY OYSTER FISHERY
24 Main Street, Dundrum, Newcastle,
Co. Down BT33 0LX
(028 4375 1810)
Established in 1984 and cultivates oysters and mussels in the pure waters of Dundrum Bay; a blend of fresh and salt water is used in the growing areas. The shellfish are supplied live.

GLEN OAK FISHERIES
Glen Oak Mill, Crumlin, Co. Antrim BT29 4XL
(02894 453173)
Established in 1977, specialises in high-quality trout and trout products distributed throughout Ireland and Britain.

HENNING BROS. FISHING CO.
The Harbour, Kilkeel, Co. Down BT34 4AX
(028 4176 2335)
www.henningfish.co.uk
A family-run business established in 1979 specialising in shellfish production, with mussel sites in Carlingford and Belfast Loughs, where the mussels are grown on the seabed, so are of high quality. Also have an oyster bed in Carlingford Lough.

MARY MCBRIDE'S PUB

2 Main Street, Cushendun,
Co. Antrim BT44 0PH
(028 2176 1511)

Specialises in serving locally caught fish – cod, whiting, sea bass and wild salmon. Open all day at weekends.

NORTHERN SALMON COMPANY LTD.

Glenarm, Co. Antrim BT44 0BD
(028 2884 1691)

Supplies organic farmed salmon worldwide, trading under the name of 'Glenarm'. Also sells smoked farmed organic salmon.

SPERRIN MOUNTAIN SPRING TROUT HATCHERY

22 Lough Fea Road, Cookstown,
Co. Tyrone BT80 9QL
(02886 765160)

Situated in a sparsely populated upland area in County Tyrone, the Hatchery breeds organic Rainbow Trout and supplies top quality disease-free trout eggs and fry world-wide

LONDON

BILLINGSGATE

Trafalgar Way, London E14 5ST
(020 7987 1118)

The country's biggest fish market, open Tuesday-Saturday, 5am-8.30am;Sunday (shellfish only), 6am-8am. NB: children not allowed on the market floor.

BLAGDEN'S

65 Paddington Street, London W1 4JA
(020 7935 8321)

A well-respected fishmonger.

STEVE HATT

88-90 Essex Road, London N1 8LU
(020 7226 3963)

One of the best fishmongers in London.

KENSINGTON PLACE FISH SHOP

201-209 Kensington Church Street
London W8 7LX
(020 7243 6626)

Small shop attached to Kensington Place Restaurant, with very fresh fish and preparation of restaurant quality.

PLANET ORGANIC

25 Effie Road, Fulham, London SW6 1EL
(020 7731 7222)
42 Westbourne Grove, London W2 5SH
(020 7727 2227)
22 Torrington Place, London WC1 7JE
(020 7436 1929)
Deliveries/Mail Order/Hampers
(020 7221 1345)
www.planetorganic.com

Sources fish including Cornish cod and bass from small-scale fisheries who do not have MSC accreditation but where the fishermen have an interest in keeping them viable.

SCOTLAND

SCOTTISH QUALITY SALMON

Durn, Isla Road, Perth PH2 7HG
(01738 587000)
www.scottishsalmon.co.uk

LOCH DUART LTD – THE SUSTAINABLE SALMON COMPANY

Badcall Salmon House, Scourie, Lairg
Sutherland IV27 4TH
(01971 502451)
www.lochduart.com

THE BILLINGSGATE SEAFOOD TRAINING SCHOOL
Based at London's Billingsgate Market, for more details:
(020 7517 3548/9)

FREEDOM FOOD LTD
Wilberforce Way, Southwater, Horsham
West Sussex RH13 9RS
(0870 754 0014)
www.freedomfood.co.uk

MARINE CONSERVATION SOCIETY
9 Gloucester Road, Ross-on-Wye
Herefordshire HR9 5BU
(01989 566017)
www.mcsuk.org
Copies of the *Good Fish Guide* are available from MCS or may be ordered online for £10.00 per copy (inc P&P). Proceeds from sales of the guide will be used to support projects to promote sustainable fisheries.

   MCS has compiled the *Good Beach Guide* for over a decade. This is now published on the internet at www.goodbeachguide.co.uk

MARINE STEWARDSHIP COUNCIL
119 Attenberg Gardens, London SW11 1JQ
(020 7350 4000)
www.msc.org

NATIONAL TRUST & FISHING
The National Trust welcomes fishing at properties, providing it is compatible with conservation of wildlife. A listing of the fishing publicly available is provided in a leaflet entitled 'Enjoy Fishing with the National Trust' which is published annually. Copies may be obtained by sending a first-class stamp to National Trust Membership Department, PO Box 39, Warrington WA5 7WD. The information is also available on the National Trust website at www.nationaltrust.org.uk/events (go to 'Recreational Activities').

NATIONAL TRUST HOLIDAY COTTAGES
Booking Office, P.O. Box 536, Melksham, Wiltshire SN12 8SX
(01225 791199) (bookings)
(01225 791133) (brochures)
www.nationaltrustcottages.co.uk
The National Trust has over three hundred holiday cottages throughout England, Wales and Northern Ireland, including many in coastal areas. At Port Isaac in Cornwall, for instance, there is a five-sided building known as the Birdcage. At Dunwich Heath in Suffolk, former coastguard cottages have been converted into apartments (see p.88). At Souter Lighthouse in Northumberland, visitors can stay in the cottages belonging formerly to the keeper and the engineer. For freshwater fisherman, there are seven cottages on the Crom Estate in Co. Fermanagah, and dozens of cottages and apartments in the Lake District. At Stackpole in South Wales, visitors can enjoy both the sea and freshwater lakes, staying in a range of no less than ten buildings converted into accommodation.

SEAFISH INDUSTRY AUTHORITY
(Seafish)
18 Logie Mill, Logie Green Road,
Edinburgh EH7 4HG
(01315 583331)
www.seafish.co.uk

SHELLFISH ASSOCIATION OF GREAT BRITAIN
Fishmongers' Hall, London Bridge
London EC4R 9EL
(020 7283 8305)
www.shellfish.org.uk

SLOW FISH
Organised by Slow Food, this sustainable seafood fair, held for the first time in Italy in June 2004, will become a biennial event in the port of Genoa. For more information, see www.slowfood.com

SOIL ASSOCIATION
Bristol House, 40-56 Victoria Street
Bristol BS1 6BY
(01179 290661)
www.soilassociation.org

WESTCOUNTRY RIVERS TRUST
Fore Street, Lifton, Devon PL16 OAA
(01566 784488)
An environmental charitable Trust formed in 1995 to conserve, maintain and restore the natural beauty and ecological integrity of rivers and streams in Devon, Cornwall and West Somerset. Very active since its inception by a small group of enthusiasts including its first President, the late Poet Laureate, Ted Hughes, who had a great love and understanding of rivers.

WORLD WIDE FUND FOR NATURE
Panda House, Weyside Park, Godalming,
Surrey GU7 1XR
(01483 426444)
www.wwf-uk.org

PLACES TO VISIT

Information current at time of going to press. The National Trust properties in the list below are just a few from a huge range of places to visit. *The National Trust Handbook for Members & Visitors*, which is published annually, will provide further details including opening arrangements where applicable, or visit www.nationaltrust.org.uk.

THE SOUTH WEST

COLETON FISHACRE HOUSE AND GARDEN

Coleton, Kingswear, Dartmouth, Devon TQ6 0OE
(01803 752466)

Spectacularly set in the stream-fed valley on a beautiful stretch of the National Trust's South Devon coastline, the house was designed in 1925 for Rupert and Lady Dorothy D'Oyly Carte, who created the 8-hectare (20-acre) luxuriant garden.

COTEHELE

St Dominick, nr Saltash, Cornwall PL12 6TA
(01579 351346)

Early Tudor granite and slatestone house, home of the Edgcumbe family for centuries. Gardens, formal and informal, run down to Cotehele Quay on the River Tamar, where the traditional sailing barge, *Shamrock*, is moored and an out-station of the National Maritime Museum is situated.

GLENDURGAN GARDEN

Mawnan Smith, nr Falmouth, Cornwall TR11 5JZ
(01326 250906)

The tiny fishing hamlet of Durgan, its waterfront dominated by the old school and chapel, is now partly owned by the National Trust. Like so many estuarine and coastal villages without harbours, Durgan still indulged in its fair share of coastal trade in the past; the old sailing barges and schooners simply beached on the foreshore to load and unload cargo between tides. Durgan's wonderful backdrop of trees is part of the wooded valley garden of Glendurgan, also owned by the National Trust and open to the public.

LEVANT STEAM ENGINE

Trewellard, Pendeen, nr St Just, Cornwall
(01736 796993)

The sight, sounds and smell of the 160-year-old engine, steaming again after 60 idle years, conjure up the feel of Cornwall's industrial past.

LOE POOL

near Porthleven, Cornwall

Along the cliff path just 1 mile east of Porthleven is Cornwall's largest natural freshwater lake, fed by the River Cober. A beautifully quiet place separated from the open sea by the shingle bank of Loe Bar, it has a 5-mile footpath around its edge and a bird hide looking out into the reed bed. The National Trust allows locals from Porthleven and Helston to fish here for the special silvery-pink strain of wild brown trout. The lake is, however, badly polluted with nitrates from farmland and sewage from Helston, although the town's sewage treatment works are due for update soon. The Cornwall Rivers Project is helping the National Trust secure European funding to clean up the lake and improve the River Cober.

Visitors at Scolt Head Island, off the North Norfolk coast. This detail comes from a photograph taken in 1923 when ownership of Scolt Head passed to the National Trust

THE NATIONAL LOBSTER HATCHERY

South Quay, Padstow, Cornwall PL28 8BL
(01841 533877)

Cornwall Sea Fisheries Committee was involved in the setting up, with Rick Stein, of this pioneering hatchery – the first commercial hatchery in England. It aims to increase stocks and production of the European lobster. There is also a child-friendly museum with quizzes, stencils and lots of fascinating lobster facts.

NATIONAL MARITIME MUSEUM CORNWALL

Discovery Quay, Falmouth,
Cornwall TR11 3QY
(01326 313388)

Opened in March 2003, the museum celebrates Cornwall's unique relationship with the sea: nowhere in the county is more than 16 miles from the coast. Three galleries are devoted to exploring Cornwall's maritime history, predominantly fishing. There is also the country's finest public collection of small boats.

BRANCASTER MILLENNIUM ACTIVITY CENTRE

Dial House, Brancaster Staithe, nr King's
Lynn, Norfolk PE31 8BW
(01485 210719)

A renovated 17th-century building with beautiful views over Brancaster Staithe Harbour, offering residential courses for schools, with cutting-edge environmental technology. Also field studies and outdoor pursuits including birdwatching, woodlands, salt-marshes, orienteering, sailing, kayaking and cycling. Programmes for adults of both day and weekend courses. Family Fun weeks in school holidays.

BLAKENEY POINT

The Warden, 35 The Cornfield, Langham,
Holt, Norfolk NR25 7DQ
(01263 740480 April to September;
01263 740241 October to March)

One of Britain's foremost bird sanctuaries protected by the National Trust. Access on foot from Cley Beach or by ferry from Morston and Blakeney. Restricted access to certain areas of the Point during the main bird-breeding season, May to July.

DUNWICH HEATH COASTAL CENTRE AND BEACH

Minsmere Road, Dunwich, Saxmundham,
Suffolk IP17 3DJ
(01728 648505 – Shop and tea-room)
(01728 648501 – Warden /Education Officer)

A remnant of the once extensive sandlings heaths, with open tracts of heather and gorse, shady woods and sandy cliffs. An important nature conservation area and home to scarce species like the nightjar, Dartford warbler and the ant-lion – thought to be extinct until it was found here recently. Shop and tea-room in Coastguard Cottages. A Batricar is available for disabled visitors.

GREAT YARMOUTH MARITIME MUSEUM

4 South Quay, Great Yarmouth,
Norfolk NR30 2QH
(01493 855746)

This museum tells the fascinating story of the East Anglian herring fishery and other local fisheries.

HERRING FESTIVAL

Hemsby, Nr Great Yarmouth, Norfolk
(01493 731606)

The annual blessing of nets and fish is followed by a herring fry-up. Charities set up stalls along the beach and a lifeboat becomes a museum of fishing history. Takes place at the beginning of September.

NORTHEY ISLAND

A nature reserve belonging to the National Trust, lying near the head of the Blackwater Estuary about 1½ miles east of the port of Maldon. Access to the island's salt-marsh, which is wonderful for birdwatching, is via a causeway, covered for 4-5 hours at high tide, by advance permit only from the Warden, Northey Cottage, Northey Island, Maldon, tel. 01621 853142.

ORFORD NESS NATIONAL NATURE RESERVE

Quay Office, Orford Quay, Orford,
Woodbridge, Suffolk IP12 2NU
(01394 450900)

The largest vegetated shingle spit in Europe, with a variety of habitats including shingle, salt-marsh, mudflat, brackish lagoons and grazing marsh, which was a secret military site from 1913 until the mid-1980s.

SUTTON HOO

Woodbridge, Suffolk IP12 3DJ
(01394 389700)

An Anglo-Saxon royal burial site where priceless treasure was discovered in a huge ship grave in 1939. Guided tours available at set times at weekends and some weekdays. Children's activities during the summer holidays and an education room/centre. Adult study days available.

THE NORTH EAST

ARCTIC CORSAIR

H320, Hull

Enjoy a guided tour of Hull's only surviving distant-water 'sidewinder' trawler, now moored permanently in the River Hull in Hull's 'old town'. Available on Wednesdays, Saturdays and Sundays. More information from Anita Waddy. Tel: 01482 351445.

COQUET ISLAND

An RSPB nature reserve is located on the island, about a mile offshore from the estuary of the River Coquet in Northumberland. In the summer, regular boat trips from Amble take bird watchers to the island to see puffins and eider ducks. On the way back, buy fresh fish from the fishing boats landing their catch at Amble, still a bustling fishing village with a large marina.

CRAG LOUGH

Hadrian's Wall & Housesteads Fort, Bardon Mill, Hexham, Northumberland

A 9-hectare (20-acre) lough, relic of the Ice Age, adjacent to Shield Crags, owned by the National Trust. The fishing for brown and rainbow trout is managed by a syndicate. Contact Barry Jones for details: 0191 251 2260

FARNE ISLANDS

(01665 720651)

For nearly 900 years, hermits and monks lived on Inner Farne, including St Cuthbert who, in 682, ended his days there. His influence made the island a place of pilgrimage and, in the 14th century, a chapel, which can still be visited, was built to his memory.

The Longstone Lighthouse, well out in the North Sea, was made famous by Grace Darling who on 7 September 1838, with her lighthouse-keeper father, rowed in appalling conditions to the wrecked SS *Forfarshire* to rescue survivors; a night that made her a national heroine.

Only the Inner Farne and Staple Islands are open to visitors; the National Trust has the awesome responsibility of managing the islands to ensure that the huge number of birds, including puffins and 'Cuddy's Ducks' (the eider ducks that St Cuthbert loved so much) and the large breeding colonies of grey seals, are protected, while visitors enjoy their stay.

LINDISFARNE CASTLE

**Holy Island, Berwick-upon-Tweed, Northumberland TD15 2SH
(01289 389244)**

Perched atop a rocky crag and accessible over a causeway at low tide only, the castle presents an exciting and alluring aspect. It was converted into a private house by Edwin Lutyens in 1903. The small rooms are full of intimate decoration and design, the windows looking down on the charming walled garden planned by Gertrude Jekyll.

Tide tables are printed in local newspapers and displayed at the causeway, so check safe crossing times to avoid disappointment.

NATIONAL TRUST COASTAL CENTRE

**Peakside, Ravenscar, Scarborough, North Yorkshire YO3 ONE
(01723 870138)
(01947 885900 (The Old Coastguard Station))**

Information Centre providing insights into the local wildlife and geology. The Ravenscar Trail, established to illustrate some of the unique geological features and land forms of the area including the nearby Peak Alum Works, starts outside the National Trust shop and takes about 2½ hours to complete at a leisurely pace. Also a rockpool aquarium.

SOUTER LIGHTHOUSE

**Coast Road, Whitburn, Sunderland, Tyne & Wear SR6 7NH
(01915 293161)**

First lighthouse to use alternating electric current, the most advanced technology of its day. A ground-floor closed-circuit TV shows views from the top for those unable to climb. Immediately to the north is The Leas, 2½ miles of beach, cliff and grassland with spectacular views, and interesting flora and fauna.

WAKEFIELD CITY COUNCIL'S RHUBARB TRAIL

200 rhubarb growers built their forcing sheds in an 8-mile 'pink' triangle between Wakefield, Bradford and Leeds. Today there are just 10 growers. Fascinating group tours of the vast forcing sheds available and a Rhubarb Festival at the end of January/beginning of February. Contact Philippa Venton (01924 305841) for details of tours. Pre-book only. 2nd week January – 2nd week March.

THE NORTH WEST

LANCASTER MARITIME MUSEUM

**Custom House, St George's Quay, Lancaster LA1 1RB
(01524 64637)**

Opened in 1985, the museum occupies the former Custom House designed by Richard Gillow of the famous local cabinet-making family for the Lancaster Port Commission in 1764. Using sound, smells, reconstructions and audio-visuals the museum tells the story of the port of Lancaster, the Lancaster Canal, fishing and the ecology of Morecambe Bay.

MUSEUM OF LAKELAND LIFE

**Abbot Hall, Kendal, Cumbria LA9 5AL
(01539 722464)**

Fascinating information available on the char and how it is fished and potted, as well as information on other traditional Cumbrian foods which you can purchase in the museum shop and taste in the Abbot Hall coffee shop.

TOWNEND

**Troutbeck, Windermere, Cumbria LA23 1LB
(015394 32628)**

A very fine example of Lake District vernacular architecture, owned by the National Trust. Contains carved woodwork, furniture and fascinating domestic implements, largely accumulated by the Browne family who farmed here from 1626 to 1943.

WALES

MELIN LLYNON
Llanddeusant, Anglesey ll61
(01407 730797)
The only working windmill in Wales, fully restored and opened to the public in 1984. Produces stoneground flour for sale. Also has an attractive craft shop and popular tea-rooms.

MUSEUM OF WELSH LIFE
St Fagans, Cardiff, Glamorgan CF5 6XB
(029 2056 6985)
A huge open-air museum showing how many Welsh people lived, worked and spent their leisure time over the last 400 years. Thirty original buildings have been carefully re-erected and furnished in period, including an early 17th-century farmhouse from Gower. Visitors can buy flour from the working corn-mill and bread and cakes baked in the original wood-fired oven of the Dderwen Bakehouse, from Aberystwyth.

PLAS NEWYDD
Llanfairpwll, Anglesey LL61 6EQ
(01248 714795)
The Marquess of Anglesey's impressive 18th-century house, designed by James Wyatt and set in unspoilt surroundings on the Menai Strait with magnificent views of Snowdonia.

PLAS YN RHIW
Rhiw, Pwllheli, Gwynedd LL53 8AB
(01758 780219)
A small manor house above Porth Neigwl, rescued from neglect by the three Keating sisters who bought it in 1938 and, having lovingly restored their 16th-century home, left it to the National Trust. The views from the delightful gardens across Cardigan Bay are among the most spectacular in Britain.

RHOSSILI VISITOR CENTRE
Coastguard Cottages, Rhossili,
Gower SA3 IPR
(01792 390707)
In 1982, the National Trust established a Visitor Centre at Rhossili to provide information about the area. Also an exhibition and shop.

NORTHERN IRELAND

CASTLE WARD
Strangford, Downpatrick,
Co. Down BT30 7LS
(028 4488 1204)
Built by the 1st Lord Bangor in 1765, the mansion is set in a beautiful 300-hectare (750–acre) walled estate in a stunning location overlooking Strangford Lough.

CURRAGH MAKING
Learn the traditional skill of curragh making with Bruce Crawford,who taught himself by studying old photographs and now demonstrates the technique at the Ulster Folk and Transport Museum near Belfast and elsewhere in Northern Ireland. This has proved very popular with all age groups. For more details contact Bruce Crawford at 23 Loughbrickland Road, Gilford, Co. Down BT63 6BL

DUNSEVERICK HARBOUR AND CASTLE
c/o The National Trust, North Antrim Office,
Innisfree Farm, 60 Causeway Road,
Bushmills, Co. Antrim BT57 8SU
(028 2073 1582)
Purchased in 1968 by the National Trust, the harbour was once involved in salmon fishing using bag nets, but today there are no commercial fishing boats. The Causeway Coastal Path runs past the ruined Castle, given to the National Trust in 1962 by local farmer Jack McCurdy, together with the peninsula on which it stands. The site is said to have been fortified since about 500BC, but the present Castle was occupied by the O'Cahans of Ulster until its capture and destruction by Cromwellian troops in the 1650s.

HILLSBOROUGH OYSTER FESTIVAL
One of Northern Ireland's premier events, held in the pretty Georgian village of Hillsborough, County Down, which attracts about 10,000 visitors from around the world. A 3-day festival promoting food and drink, including the world oyster-eating championships to raise money for a nominated charity. For details contact Sean Hall: 028 9267 3331

MURLOUGH NATIONAL NATURE RESERVE
South Down Office, Murlough NNR,
Dundrum, Co. Down BT33 0NQ
(028 4375 1467)
Murlough dune system fringes one of Northern Ireland's most popular beaches. A boardwalk, suitable for wheelchairs, leads from the National Trust car park through the dunes to the beach. An information centre is in the car park and nearby holiday cottages are available for rent throughout the year.

THE OLD BUSHMILLS DISTILLERY CO. LTD.
2 Distillery Road, Bushmills,
Co. Antrim BT57 8XH
(028 2073 1521)
Visitors can have a guided tour and tasting at the world's oldest whiskey distillery; James I granted the original licence to distil Acqua Vitae in 1608. The uniqueness of Bushmills Malt Whiskey lies in the character of Irish barley, in the special water from Saint Columb's Rill, a tributary of the River Bush which runs beside the distillery, and its distinctive triple distillation process.

RATHLIN ISLAND
Just 5 miles off the coast of Northern Ireland, the island owned by the National Trust is renowned for its rugged beauty and tranquillity. Excellent birdwatching and sea-fishing opportunities as well as scenic walks. A regular ferry from Ballycastle on the mainland takes approximately 45 minutes. Contact Caledonian MacBrayne on 028 2076 9299 for details of sailings. The Manor House is a late Georgian residence restored by the islanders and now run as a National Trust guest-house for 25 people, open all the year round (028 2076 3964).

STRANGFORD LOUGH WILDLIFE CENTRE

**Castle Ward, Near Strangford,
Co. Down BT30 7LS
(028 4488 1411)**

Situated on the shores of Strangford Lough, within the Castle Ward Estate, the centre offers information on many aspects of the Lough, with particular emphasis on its natural history.

TRADITIONAL FERMANAGH FISHING CREELS

**Ardess House and Craft Centre, Kesh,
Co. Fermanagh BT93 INX
(028 6863 1267)**

Learn how to make a traditional fishing creel with brass fastenings and a leather strap, with Tom O'Brien whose family have been basket-weavers for generations. Take a rod and line to catch a trout for your new creel!

WHITE PARK BAY

Co. Antrim (contact National Trust, see Dunseverick Castle)

Given to the National Trust by the Youth Hostel Association of Northern Ireland in 1938, this spectacular sandy bay forms part of the Causeway Coastal Path. Designated an Area of Special Scientific Interest because of its nationally important coastal grasslands, it is part of a Special Area of Conservation. The beach is backed by ancient dunes that provide rich habitats for bird and animal life.

COOKERY INDEX

Page numbers in *italics* indicate illustrations.

PICTURE CREDITS

Food photographs by Imagen

Line drawings by Eric Thomas

Photographs from the National Trust Photographic Library: Michael Allwood-Coppin 45; Matthew Antrobus 25, 62, 141; Andrew Butler 183; Joe Cornish 23, 24, 36, 52-3, 74, 75, 82, 85, 86 (above), 91, 92-3, 97, 98, 99 (above and below), 101, 102, 113, 128, 142, 150, 159, 162, 163, 166, 167, 168, 170, 172, 186-7, 190, 193, 194, 202, 205, 207, 210, 211, 213, 216; Derek Croucher 121, 137, 196; John Darley 58, 61, 181; David Dixon 48; Rod J.Edwards 76, 80; Lee Frost 6, 27, 34, 100, 117, 152-3, 176; Dennis Gilbert 191; Roger Hickman 165; Angelo Hornak 47; Rob Matheson 28; Nick Meers 175; John Miller 88; Geoff Morgan 109; David Noton 14-15, 26, 33, 122-3, 127, 129, 131, 138, 141, 145; Howard Phillips 40; Stephen Robson 87; Kevin Richardson 182;David Sellman 20, 31, 135; Ian Shaw 2-3, 41; David Tarn 105, 164; Andreas von Einsiedel 51, 179; Paul Wakefield 77, 79, 201; William Webster 208; Mike Williams 203, 212; David Woodfall 171

The author and publisher would like to thank the following who have granted permission to reproduce their material: Aberdeen Library and Information Services, 10, 65; Richard Enderby, 70; Francis Frith 8, 9, 16, 29, 37, 39, 60, 110, 111, 132, 154; George Morrison, 63, 138, 140, 188, 206, 214; Heritage Image Partnership 4, 11, 54, 94, 124, 130, 218, 224; National Library of Wales 174; National Trust 42, 181, 236; Frederick Warne 147

The photograph on page 21 is taken from *A Cornish Choice of Recipes*, and on pages 57 and 69 from *Traditional Norfolk Recipes*. All reasonable efforts have been made to contact the copyright holders of images.

Published in Great Britain in 2005 by National Trust Enterprises Ltd, 36 Queen Anne's Gate, London SW1H 9AS

www.nationaltrust.org.uk
Registered charity no. 205846

ISBN 0 7078 0357 8

Text and recipes © Sara Paston-Williams 2005
Food photographs © The National Trust 2005

Cataloguing in Publication Data is available from the British Library

Food photography: Imagen
Food styling: Maxine Clark and Maggie Jary
Editor: Margaret Willes
Indexes: Sue Bosanko
Picture research: Margaret Willes,
    Andrew Cummins and Grant Berry
Design: SMITH

Printed and bound in Singapore

US EQUIVALENT MEASURES

DRY MEASURES

1 US cup	60g	2oz of breadcrumbs
1 US cup	75g	3oz of rolled oats
1 US cup	90g	3oz of ground almonds
1 US cup	100g	3½oz of walnut pieces, frozen peas, pasta
1 US cup	110g	4oz of white flour
1 US cup	150g	5½oz of wholemeal flour, cornflour
1 US cup	175g	6oz mixed peel, sultanas
1 US cup	200g	7oz lentils, rice
1 US cup	225g	½lb of cream cheese
1 US cup	300g	11oz of mincemeat
1 US cup	350g	12oz of syrup

LIQUID MEASURES

¼ US cup	60ml	2 fluid oz
1 US cup	240ml	8 fluid oz
2 US cups (1 US pint)	480ml	16 fluid oz

BUTTER, LARD AND MARGARINE MEASURES

¼ stick	25g	2 level tablespoons	1oz
1 stick (1 US cup)	100g	8 level tablespoons	3½oz